BOOKS BY

ANNE O'HARE McCORMICK

THE WORLD AT HOME
(1956)

THE HAMMER AND THE SCYTHE
(1928)

These are BORZOI BOOKS *published in New York*
by ALFRED A. KNOPF

THE WORLD AT HOME

THE WORLD AT HOME

SELECTIONS FROM THE WRITINGS OF

ANNE O'HARE McCORMICK

EDITED BY MARION TURNER SHEEHAN

INTRODUCTION BY JAMES B. RESTON

ALFRED A. KNOPF
NEW YORK
1956

L. C. Catalog card number: 56–5792

© ALFRED A. KNOPF, INC., 1956

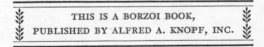

THIS IS A BORZOI BOOK,
PUBLISHED BY ALFRED A. KNOPF, INC.

FIRST EDITION

INTRODUCTION

ANNE O'HARE MCCORMICK was a great reporter in a very special sense. She had vitality, curiosity, intelligence, courage, and all the other qualities a good reporter must have, but she had something more that gave to her reporting the dimension of wisdom and prophecy. This was a rare gift of sympathy for all sorts of people, a sense of the relationships between the event of the day and the history and aspirations of her country, and, above all, a religious conviction which enabled her to see things in the ultimate perspective of life itself.

In other days and on other newspapers these qualities might not have been used to their full capacity, but Anne McCormick worked on a great paper in a time of great news. She literally made a place for herself on The New York Times by asking in 1921 to submit articles to editors she did not know, and she wrote for The Times from then until her death on May 29, 1954.

This was a period of vast convulsions at home and abroad. Just as the slower Victorian age was the era of the novelist, so this later period of wars and depressions, of dying and rising empires, of new and old ideas in conflict, of rogues, statesmen, demagogues, and dictators, was the era of the journalist.

This era demanded wider and deeper coverage of the news. For a nation and world in transition, there was not only more to be reported but much more to be explained, and Anne McCormick, endlessly fascinated by the interplay of the news on human values, human character, and human institutions, ranged across the world asking questions and reporting her facts and observations with unusual sensitivity.

Anne O'Hare McCormick was full of mirth and spunk. This

v

was the Irish in her. She literally twinkled when she talked, and what talk! Everything and everybody interested her, and she illuminated every subject she touched. I remember her showing up at the 1952 Republican convention wearing a lovely white silk dress with tiny Democratic donkeys on it, and appearing the following week at the Democratic convention in another white silk dress with small blue Republican elephants.

She was fiercely proud of the record of the American reporters in informing the world about the rising dangers of Hitler and Mussolini. She once called on Anthony Eden, then British Foreign Secretary, who remarked in a slightly condescending way that the American reporters had *also* realized the menace of the dictators. "As a matter of fact," she replied, "they were ahead of the diplomats. After all, Mr. Secretary, diplomats are only badly trained reporters."

Mrs. McCormick loved newspapers. She won every honor her profession could give her, and she was constantly besieged to write books about world affairs, but she would never stay away from her primary job long enough to do so. There was a reason for this.

She knew the hurry of this generation. She knew that people were preoccupied with their families and their jobs, and that they tended to pay attention to the news only when some great event commanded their attention. Thus, she felt that her energies could be used more effectively if she wrote on top of the news while people were listening, and this occupied all her time.

This explains the paradox of this book. Mrs. McCormick wrote primarily about foreign affairs. Her column on the editorial page of The New York Times was titled "Abroad." But because she wrote "on top of the news," because she always put the news ahead of her observations, many of her columns have lost the flavor and freshness of the time.

Thus, surprisingly, this is a book not primarily about foreign affairs but about the American scene: about the early days of the New Deal, about Franklin D. Roosevelt, whom she knew well, about America as viewed from abroad, and finally about the South.

Her articles on the South in this volume are among the finest newspaper dispatches of this century. They were written over a quarter of a century ago; yet such was her instinct for the durable things of life that they are almost as fresh now as when they were written.

Here is not only an example of human wisdom, but a style which is always clear, and often full of poetry. Anne Mc-Cormick was an extraordinary reporter primarily because she was an extraordinary human being; her writing was true and her criticism kindly because she was true and kindly; her writing was sensitive and full of spirit because Anne, even in the days shortly before her death, had all the spirit of a young and lovely girl; there was poetry in it because, like her mother, she was a poet with a sense of style about everything she did.

When Anne O'Hare McCormick died, The New York Times turned the black borders on her column and there printed on the editorial page a tribute by Robert Duffus, who worked with her for many years.

"She was a reporter," Bob Duffus wrote, "and gloried in the title. She could not understand how anyone could be satisfied with less than the personal observation on the spot. The word reporter we on this newspaper think is a beautiful name. . . .

"In spite of all her genius for seeing, understanding and reporting, she was also a deeply feminine person and could not help being so and would not have wished not to be so. She had a great tenderness for people. She had a great compassion for those who suffered. War to her was not something abstract that destroyed nations. War was the thing that destroyed individuals. War was the thing that wrecked houses in which real people lived, that left children hungry and mothers hopeless. She saw beneath the surface of the great striding events of the day and saw the effect of those events on families, on the old, on the young, on the sick.

"She shrank in horror from much that went on, but her heart was associated with a keen and logical mind. She would never have said, and never did say, that because the strife for justice was costly we must admit to injustice. She knew that there are eternal truths and eternal principles for which sacrifices must be made. She felt and showed in her writing the great pulses of history and did not deceive herself."

JAMES B. RESTON

Washington, D.C.
May 2, 1956

FOREWORD

AT A RECEPTION in Europe some years ago, an intimate friend of Anne O'Hare McCormick was in conversation with one of France's famed statesmen. The talk turned to the responsibilities of a journalist in reporting news, and the statesman said of American Anne O'Hare McCormick: "She is more than a journalist, she is a historian writing history!"

Anne O'Hare McCormick was born in Yorkshire, England, of American parents, Thomas and Teresa Beatrice O'Hare. She was brought to America as an infant. Her schooling began in Columbus, Ohio, and later she matriculated in the College of St. Mary of the Springs. After formal schooling, she received her first journalistic experience as associate editor of a weekly bulletin in Cleveland, a publication on which her mother, a poet, was once woman's-page editor. After a short time she resigned to become the young bride of a Dayton, Ohio, engineer and importer, Francis J. McCormick. She accompanied her husband on frequent buying trips to Europe, and this provided her with an opportunity she was quick to appreciate. Abroad, she studied every country they visited—hers were not the eyes of a curious sightseeing tourist, but of a young woman with sparkling mind and warm heart whose observations would someday find their way into the market places and homes of America and the marble halls and drawing-rooms of the greatest statesmen of the Continent.

In her early years of travel with her husband, Mrs. McCormick tentatively wrote a few pieces and sent them to The New York Times. More than sample vignettes, they were detailed articles about average people as she found them—their simplicity, their needs, their hopes and aspirations. Anne O'Hare McCormick never could understand how the traveler, at home or abroad, could be indifferent to surroundings that affected the lives of human beings. She had understanding and sympathy for people, a compassion for human suffering, and a mind trained to penetrate the surface. Her articles were accepted and printed in The New York Times Magazine Section. In 1921, on the eve of a trip to the Continent, she sent a timid note to the late Carr V. Van Anda, then managing editor of The Times, asking if she might send him some dispatches from abroad. Mr. Van Anda replied: "Try it!" With that quasi permission, she sent in many that captured the mind of Carr Van Anda, and she was hired.

To her publisher, Arthur Hays Sulzberger, her readers are indebted, for he saw in Anne O'Hare McCormick a woman who would not compromise her ideals, a patriot whose writings always upheld the Four Freedoms. Mr. Sulzberger invited Mrs. McCormick in 1935 to join the editorial board. "You are to be the 'freedom' editor," he said. "It will be your job to stand up and shout whenever freedom is interfered with in any part of the world." She was the first woman to serve as a regular contributor to the editorial pages of The Times. In this capacity, her writings became prolific—a thrice-weekly column, frequent editorials, special features in the Magazine Section—and the brilliance of her mind generously gave itself to history.

With the selections of her writings in this book, an important span, 1925–1945, in American history is covered. In this period, giant struggles raged in major industrial conflicts. The machine age was upon us and we were trying it on for size, using diverse economic and political experiments to try to make it fit. Men searched for moral certainties to give them conviction in the face of such complexities. Mrs. McCormick recorded all this in her own way. She excelled in making a

serious point within a framework of complete naturalnes.,
she had an ability to landscape a scene with words.

Although her background of world travel and observatio.
always revealed itself in her writings, Mrs. McCormick was
American to the core. She understood our people and she believed passionately in the American Constitution. We find her
in 1929 extolling the Senate as a precious heritage in our
democratic way of life, and her frank series on the South is of
special significance today, as she analyzed the role of the
Negro with understanding and remarkable foresight and with
her usual compassionate appraisal.

Franklin D. Roosevelt received the special attention of
Mrs. McCormick as a world figure. Perhaps nowhere has
there been a more intimate recording of his personality, or a
more detailed impression of his mind at work on the job, than
through her personal interviews with him, described as only
she could. Although her sketches of him are kindly inspired,
she remained true to the journalistic code of keeping to facts
as she reported weakness as well as strength.

Mrs. McCormick held a reading audience which included
as many men as women, yet she never sacrificed her feminine
nature in the expression of her thoughts and observations.
She kept her heart associated with a keen and logical mind.
She believed in the special role of woman to restore and
preserve spiritual and moral values to benefit the whole of society. She challenged women to this task a few months before her death in New York City, May 29, 1954, when she
took time out to make her point in the only foreword to a
book * she ever wrote: ". . . women, and particularly American women in a time when the United States is thrust into a
position of unique power and influence, have the soul of the
nation in their keeping. They have a special obligation to

* *The Spiritual Woman—Trustee of the Future* (Harper and Brothers,
1955).

emphasize, preserve, and manifest in their own lives the spiritual values that are in danger of being lost in an age in which skepticism is a virtue and faith a vice."

Mrs. McCormick believed in the goals of the United Nations and her writing on the San Francisco meeting in 1945 is a sincere appeal to the peoples of the world to make this organization work as an instrument of peace.

In the course of her life a host of honors, both journalistic and academic, came to Anne O'Hare McCormick. She received honorary degrees from many universities and colleges, including Columbia, Fordham, Ohio State, Dayton, and New York universities, Elmira, Manhattan, Middlebury, Villanova, Lafayette, Smith, Wellesley, Mount St. Vincent, Wilson, and Rollins colleges, and the New Jersey College for Women.

Among other awards, she received The New York Evening Post Medal, 1934; the American Woman's Association Medal, 1939; the Theodore Roosevelt Memorial Medal of the Woman's Roosevelt Memorial Association, 1941; and the Gold Medal of the National Institute of Social Sciences, 1942.

Other honors include the Siena Medal of Theta Phi Alpha, 1944; University of Notre Dame Laetare Medal, 1944; International Altrusa Distinguished Service Award, 1945; Women's National Press Club Achievement Award, 1945; Chi Omega National Achievement Award, 1946; Theodore Roosevelt Distinguished Service Medal, 1950; and the William the Silent Award for Journalism, 1952. She also held membership in a number of societies, including the National Institute of Arts and Letters. She was a Chevalier of the French Legion of Honor. Mrs. McCormick also was a delegate to the United Nations Educational, Scientific and Cultural Organization Conferences in 1946 and 1948.

A special word of appreciation to those at The New York Times whose co-operation helped to make this book possible: I wish to thank Mr. Arthur Hays Sulzberger for his cordiality

and encouragement; Mr. Orvil E. Dryfoos for the necessary
arrangements; Mr. Ben Dalgin for his generous assistance;
Miss Marion Andrews, Mrs. McCormick's secretary, for her
friendly help; Mr. Chester M. Lewis and his capable staff for
their special reference assistance. Also to Mr. Mack Burke,
Mrs. McCormick's nephew, for his understanding of the project, and to Blanche Knopf, a lifelong friend of Mrs. Mc-
Cormick, for her sincere interest in preserving in publication
the writings of this noted woman journalist. Grateful appreciation to Elizabeth Ann Flinn, Alicia Winn, and Anne Mc-
Carthy, and a word of tribute to the New York Newspaper
Women's Club, New York City, for establishing an annual
scholarship in journalism for a graduate girl student, in memory of Anne O'Hare McCormick.

MARION TURNER SHEEHAN

New York City
May 14, 1956

CONTENTS

xv

Contents

THE WORLD AT HOME

[1] 1 9 2 5 *March 15.* ADVENTURING IN OUR TROPICAL EMPIRE. *America's prosperous holiday makers in Florida have not outgrown the pioneering spirit.*

MIAMI

America is still an adventure. One sees it in the wheat fields of the Northwest, where the last of the original breed gambles with a single crop against the caprice of nature, the most inexorable of all monopolists, and goes down fighting only when organized industry turns the frontier into a line of business and catches the frontiersman in the trap of diversified farming. One sees it in the oil fields of the Southwest, where for a gushing decade, office men and grocer clerks camped in a desert sown with derricks, tapping the perverse veins of the earth for the newest gold. And one sees it most unexpectedly in the playgrounds of Florida, where the solid and successful, loafing in the sun, get the scent of the last wilderness and rise shouting to chase the dream of another empire.

Adventure stirs the cool blood of the safely prosperous to make a Winter sport of pioneering. They do it vicariously, of course, getting the same kind of excitement out of developing that the grain speculator gets out of the chances of the wheat crop. A clever foreigner, native of the most shaken part of the Old World, watched with me the daily parade at a fashionable bathing beach. "How secure it all is," she said. "I rest in the security of America."

"Yes, but probably the ground under you is being sold at this moment and somebody is hatching schemes to fill up the ocean. If you come back next year it will be all changed."

"That's just it," she laughed. "You are so secure that you are not afraid of risks and change. It is not only safer but

3

more thrilling than Europe because, having no fear, you plunge, and anything may happen."

Remembering the French Riviera in the year after the war, before it was repopulated by Americans, one saw the point. There the holiday makers played with a kind of guilty bravado. There was no assurance in their sad attempt at carnival. They put it on, like people donning masks to fool themselves and knowing they were counterfeit. They were in no sense typical of the life they escaped from. On the American Riviera, on the contrary, we take the sun with an air of virtue and ownership. It is not a gift or an illusion, but the natural reward of success. We are at home and ourselves. I doubt if we are ever more ourselves than in the possession of our shore frontage on the Gulf Stream.

At the height of the season, indeed, Florida has all the fascination of a moving picture, in one crowded reel, of the headlong adventure that is America. We are all here, amplified and magnified—pioneer, bushwhacker, gold-digger, dreamer, loafer, bluffer, social climber—all of us that have made Our Country, Right or Wrong. In tourist camps, Winter home towns, resorts of fashion, Florida gathers from forty-eight States the essence of all that we are, from Covered Wagon to Society Column, and presents an entire season's run of the Great American Show.

The performance is unexpected because resorts are the last place in the world to look for any enterprise beyond the exploitation of tourists. The resort is the most nearly international of all human institutions. If there are any two things on earth more alike than two resorts, it is the ritual observed in both. In resorts, wherever they are, people who deny every other sort of dogma are thrilled by dogmatic custom into doing the same things in the same way at the same hour. Their remarks while doing it are inevitably the same in any language. The tables of the law regulating the life of resorters, from Deauville to Luxor, from Cannes to Palm Beach, must antedate the Ten Commandments, and are far less often broken.

Of all who conform to these universal ordinances, the American is perhaps the most rigid conformist. The Briton follows customs chiefly because he has made most of them. The Latin breaks loose whenever his individualism gets the better of his indolence. The Slav is a fatalist, moving only in revolutions. The Teuton is orderly by nature and training; but no one of them goes so far as the American when he makes a business of doing and saying the proper thing at the proper time.

The typical resorter is the lady visitor at Palm Beach who was dragged down on a recent glistening night to see the moonlight on Lake Worth. She brightened up when she saw other witnesses out for the spectacle. "After all," she sighed, gratified, "it is the thing to do. Everybody is here."

All resorters are gregarious, whether they herd in tourist camps or in the biggest hotels. Otherwise they would not be resorters. At Deauville, Biarritz and the Lido, bathers affect the same hour and congest the same small strips of sand and sea, no matter how long and silken is the available shore. But nowhere have I ever seen them more nearly unanimous and synchronous than at Miami and Palm Beach. It is now 12 o'clock and the bathing hour. The short shelf of beach directly in front of the Casino is covered with swimmers and spectators, mostly spectators, like a runner of bright Balkan embroidery cut off so shapely at the ends that, though I sit in the sands less than a hundred yards away, I am as much alone as if I were miles up the coast. No one strays from the corral, and by 1:30 the corral itself will be as empty for the rest of the day as if the ocean had been turned off.

All resorters dress alike. Their sartorial function is to march first in the profession of fashion, and they do it with military precision. They are in white when white is indicated; they gather themselves like Spartans into a single specified line; they split their costumes into one, two or three pieces, according to orders. I admit that Americans achieve by their greater regularity the best effect as spectacle, like a set costumed by one designer, and that no other people in the world dress so perfectly the part of the perfect resorter.

Americans shine at resorts. They are good at observing rules, particularly if the rules are not of their own making. They do not always look so happy and at ease as others, but they always look more correct. Watching them keeping step at the fashionable resorts of Europe, I have often wondered if, at that stage of our social progress, we really have any characteristic national gait.

Well, we have. Observing the same people, or their counterparts, back at Palm Beach and Miami, Ormond and Bellair, one makes the interesting discovery that Americans have neither Americanized European resorts, as Europe is fond of charging, nor Europeanized American resorts, as is often feared in the midlands. It is the inconsistent complaint of the French and Italians that we take possession of their paradises with the idea of making an America out of Europe, or that we buy up their old furniture in order to make a Europe out of America. Until they see us at home they can never realize how we suppress ourselves abroad to conform to their traditions, or how little Europe can be translated to this wide young world with a few shipments of Spanish tiles, Italian grilles and French tapestries.

Take Palm Beach, the most finished and reminiscent of our Winter colonies, the only retreat from boosters selling Florida climate by the acre. Palm Beach has imported successfully a great deal of Latin charm. Its Spanish and Italian villas are more consistently Spanish and Italian than anything in Italy or Spain. It has aged graciously and amazingly in the last five

years. Between the buildings so skilfully made old, and the
people so skilfully made young, it is a fine exhibit of the possi-
bilities of art. The cottagers have adopted the style that suits
the palm trees and the sky, used it with taste, and succeed
rather better than the Old World nowadays in living up to
their surroundings. Miami Beach is newer, bigger, less grave
and pretentious, but in another ten years it, too, will be old
and beautiful in the Mediterranean manner.

They will be, nevertheless, only more or less lovely and
exotic backgrounds for a life and an attitude toward life that
are peculiarly our own. Florida offers the best assurance that
we do not become Mediterranean by living in Mediterranean
houses in a Mediterranean climate. In the most charming
cloisters we remain an utterly uncloistered people. Our life
becomes the more public when we play. The enterprise of
our newspapers, added to something native and ingenuous in
ourselves, makes us the most reported and illustrated population on earth, and explains, perhaps, the pose and self-consciousness that distinguish us in our hours of ease.

All kinds of "prominents"—millionaires, politicians, prize-
fighters, movie stars, cartoonists, Ambassadors, society folk—
are gathered into the revolving show case by industrious reporters and camera men. We begin early. At the annual Children's Party at Palm Beach, where lovely babies appeared as
delectable valentines, it seemed to me the youngsters spent
most of their time having their pictures taken for the papers.
They accepted it as a matter of course. Five-year-olds posed
as easily for the photographer, and gave their names and
pedigree as nonchalantly to busy reporters, as if they were
at the end instead of the beginning of a career in the public
eye.

Even more distinguishing is our passion for improvement.
Our worst enemies—seeing Americans here at rest!—cannot
accuse us of being satisfied with things as they are. The gods

of our machine are effort and enterprise. It does not occur to us to sit down idly in places that may be turned to better account. Not since the days of the Corsairs, at least, has it been borne in upon the unimaginative Europeans relaxing on the French and Italian Rivieras that they might auction off the climate, sell the mountain sides and turn their beaches into allotments. People of that sort, said a St. Petersburg booster to whom I mentioned this damning fact, never will be able to pay their debts. He reminded me of the impoverished Frenchman urged by an American friend to cut up his estate at Cape Ferrat into salable lots. "But then it will be a business," he protested. "Where shall I take my repose?"

Resorts are exploited as much in other parts of the world as they are here, but they are exploited merely as resorts. The reason for the difference may be that the Old World has long ago exhausted its capacity to boom and has tapped all its known resources; it is more probable that we develop because we do not enjoy our repose. We are not more industrious than other peoples; we are only younger and less tired. It is impossible for us to see potential building sites anywhere and not start developing. When there is no scenery, as in Florida, we make it, and when there is, we sell it.

Are we then a young people that can neither rest nor play? Do we flock to the most expensive playgrounds in the world only to demonstrate that we are not at home en plaisances? To the categories of the frustrated who depress and prosper the rising novelist must we add these colonies of the pleasure-seekers who cannot enjoy?

The answer to all these questions is an emphatic no. Contradicting our display of nervous energy and speculative enterprise, it remains true that the spectators far outnumber the performers at any of our shows. The side lines, especially at resorts, are superlatively long and overweighted. We have the biggest gallery to be seen anywhere. American hotel

verandas are on a scale unique in the world: they must be
built to accommodate the crowds constantly engaged in "sitting around." The crowds do not even read.

Evidently we can relax! We can do nothing as consecu-
tively and ponderously as anybody. And we can frivol. Witness the swarms of the middle-aged cavorting day and night
on the dancing floor of every equivalent of the Cocoanut
Grove and the Club de Montmartre. What we cannot do is
sparkle at these occupations. Our animation is reserved for
the auction and the bally-hoo. When we get down to business
we are about the only tomboys left in the world. Compared
to these booming coasts, the Riviera is sober and settled
down. The maritime Alps have beckoned adventurers since
the days of the Chaldeans; the remains of Roman boosting
break into the golf course at Monte Carlo, and what is left
of Phoenician enterprise paves terraces for modern villas at
Beaulieu.

But it is all over. Of the go-getters of the Valley of the Nile
there remains only the buried loot. Deauville and the Lido
are cynical and sophisticated in ways beyond our understanding. The sports of St. Moritz demand too much muscle of a
people fast forgetting how to walk. We are not really at home
among these embers and these aliens, though our talent for
mimicry enables us to give them on their own ground an imi-
tation almost better than the real thing.

Can we play? Look at us on the home fields. A few hundreds take to the surf on the Southern beaches; a few thousands play the golf courses, which are the first thing provided
in every new development; some fish in the sporting waters
along the keys; others amuse themselves with launches and
yachts and sailing boats. The second-best sport is spending
money.

But development, and watching development, is our real
game. The foreigner who sees us reveling in business and

thence concludes that we do not know how to play fails to understand that business is our true level.

Of course, there is a corollary to these random impressions of American Winter resorts and resorters. It may be that our delight in building docks and development projects in the sands where we go to play, our hilarity in money-making and our somewhat dull extravagance in money-spending are signs not only of the energy but also of the limitations of youth. Perhaps we lack the English content in pure holiday and the French seriousness in pleasure because our interests are too shallow and our experience is too circumscribed. One may draw the usual indictment. One may wonder that with all its suavity, luxury and Winter bloom Florida should remain an intellectual desert. This visitor's only conclusion is that it is a great show.

[2] 1 9 2 9 *November 10*. IN DEFENSE OF A SCORNED SENATE. *Despite the fact that it serves as a Forum for perverse and long-winded oratory, the upper house remains our one assembly that functions as a deliberative body of government.*

WASHINGTON

The Senate goes on talking. As the debate on tariff rates drags along, day after weary day, the gallery grows thinner. The conducted groups of sightseers constantly circulating around the Capitol stumble into rows of empty seats, sit for a few minutes, sigh, and shuffle out again. No mind but a Senator's can focus for three hours on agar-agar, even though the Senator enlivens a grim discourse on seaweeds with gestures like an Egyptian frieze come to life. From schedule to schedule the argument drones on. It is in-

terrupted at regular intervals by Senator La Follette,* official
objector for the farm belt, who asks questions with the effect
of a smart boy teasing his elders. When a Senator on the right
wakes up suddenly and inquires what paragraph is under
discussion, no one but the speaker can answer.

Digressions are fewer than usual, Senator Heflin * has
heard about the Fascists; he introduces a resolution against
the Romanization of the United States. Senator Cole Blease *
shakes his fist over conditions in the District of Columbia. Or
a sharp squall blows up over the lobby investigation and the
case of Senator Bingham.* No more is needed to emphasize
the obituary character of the debate. Senator Reed * saddens
Senator Smoot * by admitting that the tariff bill is dead, but
he fights on doggedly in a lost cause, head hunched forward
and jaw set, sole defender on the floor of the industrial interests of Pennsylvania. The rest of the Republican regulars
slump behind their desks; all the jauntiness of the first days of
this session is long since departed.

A clerk in a cinnamon-colored suit comes in with a sheaf of
papers. "A message from the President of the United States,"
he intones gloomily. Pages distribute the sheets among the
Senators, who learn without interest that the American Minister to Albania, once a reporter in the press gallery, is to be
transferred to Persia. That faraway event does not pull them
down the long desert trek from one incredible court to another, nor drag into the Senate Chamber all the tenses and
tensions that lie between the heart of Europe and the heart
of Asia. The Senators go on talking about tariffs, wrestling in
their own way to measure and adjust, by 6 per cent here and
100 per cent there, the same unbridgable differences between centuries and civilizations.

* Senator Robert La Follette (R), Wisconsin; Senator James T. Heflin
(D), Alabama; Senator Coleman L. Blease (D), South Carolina; Senator
Hiram Bingham (R), Connecticut; Senator David A. Reed (R), Pennsyl-
vania; Senator Reed Smoot (R), Utah.

The session of the Senate here suggested—and it is not one session only—is not typical for the reason that attention is too concentrated on one subject. The Senate is just now attending more strictly than is its custom to the business of rewriting the tariff. But it is sufficiently typical of the desultory habits of the upper house of Congress, its slow tempo, its unregulated range and freedom of debate, its general unruliness, to explain why it is so often and so vainly called to order. The Senate is perverse, long-winded, vain, unmanageable. It obstructs the orderly processes of legislation and embarrasses the Executive. It particularly exasperates the American business men, who hold conventions every year and noontide meetings every day to discuss the wastefulness of talk.

The more thoroughly the business mind prevails in this country the more it inclines to regard politics as a species of unnecessary noise. Listen to the comment of the business executive on the lobby investigation: "You can't expect a politician to understand business." Observe the captains of commerce reacting to debate on legislative issues. "Oh, politics!" they shrug, as if politics were a form of juvenile delinquency beneath the notice of makers of ice-cream cones or sellers of radio sets. Business observes the House dispatching its business and the Senate going on forever. The Senate, it says, as some one remarks of Senator Borah,* is always in session; moreover, it lives on wind and limelight. The persistent vitality of the Senate is like a violation of economic law.

It is true. Regard these elders of the people and explain if you can why a Senate continues to thunder in America, completely overshadowing the lower house, while in every other country it is reduced to silence and shorn of power. They are not decorative, they are often dull; for useless sound they merit all the gibes of the paragraphers and for lost motion all the irritation of the efficiency experts. But if these heads sur-

---

* Senator William E. Borah (R), Idaho.

mounted togas instead of nondescript sack suits and assorted collars, the Senators would look very like the old Romans dug out of the Forum and assembled once again in a room in the Capitoline Museum. The Roman Senators were not supplanted; as long as the Roman people had power, so had they. Perhaps the parallel holds for the American Senators. They hang onto their power, to prerogatives, with the same tenacity you see in the bulldog heads of Rome, those unmistakable masks of politicians, men who dominated by talk.

And if the Senate did not talk, who would? If this incessant voice were still, where now would public issues be debated? Where especially would the contrary mind in government be expressed in this country? There is little enough interest in politics in the United States, and if the Senate did not force the public business into the headlines by investigations, oppositions, gallery playing, no one would. In justice to the Senate it must be said that it is the only Parliament we have left, the one assembly that functions as a deliberative body. It is small enough to move without moving en masse. It resists the logical development of the modern Legislature, which must work like a machine if it is to work at all in a machine system, by an overemphasis on the individual. It makes a virtue of negation and delay. Only in the Senate can the Noes ever have it, or the independent stand alone, or the minority manoeuvre itself into a majority.

No doubt the House is more representative of the country at large. It is certainly more popular. The very transiency of the tenure of its members, elected oftener and by smaller units of population, makes the House more responsive to the currents of change in the national life. It reflects the increasing size of cities and the consequent weight in government of business and industry. With the passage of the reapportionment act, it will reflect this transition even more accurately. The House is a machine, steered by the Rules and

Ways and Means Committees and easily controlled by the Speaker. It is the legislative machine of the administration in power, and passes the laws it is supposed to pass, in the time in which it is expected to pass them.

The House is realist and gets things done. Just what the House gets done seems of less importance. In our impatience of delay we prefer to correct rather than prevent mistakes. That is the method of many successful executives, who act on the theory that quick decisions that may turn out wrong are less wasteful than the deliberation necessary for right decisions.

The Senate represents the older method of looking before you leap. What the Senate really represents, of course, is the earlier conception of the United States as forty-eight equal and sovereign Commonwealths. It is a league of nations. But it expresses, too, an earlier America, a country wide spaced, leisurely, agricultural and conversational, a land of corner saloons and crossroads groceries dedicated to political argument. The Senate is no economic parliament; it is an old-fashioned political democracy, wherein the best talker wins. It struggles to preserve the American tradition; valiantly, and sometimes with astonishing success, it swims against the tide.

The paradox of its position is that the harder it fights to conserve, the more "radical" it is considered. The House, so modern that it is a kind of legislative collective, is the right arm of the government. The Senate, so traditional that it plays up the individual and shouts for all the dogmas of the founders, is by that tradition turned to the left. There could be no more suggestive indication of the political direction we are taking than this emergence of the Senate as the last hope of the liberals.

The pending tariff bill furnishes a perfect illustration of the function of the Senate and poses at the same time a very interesting question. With few changes, it will be remembered, the Hawley bill was passed in record time by the House. There was a good deal of editorial approbation of the promptitude and efficiency of the procedure. The Senate, on the contrary, has been sharply taken to task because it argued about tariff all Summer. After rejecting practically all the administrative features of the bill, adding the debenture feature, haggling over the question of the "American valuation" of imports, which Mr. Grundy testifies is the really important provision, and voting to take away from the President the power he now has to change duties at will, the Senate did not get down to a discussion of rates and schedules until after the middle of October. Meantime, as a sideline, it launched an investigation of the tariff lobby, confounding the tariff-makers by broadcasting the well-known methods by which tariffs are made.

By the Senate is here meant the Senate majority, the coalition of Democrats and Progressives, now at last attacking rates in its own leisurely and loquacious fashion. The point is that without the inefficiency and contrariness of the Senate, we should now enjoy the lobbyists' tariff the House passed so promptly. And the question is: What and where is representative government? Do we elect leaders to shape our opinions or followers to enact them into laws? Because it now transpires, what nobody seemed to guess until the Senate started making trouble and delay, that only the manufacturers wanted the new tariff, anyway!

It begins to look as if the issue were to be sharply drawn between those business interests known as Big Business and the powers now controlling the Senate. Business does not like the three-party picture presented by the upper house. It is irritated by uncertain and shifting majorities. It distrusts and disdains the political tactics and the political mentality. Everybody shares the idea that the politician is of a lower order of intellect than the commercial and industrial geniuses who are the architects of our prosperity. Yet somehow it happens, as it has happened recently, that when the mind of the great business executive is pitted against the minds of the Senate, the politician does not suffer by comparison. At its worst, the Senatorial mind can be trivial, sentimental and complacent beyond belief. Discussion in the Senate Chamber is often as shallow and unreal as a high school debate. But at that the political view is seldom as narrow as the business view, and never as credulous.

At its best the debate is very good indeed. When the Senate listened to Ramsay MacDonald, a Briton as self-made as the best American, it learned that there is no parity between England and the United States in the use and inflection of the mother tongue. The Socialist Prime Minister speaks English more beautifully than any Senator. A good many Senatorial speakers carry independence to the point of rebelling against the rules of grammar and indulging in vagaries of pronunciation one hopes will not be adopted by the young students of political science in the galleries. Old-timers say that the literary level of the speeches is not what it used to be. The general comment on the wide knowledge of literature displayed by Senator Cutting * in his protest against tariff censorship indicates how few "literary treats" the Senate enjoys. Senator Glass * and Senator Borah are distinguished as readers and scholars, Senator Walsh *, Senator Norris * and Senator La Follette for the thoroughness of their preparation of the subjects they discuss, Senator Reed for his force and tenacity, Senator Caraway * for the biting sarcasm of his rejoinders. In devastating invective Senator Reed * of Missouri has no successor, but the impromptu give-and-take debate is often

---

* Senator Bronson M. Cutting (R), New Mexico; Senator Carter Glass (D), Virginia; Senator David I. Walsh (D), Massachusetts; Senator George W. Norris (R), Nebraska; Senator Thaddeus H. Caraway (D), Arkansas; Senator James A. Reed (D), Missouri.

witty and pungent. All the Senators are fluent, many are eloquent; what one misses most is the glow and heat of ideas.

Two observers relieved the tedium of a recent session by checking over the roll-call and attempting to rank the Senators according to their ability. Out of the ninety-five on the list they put ten in the first rank and sixteen in the second, a fair enough proportion of topnotchers in any such assembly. The idle classification became interesting when a dozen others were asked to pick out the first ten, and in each case made the same choice. They always began with Borah and ended with Walsh. It is worth noting that the political parties are about equally represented in the lists, and that some of the elect—like the late Senator Burton * and the dean of the Senate, Senator Warren *—are almost never heard upon the floor. Probably the best brains of the Senate show up in the work done in committee rooms.

"In the days before Senators were elected by popular vote," said one of the observers, "perhaps two-thirds were above the average in ability and one-third were below. Now I should reverse the proportion. But I should say the ten first-class minds in the Senate are equal to the best minds in any profession. Moreover, the standard of integrity is higher than the level of ability. Some Senators represent 'interests' and are subject to influence of one kind or another, but not more than two members of this body could be imagined as corruptible."

"Old boys" the Senators seem from the gallery, sometimes vain and pompous old boys, enormously pleased with themselves and their position. Interviewed one by one—and they are almost invariably approachable and friendly—they seem abler than when on the floor. Often they are abler than they dare to appear; such is the debasing effect of popular election

---

* Senator Theodore E. Burton (R), Ohio; Senator Lindsay C. Warren (D), North Carolina.

and the Congressional Record. The chamber is a debating club, and the "old boys" are decidedly clubby. In general their attitude toward one another is one of demonstrative affection. They are always literally patting one another on the back and the opponents in the most caustic arguments usually leave the scene of hostilities arm in arm.

Since the Senate renews itself slowly, only one-third of its membership changing at a time, it has an effect of continuity lacking in the House, which can be completely transformed every two years. The six-year term makes for independence; for several years the Senators need not concentrate on re-election. Trammeled by no rules except the rules they impose upon themselves, they are at liberty to be as irrelevant and out of order as they please. It is the presence of the irregulars, however, which gives the assembly its great effect of anarchy and independence. That mobile column swinging between the two sides of the Chamber has power at any moment to change its political character. The Progressives are the goad of the majority, and its despair. Members of this same group cut into the Democratic strength in Wilson's time and kept us out of the League of Nations. Now in Hoover's they turn the Republicans into a minority to block the industrial East in its attempt to reap special benefits out of farmers' Congress. They have kept three Presidents in their place, and the fourth may find that the best technical equipment is no match for expert political strategy.

Only ultra-conservatives could call this group radical. Its leader, now therefore the real leader of the Senate, is one of the most conservative men in public life. Senator Borah is so strong a nationalist that his whole strength as Chairman of the Foreign Relations Committee has been exerted to save us from any international commitments. The one consistent motive of his career in the Senate is the determination to maintain in their pristine purity the doctrines and traditions of the Fathers of the Republic. Of all the Senators he is the inflexible constitutionalist and legalist, the keenest to discover and resist encroachments of the Executive on the legislative branch of the government. He opposed the flexible provision of the tariff bill because it is not his idea, he told the President, of "the division of the departments of the government under the Constitution." His objection to our adherence to the World Court is primarily the objection of a careful and canny lawyer.

The Senate, too, like its present chief, clings stubbornly to its traditional prerogatives in a political structure in which all such traditions are weakening. It holds out for the political as opposed to the economic, solutions for independence against efficiency, for democracy between the States, democracy between classes. It upholds principles, now under question that one day we may be eager to reaffirm.

In defense of the Senate, one might go so far as to say that its virtue is verbosity and its function is obstruction. Better that the most enlightened legislation should be lost or delayed than that, as in the House, it should never be debated. So let the Senate go on talking. If its talk is hard to bear, think how much more unendurable would be its silence!

[3]   1 9 2 9   *December 1*. THE WEST CHALLENGES THE EAST. *The clash of two states of mind, with industry on one side and, on the other, agriculture seeking political equality, has swept over the Senate to confound the lawmakers.*

WASHINGTON

On a weary day when the Senate was diagnosed as a case of nerves, and reckless allusions to Communists and wild jackasses, common and preferred Senators, were cited in proof of Senatorial brain fag, it happened that an official air-tester man was called into the Chamber to analyze the exhausted atmosphere. Armed with an apparatus resembling a nursery bottle screwed on top of a long rod, he proceeded from left to right, from chair to cloakroom, sampling impartially the dry, devitalized air. The test had no comic significance. It was not a boyish prank of the wrinkled "freshmen" kicking over the traces and adding a new bloc to the confused pattern of the session. It was not intended to measure how much moisture and fresh oxygen are used up on a tariff schedule, or burned up in the heat of personal remarks. It was intended for nothing at all—alas!—but a check on the ventilating system.

But what if there were an instrument for taking soundings in the stale air of debate! What if some accurate gauge could register the humidity of the political atmosphere! One sat in the gallery, bemused by the idea, pondering what the magic bottle would reveal if it were plunged in the currents and counter-currents blown into this hall from so many local climates. In the beginning there were forecasters in plenty to predict that this Congress would run into storms, but none to foresee that they would be so violent as to blow down party walls and tie up traffic. And now that it ends, as inconclusively as life itself, where is the handy mechanism to point the meaning and direction of its confused and unexpected course?

It may well be that this abortive parliament has written a chapter as searching and significant as any in our recent history. The fulfillment of a campaign promise, it became in fact a platform of debate for the real issues swept aside by the passions of the campaign. All the vital questions which nobody bothered to discuss then have since invaded the Senate. Like a slow yeast working in a heavy dough, these questions have finally leavened the lump, so that at last, as in

Russia after the revolution, everything that was at the bottom is on top, and all that was on top sinks to the bottom.

The session was not fruitless. Between April and the last week of November it established and financed a Federal Farm Board which is leading us into the largest experiment in cooperative marketing of farm products ever attempted except by the Soviets. It changed the complexion of our immigration. It argued a tariff bill nearly to death and exposed the processes of tariff making, to the end that the old whole-sale, high-pressure, grab-bag methods of rate-raising will never again be safe and successful, and tariff policy as a whole is bound to be re-examined in what scientists would call the light of modern discoveries. It changed the outlook of the Administration by revealing the awkwardness and uncertainty of Mr. Hoover in handling the primary implements of politics, which are politicians.

Finally—and this is where the action begins for the top gallery—it proved that the oldest and raciest issue in the national life, the clash between two states of mind, known loosely and variously as East and West, industry and agriculture, city and country, is as loud and hearty as ever. Heartier, in fact, because not in years has Young Lochinvar tilted with the belted earls of the factories with such a show of prowess and victory. The weight in the unequal contest has strangely shifted. You have only to listen to the gaudy epithets hurled from East to West instead of in the contrary direction to recognize that this anger is the shocked anger of defeat.

The industrial States reel between two lines of attack; on one side are solid earthworks against any increased duties on manufactured goods, on the other a joyous skyrocketing of all tariffs on foodstuffs. They reel into a political abyss. "Behold the new campaign committee for the Progressives: Moses,* Reed and Bingham!" chuckles Senator La Follette.

* Senator George H. Moses (R), New Hampshire.

And Senators who all through the session sat tight and voted straight with the Old Guard toward the last stampeded in a kind of panic to "the Western crowd." It is now literally "the Western crowd." The East is for the moment reduced to its geographical size in a continent where all the rolling leagues beyond the Alleghenies, remember, are psychologically "West." Even the brigaded members of the House, who passed the Hawley bill with hardly a murmur, return from their constituencies ready to "talk small" on tariff in a sense that Mr. Grundy did not dream of.

The question is: Is it real, this exciting prologue of thud and blunder? When the Senators fling verbal brickbats across the chamber, New Hampshire against Nebraska, Pennsylvania against Dakota, Connecticut against the field and the field against Connecticut; when the big round whole of the Republican majority cracks into three local fractions, is it politics, nerves or the irresistible ferment of truth? In a word, is the cleavage between two powerful geographic abstractions as actual as it is political, and if actual, what is the meaning of the astonishing swagger of agriculture in the mother country of the machine?

Actual? But nothing in the world is as real as local patriotism; most of us have so little else to shout about that we cheer for the self-projection which is the town and State of our business and abode. As much as the name we are the address on the envelope. To think of politics as anything but life reduced to formula, sometimes indeed to absurdity, is to miss the massive drama of the most human of the arts. Alone among them all, politics has for its raw material men; it selects and groups and orders men as the painter in his smaller fashion composes the elements of his landscape or the musician picks out of the vibrating air the sounds he harmonizes. Be sure that only the actual has lasting political vitality. No issue comes hammering into Parliaments, much less stays there generation after generation, unless it is an organic issue, tangled in the structure of life itself.

Such is the classic issue that in its latest incarnation upsets the efficient schedule of the Hoover Administration. It was first raised when our ancestors began to feel herded in the original Colonies and struck out into the open spaces of the Northwest Territory. With every subsequent migration the political and moral distance lengthened between the pioneers into new country and the towns they left behind. To the prairie, though the American frontier has long since passed back to the roaring furnaces of Detroit and Pittsburgh, the restless jungles of New York, the No Man's Land of the Chicago Loop, the East and the city are still the zones of soft living, special privilege and easy money. To the East the settled and solid prairie is the back country of Mr. Grundy, unstable, rustic, half-tamed, with no stake in big business and no competence to legislate for industry.

Before the Civil War our industries were really infants, but they grew so fast during that struggle that at its close the contest between agriculture and industry developed an animus second only to the antagonism between North and South and ranged itself on the same lines and on nearly the same terrain it agitates today. The decade after Versailles is so like the decade after Appomattox that our magic era, the breathless period when we motored en masse to the top of the world, is almost literally described in "The Tragic Era" of Claude Bowers. Agents of interests seeking special government favors swarmed the lobbies and corridors of the Capitol during the Congress of 1865. The new industrialists were aggressively self-assertive and log rolling for higher tariffs was so impudent that Godkin * in The Nation denounced the lobby and the unscientific method of fixing rates, "secretly as

* E. L. Godkin, first editor of The Nation, a weekly journal devoted to politics, literature, science, and art.

Congress does," as "one of the most fertile sources of corruption ever opened in any age or country." In the same language heard in the Senate yesterday, the New York Chamber of Commerce of the 1860's protests that increased tariffs "would mar the prosperity of agriculture by increasing the cost of its supplies without enhancing the cost of its products."

Listen to Mr. Bowers, reporting not the special session of Mr. Hoover but that of Andrew Johnson:

"The penetrating could easily see the significance of it all —the passing of influence in government from the agricultural to the industrial element. One day an Iowa representative warned Thad Stevens 'of a great storm coming from the West.' So stubborn was the protest of the farmers that a gesture of conciliation was made to them by abandoning the plan to increase the duty on pig iron $6 a ton. . . .

"But it was in the Senate where the most bitter battles between the industrialists and the agriculturists were staged, and there Senator Grimes of Iowa led for the farmers, strongly supported by the Midwestern Republican press. When a tariff measure seemed certain of passage, The Chicago Tribune said, 'If Andrew Johnson has a grain of political sagacity he will veto the bill and set himself up as the champion of the people against extortion and robbery.' With Hendricks interpolating, to encourage the rumpus, the Democrats sat back and watched the enemy clawing at one another. Henderson of Missouri ridiculed the argument that the tariff would help the farmers who were then burning their corn because they could not find a market. But it was Grimes of Iowa who bore the brunt of the battle. His insurgency enraged the protectionists. . . ."

The deadly parallel is worth pointing because it accentuates the most striking aspect of the present situation. The penetrating ones who saw so clearly in 1865 that agriculture was losing influence in government would be confused to see the same storm from the West blowing strongly on the same scene sixty years later. The historian noted the farming interests passing from the political stage in what he calls our "counter-revolutionary" epoch. Yet here they are, in 1929, as vehement as when industry was young, exerting more power than they did seven or eight years ago, when the farmer was as flat as the stock gambler is today and no one thought to lower his taxes or call high-power conferences to break his fall.

For this phenomenon there is no present parallel. In other countries the agrarians lose to the extent that industry gains. In England the once domineering land is now a mere background for another struggle. In Germany, second to the United States in industrial development, the fight for power is between the employers and employees of industry. Even in France, last stronghold of the small and independent farmer, the contest, so far as it can be defined, is waged within the industrial blocs, Left and Right. The Russian Revolution is slowly and ruthlessly industrializing itself against the power of the land; the Soviets are packed against the peasants as a defense of the urban proletariat from agrarian reaction. That is the inevitable path. Only Mussolini, with an intuition that may be prescience, strives to avert the common fate of nations by restoring prestige to the husbandman.

What does it signify, then, that in the United States, where industry has attained a kind of supernatural productiveness, and the city has become a mountain of smoke and steel upon every sky, the agricultural regions are able to win even strategic battles? The obvious answer would be that this is not a clean-cut struggle between agriculture and industry. The West is full of factories and the East is full of farms. Our greatest industrial concentration is on the Eastern borders of the West. New England contains as much primeval forest as Montana, and within fifty miles of the national capital are sections more backward and primitive than any to be found in the West. There is no place where pavement ends in this macadamized land. The country is so urbanized and the city so suburbanized that the rural population spends half its time in the city and half the urban population lives in the country.

Yet it is also obvious that the main business of the narrow and populous strip called East is manufacturing and the main business of all the rest of the country is farming, and that the two sections look upon economic and social landscapes as distinct as the pinnacles of Manhattan from the peaks of Idaho, and breathe a political atmosphere as different as the relaxing breath of Washington from the keen air of Minnesota. Space alone makes separate worlds for the Texan and the Rhode Islander; the dwellers in little mill valleys cannot see eye to eye with plainsmen whose fields are a hundred miles square. Space, and the fact that in these spaces live people more nearly 100 per cent American than in the East, less diluted by Europe, transplanted Puritans preoccupied with political liberty and moral law and precept. As in America the machine has not made the industrial States Socialist, so the farm has not made the prairie States conservative; to the "backward States" the manufacturing areas seem sunk in political reaction. The "West"—and this includes the South— is strong in a sense of injustice, and also because it has a livelier faith in all American institutions.

Still the focal question is unanswered. One hesitates to offer an explanation that seems to run counter to the natural course of progress, but after checking findings in the field against observations in Washington, the only place in America where East and West really meet, it seems to me that we are witnessing the beginning of the come-back of agriculture. If true, that is a sensational statement. It implies that the Senate reveals a real tendency no one has yet formulated. I believe we can go further and say that the West is not only growing in power but that it will grow stronger yet, so that the East will find itself forced to make terms on a new basis of equality. And by the West is here meant not a state of mind, or a geographical division, but the agricultural interests as such. And this in spite of several well-known facts: that farmers are fewer by millions than they were fifteen years ago and that their number must continue to decrease; that towns grow larger and villages disappear; that the small farm is profitless and fading from the picture; above all that the march of industry is inexorable and that factory smokestacks are winning over grain elevators in every rural region.

Against these facts may be ranged others, more prophetic. The first is the American farmer himself. He is not and never has been a peasant in the European sense, a being rooted in the soil and instinctively attached to it. Such peasantry as settled on this land has for the most part been squeezed out in the slow grind of a disastrous decade. The fittest survive. To the West the farm is more and more a business, endurable only if it can be worked to pay, pooled to pay, mechanized to pay, or held until the spreading town turns it into a happy homes allotment. In any case it must pay. The second fact is the corporation farm, the experimental farm, the specialty farm, the rise in every agricultural State of a generation educated to operate and manage collective farm enterprises. Added to these, the result of agitation, education, macadam and motor cars, is the new and enormous self-consciousness of the farm as an industry. The 1930 farm State is no more like that of 1865, or 1920, than the plowshare is like the combine.

It follows that the fewer farms and farmers the more powerful they will be! That is to say that the more organized, enlarged, mechanized, incorporated the farm becomes the more its influence will be felt in politics. Industrialized, the farm can assert itself against all other industries; as factories increase in the farm States, more industries will depend on the farm and vote with the farm. In the last twenty-five years this country has evolved the new factory standard of mass production and thereby manacled or liberated humanity— the word depends on whether you find the present pace of life monstrous or thrilling. It is not impossible to imagine that in the next two or three decades we shall have reduced the more stubborn soil to the same regimentation and developed in the process a breed of land lords before whom the steel kings will be as helpless as is their representative in the Senate today.

If the air tester in the Senate could take spiritual soundings, perhaps he could detect, rolling in from dim fields like a broken and fabulous tide, the first wave of the new agriculture—the West driving its Eastern machines against the East. Only yesterday most of the rebellions in the world were against the landed interests; from feudal times until yesterday power has always resided in land. Today's revolt is against the barons of industry. The deep instinct of the human race for equilibrium strikes against unbalanced power wherever it is concentrated. Therefore, when agriculture takes a fresh spurt of political power in the very system in which industry has reached its highest development, we may regard it not as a brake on progress but as one of those reactions that act as correctives to progress.

As a final indication that there is life in the old farm yet and that as an issue it has indestructible vitality, take the attitude of Mr. Hoover. As the special session closed, it belatedly appeared that he favored the agricultural tariff bill insisted upon by the Progressives from the beginning. He it was who gave the impulse to the action of the Young Guard in deserting the old regulars and practically joining the rest of the Chamber in raising the duties on farm products and leaving the industrial schedules as they were in the Fordney-

McCumber Bill.* There are two possible explanations of this last-minute change of tactics. Either Mr. Hoover was all along in sympathy with the Progressives and the Democrats and was placed in a false position in having to stand by the old-line high protectionists, an interpretation hardly supported by the smooth passage of the bill through the administration House. Or, like the "Western crowd" in House and Senate, the President has also heard the voice of the country. Both reasons for the revised and happier ending of his extra session are probably true. For Mr. Hoover himself belongs to the "Western crowd." Temperamentally, he stands somewhere between Ohio and Kansas. His move away from the tariff die-hards is one of the most significant circumstances in the whole situation. Uncertain and impatient in dealing with politicians, in reading the mind of the country, perhaps one should say in thinking with the mind of the country, Mr. Hoover is almost as good as the humidity gauge applied to the dried-up air in the Senate Chamber.

It is now fairly clear that the President will never be a great party leader, because he is not a party man; his mind is essentially non-partisan, which explains his strength in the country and his weakness in Congress. The regular session will be marked by continued lack of team-work between the Executive and the Legislature. It is clear also that tariff is dead as a popular issue; any further tinkering with tariff in this or future administrations will be a downward revision of all schedules, agricultural as well as industrial, to bring our trade policy into some relation with the world we live in. Clearest of all is that the political center of this country moves further West. In the new American countryside, which is neither truly rural nor truly urban, and unlike any other that

* The Fordney-McCumber Bill, enacted September 21, 1922, gave the Tariff Commission power to suggest that the President increase or decrease rates not more than 50% of original rate on any item to meet competition.

ever was—a countryside factory-made and forever listening in—the national policies will more and more be tested. That is the news the special "extra" of Congress has managed to convey.

[4] 1 9 3 0 *May 25*. THE SOUTH: EMPIRE AND PROVINCE. *The new industrial system assaulting the traditional citadels of a tenacious provincialism.*

NEW ORLEANS

From the Potomac to the Mississippi is no great journey. New motor highways run straight and smooth most of the way. "Specials" and "Limiteds" with alluring names make nothing of the distance but a blur of spreading towns, shacks scattered in weedy cotton fields, cypress trees wading in swamps, broomsedge fading into palmetto, ragged canebrake, and finally the brilliant rotogravure beaches of the American tropics. Going South by that route is hardly more than an overnight change of scene and climate, but it has the cardinal advantage of all short cuts; it gets there.

There is another road. It zigzags on locals between the mountains and the sea; shoots off on tangents across tobacco fields and cotton fields and into the magic mildew of the swamp; stops to listen to towns talking, towns with a Past and towns with a Future, the first filled with tourists and the second with conventions, and towns crowded enough without any visitor but the Present, harrowing the elders like the "rousin'ment" of the Summer revival.

By that route you can go South forever without arriving anywhere that might be called a conclusion. But you will have the hardy experience of seeing the oldest, most conservative, most American America in a panoramic confusion of change. This America claims to be the only homogeneous

section of the United States, and it is, uncorrupted by foreign
blood, unmarked even by those migrations from one part of
the country to another by which New England, for instance,
is set in waves across the continent, from Lake Erie to the
Rockies. The South has trickled out of its borders, mostly
toward big cities and the East. It has milled back and forth
within its own limits, the Georgian to Carolina, the Missis-
sippian to Georgia and vice versa. On the whole, it has remained static compared to other sections, and, aside from
the push to Florida and the commercial centers, the rest of
the country has moved in every direction but south.

Yet in this homogeneous country you meet strange peoples,
and all varieties of mental and physical climate. The two
races who live side by side and worlds apart, in a relativity
as subtle as Einstein's, are hardly more separate than are the
mill villages from other communities, the cropper from the
landlord, the mountaineer from the lowlander, the bayou
from the Piedmont. Living in the South attains a grace and
dignity that inspire foreign critics to acclaim it the spiritual
oasis of modern America and sinks to a level so far below the
national standard that vast areas are as poor and primitive,
as out of touch with the Machine Age, as if they were in
Albania. In general, the South may be explained as a difference of time as much as of geography. The zigzag takes you
not only from plane to plane but from century to century.
Epochs clash, not only the old South and the new, but America as it is and as it used to be.

The Spring flowered all along the way and was nowhere in
full bloom. I was too early for the azaleas in the enchanted
gardens of Charleston and too late for the Azalea Trail at
Mobile. The magnolias did not oblige with the romantic aisles
they can create when all the glossy trees put forth their
waxen petals at the same hour. In Savannah the dogwood
died in the little parks that break into the loveliest of South-

ern Main Streets, while the buds were only beginning to glimmer in a thicket behind a mill village in Middle Georgia. The wild iris and crocus of the North embroidered the slopes of Lookout Mountain at the same time that japonica braved the smoke of Birmingham, and April roses, cream and crimson, were already overblown in the gardens of Mississippi.

Always the prime of the Spring was just behind or just ahead, until at New Orleans it was gone, and Summer baked the levees and filled with heavy shade and scent the gardens of Prytania Street and the courtyards in the French Quarter. It is the traveler's usual fate to miss the local perfection, but in this case, besides giving me a dozen Springs instead of one, the moving and elusive season had the value of a symbol. For there are as many Souths as there were Springs, as many stages of development and as much local color. This is no flat and narrow land, of uniform topography and simultaneous fruitfulness, like the prairie States of the West. Much less is the human landscape on that level. A one-crop belt as even the wheat and corn belts are not, for this one crop more than anything else has the South been stratified into classes, and the communities outside its kingdom have been isolated, pushed off the best land and far into the hills.

The South is an empire. My own observations were confined to the field fenced in by the Mississippi and the Potomac, the Atlantic Ocean and the Appalachian Mountains. These boundaries include the States of Virginia, North and South Carolina, Eastern Tennessee, Georgia, Alabama, Mississippi, Louisiana and Florida. Roughly, these States occupy three geographic planes, each distinct as a shelf, and as separately populated and furnished. On the top shelf, at altitudes as high as any inhabited in this country, in deep coves or on fertile shoulders of the mountains, in the enclosed high countries called the Great Valley and the Cumberland Plateau, live those Rip Van Winkle clans, forgotten in their crannies

for nearly 200 years, an ancient blend of English, Scotch and
Irish, now supposed to be intermixed with Germans long ago
sifted down through the Shenandoah Valley from Pennsylvania. Precious to ethnologists as the purest Anglo-Saxons
left in the world, certainly the most uncorrupted by progress,
these highlanders are hardly discovered when corruption begins. Like a gold rush they are descending to the mill villages
of the Piedmont. Without batting an eye, the Elizabethans
relinquish the handloom for the fastest and most intricate
machines of the modern textile factory. The last to speak the
speech of Shakespeare flock to the talkies.

The Piedmont area is the middle ground of the South. A
rolling plateau extending from Western Virginia to Central
Alabama, it is, in general, the zone of the new industry. In the
narrow span between two censuses, more water power has
been harnessed and more factories have been established in
this area than in any part of the United States. In these factories the highlander first meets that other "defeated farmer,"
the lowlander, struggling up from the coastal plains to exchange his mule and his tongue plow for a machine tender's
job. However thin and precarious the pay envelope of the unskilled industrial worker, it can never be as thin and uncertain
as the living either mountaineer or plainsman was able to
pull out of the land. Thus the Piedmont is a kind of mortar
in which sand rubs against flint—and slowly generates a spark.

The coastal plain is sand and swamp. The sand hills run
with the wind and the swamps are threaded by wandering
creeks. Here are the abandoned rice and indigo fields of the
Carolinas, leagues of loblolly pines, recklessly undercut, the
rich black belt of Alabama, black in soil and population, a
large proportion of the cotton acreage, the fertile truck gardens of Mississippi and Louisiana. Florida is nothing but
coastal plain. Though for a time it set a dizzy value on sand
and sun, phosphate and marsh, there is no doubt that the

Florida ballyhoo did as much as anything to drum up the South and set it marching.

This three-tiered empire is by no means, of course, the whole South. The nine States it comprises form parts of three of the nine regions into which the United States is divided by the Department of Commerce. When I outlined my itinerary to an official of the department before making the trip, he made only one comment. "Include as much as you like," he said, "but be careful what you exclude. You'd have to do a lot of explaining to a Kentuckian or a Texan if you left him out of the South."

That statement is as significant as it is true. At least six other States, in addition to those nine, think of themselves as belonging to the South. In no other section except that considered the poorest and most backward of them all does half the country insist on being included! The Middle Westerners who populate the narrow native quarters of New York make no boast of their origin. Neither do the Easterners who people the West. Both, on the contrary, are pathetically eager to "belong" where they are. But the Southerner, wherever he goes, carries the South like a flag, and the outlander in the South, wherever he comes from, is for the first time in his life a "Northerner."

More than that, if the Southerner has made money, if you catch him hustling, and a good many Southerners nowadays are caught affluent and energetic, he is as apologetic as a man used to be who had fallen from grace or strayed from the fold. Surprised at work hours before a New York executive would be at his desk, he blames it on the climate. "Have to start early down here," he explains. "After noon we loaf." At 5:30 this particular loafer was still at it. "This is Southern sloth," he boasted then, "no business efficiency. I've been fussing all day over one little job." The little job was a $100,000 contract, but this is the South's way of flouting the Northern virtues even while it practices them. Working ten hours a day, it can still insist that it is easy-going and indolent. Willing to sell its labor at any price to attract industry, it believes it has no "money standard."

The South is an empire, but it is also still a province. Its self-consciousness as a section perpetuates the most glamorous tradition in America. In its most pontifical days, before the barbarian invasion, New England never had the local patriotism of the South, a loyalty to an idea that outlasts the idea itself. What confederated the Confederacy into a secession is easily explained, but not what confederated these States into a South that for seventy years has maintained a solidarity almost as much social and spiritual as political. Today that powerful provincialism, one of the most striking phenomena of our history, is powerfully assaulted. The empire may be said to be at war with the province. The undeveloped resources of the South, human and material, are too conveniently located not to be exploited and their exploitation plows fast—carelessly through local patterns. When I spoke of the South being as elusive as the Spring, I meant the South as a separate entity. It is there, but it appears and disappears, here one moment and gone the next, like the beautiful lady roped in the magician's box who turns out to be a flock of pigeons.

In Virginia, in another air from that on the north side of the Potomac, you are sure there is a South. The North, or the world for that matter, has no place for meditation like the incomparable lawn of the university at Charlottesville— that close of old green terraces looking up to blue hills—between the quiet colonnades of Jefferson. Jamestown, tranquil, too, on its wide and lonely river, to an American evocative beyond all other sites, is infinitely remote from Plymouth Rock; this is the perfect landing place for a gentleman! In the porticoes of old houses, set early in this soil and mellowed

by generations of ample and simple living, you can agree with
Keyserling that here is "the only really cultural atmosphere
in America today." It is perhaps prophetic that he found this
atmosphere at its best at Westover, where a great tradition is
restored by the profits of one of the most modern and practical of American arts, the art of plumbing. You may suspect
that what he savored, what Virginia offers more generously
than any other State, is something that antedates the ante-
bellum, not the South so much as the American past. No matter; the South was the scene of that epoch. Probably that is
the only reason it has been saved for restoration.

What is true of Virginia is truer of Charleston, where the
epoch is kept alive by the same society that created it, and in
lesser degree of other of the old coast towns, Savannah, Mobile, even New Orleans, though there the blond, inbred and
delicate civilization of Charleston has more color and dimension, the South darkened and deepened by the older South
of the Latins. Louisiana serves to prove how natural is that
blend, helps to define an impression produced by all these
ports, and that is that they are more closely related to the
Old World than to their own hinterland—the Old World that
vanishes faster than they, because often one is flicked by the
thought that the old South is about the only place left that
has resisted "Americanization."

The South was rural, is rural yet; for that reason one recognizes it oftenest in the country. Where the pattern appears
most unchanged, curiously enough, is where a war was
waged to change it. The plantation is not modernized. The
same old Negro and the same old mule plow up the ground
for the cotton planting. The farmhands are paid, in one way
or another, but they belong to cotton in the same sense, with
much the same effect, as once they belonged to the planter.
In his lodge on the Congaree swamp, one moonlight night,
Dr. E. C. L. Adams introduced me to the gullah Negroes he

has celebrated in his Congaree sketches. In their thundering spirituals, their chuckling stories, their jungle dances, you catch in such an environment what is lost when the scene is changed. You recognize that this is the haunting undertone of the South. It echoes in the fields. It is now the accompaniment of machines. In the brand new State docks at Mobile the beat of the most modern cotton presses chimes in naturally with the rhythm of the chanting Negroes.

Yes, there is a South! It is compounded of early America, a tenacious aristocratic tradition, local loyalty, the enormous passive influence of the Negro, the culture of cotton. Cotton has changed its habits less than any American industry. In Vicksburg, once the capital of the kingdom, brokers in dusty offices up rickety stairs tilt their chairs at tall windows looking up the Yazoo Delta and talk a kind of dead language of trade. They are less changed than the cropper. The main difference between today and yesterday is that the cropper now moves about from plantation to plantation. He has become a nomad; often he escapes altogether. New on the landscape is the Negro careering along the roads in rusty Fords that clatter like a chain gang moving. Perhaps that is what this movement is.

There is a South, and then again there isn't. You lose it in the towns, particularly in the Piedmont. Some of these towns are wholly new, like the latest mill villages, built from the ground up as part of the factory equipment. Others are transformed, like Elizabethton, Tenn., which has quadrupled its population in the four years since the opening of the first rayon plant. Others have built out what local distinction they possessed. It was not great; the civilization of the old South was not an urban civilization and its spirit was never civic spirit. The antebellum villages were plantations; a few cities sufficed for politics and trade. The Atlanta Sherman left in ashes was a strategic railway terminal, a small town com-

pared to the present metropolis of the Southeast. It would
have been new, anyway, by now. Birmingham is newer, and
immensely proud of it; it boasts that it is the youngest city of
its size in the world, and already makes almost as much
smoke as Pittsburgh. Chattanooga, shooting up between her
embattled mountains, shows no mark of age except her amazing collection of battle markers. Charlotte, N. C., the cotton
mill capital, might be anywhere. The Elks I heard orating in
the hotel dining room did not vary their nation-wide sentiments by so much as a Southern accent.

You move from one chain-store Main Street to another,
from one new hotel to the next. All the domes of the State
Capitols are lighted at night. Churches of the same dominant
denominations occupy the best corners. In the blocks between, all the rest of the entertainment is provided by the
same stars who twinkle simultaneously on Broadway. Contrary to expectations, the South grows no "deeper" as you
proceed. South Carolina is really the southernmost State as
North Carolina is the most northern. If there is any truth in
that dangerous generalization, it may be because South Carolina had further to fall from her proud height in the old
South, and North Carolina, "the valley of humiliation between two mountains of conceit," had a middle class with
which to build a new economy. Largely it is due to Chapel
Hill, which more than any Southern university stirs up the
mind of its State and relates the local problems to the general
complex of change.

Beyond South Carolina, I was more and more teased by
the presence of something familiar. At Montgomery, Ala., no
longer the sleepy capital of a dozen years ago, Governor Bibb
Graves's paraphrase of Bishop Berkeley,* "Southward the
course of empire," supplied a clue. The paraphrase is not
original with the Governor, but it is probably true and cer-

* George Berkeley, 1685–1753, Bishop of Anglican Church, Ireland.

tainly expresses the empire-making spirit sweeping down the South, gathering force as it goes. It was Jackson, Miss., however, that formulated what this South kept suggesting. The capital of what has been called the most backward State is the most surprising town of them all. One descends into a new station from the new overhead tracks and looks down a blazing, newly paved main street on which not one of the skyscrapers is more than five years old. There is a new Capitol, now buzzing with impeachments of various State officers —not so new!—and new residential developments, Tudor, Tuscan, early American, transforming the encircling woods and housing a population that in ten years has more than doubled. There was not a vacant room in the three new hotels, which swarmed with a State convention of teachers, all young, mostly long-skirted, high-waisted girls, deafeningly alive. Jackson shouted what has happened to the South: it has gone Middle West!

Further, indeed. The Middle West has no longer this fine fresh fervor of Southern go-getting. The South has the industrial complex; it worships industrialization as rhapsodically and recklessly as Russia in her five-year plan. It makes blanket inducements to new factories—free land, no taxes, no hampering laws, cheap labor. Alabama has a tireless development board, subsidized by the State itself, to make contacts for new industries. The railroads, the chambers of commerce, above all the power companies, work early and late in this sectional enterprise. The most frequent argument advanced against government operation of the power site at Muscle Shoals was that the government would not go out like the power companies and solicit for new plants.

You can look on one picture or the other. If you choose the first, remember that Virginia has no such pride in a reconstruction of the eighteenth century at Williamsburg as in her new treasures, the greatest rayon plants and the biggest coal

dump in the world, and that Vicksburg dedicates with ho-
sannas the latest marvel in bridge-building, the southernmost
span across the Mississippi. If you take the second, observe
that Jackson rose in arms when it was proposed to destroy
the old Capitol after the new was built and that Charlotte
takes her new courthouse a half mile out but manages to
afford to keep a $1,000,000 lawn around an old church in the
middle of the town. Either South you look at is confused and
contradictory. Often you seem to see the South vanishing
and reasserting itself in the same movement. Either way you
look, look quickly, because both pictures are composing into
one. Very soon "the South," either as it was or as it is, will be
visible no more.

I can do no more than suggest the bright mix-up of the
kaleidoscope. Even this hurried and broken view reveals what
special problems are faced by the South in coming late and
handicapped into the industrial belt. The first is that she is
so late. Entering industry on a large scale at a point so much
further along the road than the rest of the country, she has
to make at the same time the adjustments of the first stage
of the industrial revolution and the readjustments of the present stage. Her surplus rural population must be broken to
the machine at a time when the machine itself, by its new
speed and perfection, is discharging skilled workers everywhere.

In this process her old handicap becomes a new irritant.
The rural Negroes must be industrialized as well as the rural
whites, and the color conflict of the future, far more searching
than the social problem of the past, threatens to take the form
of economic competition between the races. Already the
Negro begins to complain that the whites are pushing him out
of the few lines of work in which he has hitherto enjoyed a
monopoly. Thus the South becomes the point of collision of
two major problems.

Rationalization and modernization of the cotton industry from top to bottom is perhaps the most immediate step. No one can look upon the Southern landscape without realizing that the rehabilitation of what Dr. Carl Taylor of North Carolina calls "the great rural slum of America" is fundamental to the progress of the new South. These slums are the tenant cotton farms; they represent the lowest level of American life. There is something feudal about cotton. Its roots are in slavery and it cannot outgrow them; it has created in these croppers, colored and white, the only American peasantry. Further along the line is the mill village, the plantation of the cotton mill, also a feudal institution, often benevolent, necessary to the establishment of the textile industry in a wholly rural environment, but out of place in a democracy and out of date in a modern industrial system. The mill village illustrates better than anything else the peculiar, traditional and personal relationship between employer and employee in the South. It focuses the labor problem, which must become a larger factor as industry passes out of the present crisis, as organization proceeds, as industrial legislation is forced upon States reluctant to enact any restrictions that would halt the inflow of a single dollar of new capital.

It has never happened yet that the conditions that tempt industry to enter an undeveloped field survive very long the establishment of industry. The South is no exception to this rule. It is written in the stars that the theater of the war between the States will be in time the chief productive area of the Union. Only the effects of that conflict have delayed the development of the southeastern half of the country; more and more it attracts Americans tired of rigor and ready at last to negotiate the business of life on the easiest instead of the hardest terms.

The question is, What will happen to the South in this transformation? Will the Southern mind survive when all the material differences that shaped it have disappeared? Is provincialism possible when the cotton, the corn and the wheat belts all become industrial belts? In a word, can the South hold out? If it can, what will be the effect of this mind, fusing now for the first time with the general mind, on American civilization? I have tried here only to picture the present confusion. The elements creating this confusion and what order will come out of it suggest the most interesting studies to be made in America today.

[5]   1 9 3 0   *July 13*. THE SOUTH: IMPACT OF STRANGE FORCES. *An industry and society, a struggle of old ideas and new goes on.*

EN ROUTE

The village lay among ranging hills, in a setting of Alpine beauty; Mount Mitchell was a blurred cone in the dim distance and the nearer slopes were misty green in a Spring rain. Drenched peach trees blossomed on the hillsides, aslant like the cottages, which straggled on stilts along climbing roads of red clay, now wet and slippery. White bath tubs in wooden crates were dumped in front of the houses, while little ells, evidently intended to be bathrooms, were being hammered up at the back.

This is one of many Southern towns feeling the impact of strange forces, but it is among the first to show the old mold cracking under the pressure.

If one is looking for signs of social change in the South, here undoubtedly is the place to begin. The cotton mill workers are a kind of separate caste. In the stratification that has been built up in this society on its solid black foundation—and how that permanent underpinning has shaped the whole structure!—they occupy the lowest white level. Their segrega-

tion in their own colonies is accepted as a settlement of their
social status that is comfortable for everybody. It is almost
an axiom, heard again and again, that leading citizens may
be bred on the poorest tenant farms, but never in the mill village. I was reminded of it by the assistant secretary of the
Chamber of Commerce in a Virginia town who announced
that he was a spinner's son. "Look out for us, because we are
something new," he boasted, with the pride of any pioneer.
"There are not many of us yet who have had schooling or
ambition enough to head away from the mills into stores and
offices outside. My generation is the first. We are educated
in the mill schools. Now, of course, I don't like the labor organizers who are stirring things up in this town. They give
the place a bad name and hurt business." He smiled, the assistant secretary of the Chamber of Commerce. It was the
spinner's son who added: "Say, though, they sure do help to
break down our inferiority complex."

If signs of social ferment reach the level of the mill village,
it can be taken for granted that the leaven has touched
bottom and that nothing in the whole edifice is safe from
change. And that is true; on every other plane the signs are
clear as print. In fact, you may read them in print if you
study the society columns of the local newspapers, always
remembering that there was a time, and not so long ago, when
there was no such thing as a society page in these convivial
provinces. Social entertainments in the older South were
strictly private affairs. It was considered vulgar to advertise
one's hospitality. A reporter at a wedding was a social error.
To publish an account of a ball was to let outsiders into the
inner circle, destroying its exclusiveness. Where were the
point and piquancy of social conversation if the tidbits of
gossip could be baldly chronicled in the public press?

Now, save in Charleston—and may Charleston never fail
us as the present exception which proves the ancient rule—

the society sections swamp the newspapers. Nowhere is the social item so copious, fulsome and explicit. If the paramount interests of a community were gauged by the space allotment in the morning paper one would judge that the social and the personal are the chief preoccupations of the South. But, however true that may be, it is proved no truer by the spread now than by the former taboo. The storm that broke out in Charleston a few years ago when an irreverent editor from the North presumed to print an account of the St. Cecelia Ball, that annual gala of the Last of the Privates, demonstrates the importance of the social as much as does the splurge of society news today. The two codes are but different fashions of expressing the same emphasis. And even Charleston falters; the social collective impinges even here. For it belongs to the Junior League, and between the publicity policy of that dashing organization and the Charleston tradition the local branch suffers all the strain of a house divided.

Between the two codes lies a whole epoch of social evolution. Industry intervenes, and because it has not yet gone far you can see here better than anywhere else just how it works on the manners and tastes of a people. The machine breaks through superiority complexes as easily as inferiority complexes. It is neither fastidious nor reticent. It vulgarizes because it communizes. Like noise, speed, smoke, crowds, publicity is part of its sweeping crescendo. It is its nature to invade privacies and drive through quiet and seclusion. No sooner does it appear on any scene than the tempo quickens, the scale enlarges, the old social patterns waver and warp.

The selective processes of an agricultural society are slow; its aristocracy is composed of the patient, those who stick for generations on the same land; its note is continuity. The selective processes of industry, on the other hand, are sudden and swift; it lives by movement, scraps as much as it produces; its food is change. The material rewards of the two systems are, of course, incomparable. You have only to look at the landlord and the figure he cuts in the modern world. The most powerful and opulent figure of the past, today he is diminished, outclassed, overwhelmed by the industrial magnate.

All this is not a commonplace in the South, nor can it be a commonplace to any one who sees this revolution in process. Here you have the social scene as it was set by a landed aristocracy, the only one America ever had, and against that background, still largely rural, smokeless and tranquil, a perfect exhibition of all the transforming tricks of the machine. The planters of the golden age were a minority, as ruling castes always are, but their empire was undisputed. They were supported by slave labor, and thereby confirmed in the sense of superiority that has determined the course of Southern history. The Negro was a courtier whose servility influenced the destiny of his master as much as his own, just as that other form of mastery called chivalry, equally bound up with the romantic feudalism of the ante-bellum system, in the long run weakens the protector more than the protected. But that comes later.

What strikes you first on this scene is how very simple, after all, was that vanished grandeur. The land at its lordliest, as proud as the estate of the English earls or the grand seigneurs of France, beside the machine-made magnificence that supersedes it looks as modest as a pyramid or a Parthenon might look if set down beside the Chrysler Building. The hopeless struggle to save the farm has taught us that millions cannot be pulled out of the soil as they are drawn out of rolling mills and automobile factories. Here we learn that they never were!

Industrial wealth as a social factor introduces the new note of luxury into the South, but is still so far from dominant that it is modulated to the prevailing key. The scale remains the country scale. It does not rise to 300-foot yachts or collections of Rembrandts. The houses of the new rich are modeled after the old, for the most part. The pleasant homes that multiply among the pine woods around Atlanta or on the mountainsides above Birmingham are nothing like the palaces of Lake Forest or the great manors of Cleveland and Detroit. The people who live in these homes are as complacent as the successful elsewhere, but they assume a half-humorous astonishment at their prosperity.

It is the fashion to apologize for wealth. Whatever form pretense takes in the South, ancestor worship, social veneer, the ostrich attitude towards unpleasant truths, it does not run to display or swank. Charleston enjoys pretending that invitations to the St. Cecelia Ball have to be addressed to the poorhouse. During the season ladies of the first families like to boast about their "paying guests." But compare the countrified jumble in the shop windows of most Southern main streets with the austere elegance now the mode in other main streets, the stock inside being in both cases the same, and you will deduce that putting its best goods in the show windows is not this section's particular form of bluff. Therefore, the South, though so much poorer, seems less strained and anxious than the North. The aristocracy is easier to live up to than the plutocracy.

Life is simpler, less sophisticated. Hospitality, for all its warmth and effusiveness, is less lavish and more discriminating. If you are asked to "supper" you are given supper when you arrive, an old-fashioned meal, well-cooked and plentiful, but not a formal dinner. The whole scheme of entertainment is easy and informal, and that is partly due, no doubt, to the familiar, friendly presence of the Negro servitor, as he is not known in the North. One of the prime advantages of the newly rich in this section is that they can expand in a domestic atmosphere created by a colored house man instead of an English butler!

The relationship between master and servant is personal, as all relationships are personal. It would be as difficult to be formal among Southern servants as it was in the old patriarchal days in Russia, when the peasants waiting on the guests in the greatest houses so often took part in the table conversation. Housekeepers here echo the usual complaints; wages are three times higher than they were ten years ago, and white girls are replacing Negroes as domestic help. Nevertheless, the South is better, more cheaply, above all more cheerfully served than the rest of the country. That may be one reason why it stays at home, enjoying a cuisine justly acclaimed for its excellence and leaving to the stranger the casual and indifferent fare of the restaurants and hotels.

One gets the impression that Southern emphasis on the social and personal expresses an actual pleasure in human intercourse. It would be too much to say that the young people do not prefer the talkies and the sports car, but at one party I did witness the unusual phenomenon of groups of boys and girls engaged in general and apparently enjoyable conversation. Among their elders there seems to be relish for talk for its own sake, and a real interest in people reminiscent of an older world, one less perfectly wired and motored. Sometimes the interest is in ideas; more often it is in gossip, politics, above all just now in matters touched on in this article: social changes turning things upside down. The South has not lost the fresh faculty of wonder; it wonders now, and is excited, a society in a state of voluble astonishment. This, too, one guesses, is an inherited habit. The old South was gregarious. It was not a particularly intellectual or artistic society, but it cultivated one fine art, the art of living; it savored to the full the daily event, graced and rejoiced in the human spectacle. It had, and still retains, what we lose with every hour the machine saves us—the time to talk things over.

Listening to this talk over a fairly wide range of territory, one gains a further impression. The South specializes, as every one knows, in "feminine charm." The last stronghold of the Age of Chivalry, it has developed coquetry, clinging vines, languishing and lovely ladies. The old taboo against social publicity was fundamentally a kind of purdah designed to keep this charm in its proper pigeonhole and to interpose a veil of sentiment between the women of the protected class and the other women of the old South, the faded drudges of the farms, and the still darker sides of chivalry. From top to bottom, nevertheless, the old ideal prevailed. Therefore it is particularly interesting to observe the reactions of women emerging from a tradition that was cherished as a fiction long after it ceased to be a fact.

It goes without saying that Southern women have for years past been doing everything that women do everywhere in the twentieth century. They work all night in factories, direct businesses, edit newspapers, practice all the professions, run Gubernatorial offices. Though co-education is far from an established principle in Southern States, they engage in important economic research work in all the universities. They manage some of the biggest plantations. At least two women operate model industrial farms in the Mississippi Delta. I found a woman acting as head of the Mississippi State Chamber of Commerce. And whatever they do, it must be said for them that they do it like ladies!

The Northerners are business women, but the Southerners are women in business. They make the conjunction with more grace; they are more feminine. With their gentle, half-plaintive drawl, their suggestion of softness and amiability, they are never quite lost in the job. When you ask the telephone girl at your hotel to call you at seven, "I suah will, honey," she answers sweetly. They all answer sweetly. You are called at seven, but there is no depersonalized, stereotyped service. The Southern girl doesn't "make it snappy." Whether it is art or artlessness, the ladylike manner of this adjustment is a triumph of adaptability. It comes near to being a conquest of the machine!

The famous feminine charm remains, but the women impress one as being more adventurous than the men, less afraid of change. Naturally this does not apply to all women; there are vast valleys of inertia and prejudice. But if the leading citizens of any town were divided into liberals and conservatives, a greater proportion of the former would be women. This impression I heard confirmed in Richmond by Mrs. Beverly Munford and Miss Lucy Mason, both militant liberals and both of the oldest Southern tradition. Louis Jaffe of The Norfolk Virginian-Pilot, winner of one of the Pulitzer editorial prizes, gave it as his opinion that the women's clubs represented the most liberalizing influence in the South. From white women have come the strongest protests against lynching, also the initiative in the movements for rural schools and rural public health work for the Negroes. In two cities I attended round-table conferences of the Urban League dealing with Negro unemployment. At both, the white citizens were women and the Negro leaders were men. I mention this because participation in such movements of racial cooperation is here the final test of "liberalism."

Yet the Negro has kept the South rural, and it is clear that his adjustment to a changing environment necessitates a readjustment of the whole modus vivendi as it has been developed between the races. The Negro is probably most responsible for the social structure of the South. The civilization which gave it form flowered upon his labor; most of the unwritten laws that constitute a social code are the outgrowth of the slave system. The Negro has kept the South socially conservative as he has kept it politically Democratic and dry. The Negro has softened its manners and its speech; if it is indolent, which anyone must doubt who sees its capacity to hustle, it is because it has been served too obsequiously and too well. Sometimes one wonders if without the black men there could have been a romantic South, that glamorous land of country gentlemen. He was the acolyte of the social ritual, just as today he is the source, or at least the "memory," as someone has said, of its poetry, its music and its humor. "With all your troubles, you are still more light-hearted than the rest of these United States," I said one day to a Southern poet. "We have lived side by side with a race that laughs," was his answer. Perhaps that gayety is itself an illusion created by the Negro. Certainly in the new South he is the only one who sings.

In the newest skyscrapers I have seen elevators marked "Colored," which seem designed to segregate on the way up Negro clients who are going to transact business in the offices of white firms.

If anything, therefore, there is a tendency to strengthen the social barriers. But the Negro can no more be segregated from the movements of his time than can the Hindu and the Chinese; less, indeed, because it is his fate to be planted in the very track of the industrial Juggernaut. He also is subject to machine pressure, to social change; he experiences his own revolution. A Negro college girl investigating for the Rosenwald Foundation reported many instances of the sharpening competition between blacks and whites on the lower rungs of industry. "But the Negro moves a step higher when he is pushed out," she said. "He has to be prodded into learning a trade." She had figures to show how his economic level is slowly, very slowly, rising, as without figures one can see by watching how, North and South, the Negro is edging into better residence districts. The most notable of all the improvements in the South, and the least noted in these articles, are the magnificent network of new State highways and the multiplication of modern country schools. They are like open doors upon the world for millions heretofore sequestered, millions of Negroes as well as millions of whites. The Southern darky has a range and freedom of movement he never knew before. How he enjoys it is evident enough in the black caravans rolling along the smooth roads, visiting, prospecting, or "jes' explorationin' of this big ole worl'," said the chuckling father of a family of eight pickaninnies packed in an old flivver and wholly undismayed by the lack of any other habitation. The South is educating the Negro, not as zealously as it educates the white, but more systematically than ever before. To what end it hardly knows, it raises his standard with the rest.

So the Negroes move, too, as at the hand of a colossal scene shifter. They are a patient race and the South treats them with patience rather than with abstract justice. In general, its policy has been one of temporizing, punctuated with exclamations of anger and periods of generosity. Everybody vaguely realizes that the outlines of the problem are changing, and will change beyond recognition as the cotton field is mechanized. The real crisis, it is acknowledged, lies ahead. That is another shadow, and the greatest, to add to the picture of confusion.

In the South, as was said in the beginning, you see how the coming of industry plows through every social stratum and puts a whole population to the stop-watch and stretch-out system. In the same gesture the population submits and resists. The manufacturer, the merchant, the business woman, the whole social and domestic organism, the wandering black, all strike against being robotized as instinctively as does the cotton mill operative. For drama in the Greek manner, where the dramatis personae are always fates and great forces at war, there is nothing on the contemporary scene more absorbing than the conflict going on in the mind of the South between—well, let us say, not to go too far—between collectivism and Jeffersonian individualism.

[6]   1 9 3 0   *July 20.* THE PROMISE OF THE NEW SOUTH. *Swept by economic revolution, it is emerging from isolation to swing into the stride of America.*

ENROUTE

Seen in perspective, the changes transforming the South today are but the variations or the effects of one change. The Southern States are going through, late, what all the States have gone through. Out of step for nearly three generations, they now swing into the stride of America. They join the Union in the only sense that any longer matters, swept at last into that economic revolution, made by machines rather than by men, which we have carried so far that all concurrent revolutions, whatever their manifestos, are only violent efforts to speed up the mechanization of life to the American standard.

That is true of the revolution in the South, where one of the most fertile fields in the world awaits the application of the American standard. In this region which a real estate promoter would undoubtedly pick out as the best location in the United States, at the front door and on the sunny side of the continent, close to the markets of the East and Middle West, favored by climate, soil, mineral wealth, water power, every circumstance to make a nation prosperous and self-sufficient, nearly half the population exists at levels we airily ignore when we talk about American civilization. The tenant farms maintain a peasantry, white and colored, whose lives are poorer and more drab than those of Balkan peasants; the norm of domestic architecture is not much better than the temporary huts of the refugees deported from Turkey into Greece. If by proletariat is meant a permanent and hereditary laboring class, here, too, in the inhabitants of the cotton mill villages, is an American proletariat. No country has a right to be called rich which contains this poverty; none may be said to be mechanized, much less overmechanized, where so many millions live without benefit of any machinery whatever.

This is the base of the pyramid. It represents the weight of poverty, and of inertia born of poverty, the South has to drag along on its upward march. It explains why the rural-mindedness of this section differs from the rural-mindedness of the farming States of the West. Though the Western States are labeled progressive and the Southern States are called conservative, Nebraska as much as Georgia, the Dakotas as much as the Carolinas, express the agricultural point of view and struggle to maintain it. Both sections uphold the tradition for which the Constitution was written, embody the mind of the land as opposed to the conquering mind of industry.

But what different lands they are, and from what contrary experiences they derive their mental slant! The Western farmer has always moved on; he started far East, or in Europe, and he has the energy and discontent of the emigrant. A landowner working his own acres, his is the great protestant voice of politics. But he sounds radical only because all protests do; his revolts are, in fact, the sorties of the profoundly conservative, fighting the "predatory interests" that threaten the safe old world of the independents. The Southern farmer is born and bred in his own State. He belongs to the soil more than the soil belongs to him. Even when he is a landlord, he is the subject of a dynasty created by cotton culture, the plantation and slave labor. Usually, however, he is a tenant on his few acres, a dependent instead of an independent. Too much of this land is voiceless; what you hear is the system creaking.

It is easy to understand why European intellectuals, discovering the South in increasing numbers, find themselves more at home there than in other parts of this country. The oldest and most native America is nearer and more intelligible to Europe than is the wild ethnic mixture of the newer America, made out of so many Europes that it is as strange to any as rayon must be to a silk worm—a chemical reaction rather than a race. The South conforms to an order the European recognizes. It is individualist, traditional, stratified, leisurely, homogeneous, as nations are.

For the same reasons the American finds it different from the rest of America. He understands the historic why better than the foreigner, knows that much of the distinction is manner and accent, perceives that what the Keyserlings and the Siegfrieds savor so happily is the old aristocratic mind of the country rather than the new middle-class mentality of the towns. Yet he feels, also, that while other regions of the United States are geographical divisions, this is spiritually a province. As the rural pattern is unlike any other, so is the mental attitude. And as he watches the revolutionary forces of industry and prosperity plowing through the pattern, he wonders what will happen to this distinct and reluctant mind.

When one interviews the South, no question is more interesting than this, nor more important in any forecast of that American tomorrow toward which we are whirling with such momentum and so little control. For the psychologic effects of industrialization are as profound as the economic; as industrial contacts are more widely established, the industrial mind of America works on the South as never before, while at the same time the mind of the South, emerging from the isolation of too many years, once more becomes an active part of the national mind. When you consider that for a hundred years the political and intellectual leadership of this country came from a section that since the Civil War has exerted almost no influence, you realize that in this possible come-back the new South may mean as much to the nation as the nation does to the South.

As these States grow richer and more urban, as the submerged masses, moving from cotton field to factory, acquire the industrial outlook and become articulate, the country below the Potomac is bound to be more powerful. An industrialized South stands in a new relation to the North. If the only national leader produced by this section in fifty years deflected the course of America as Woodrow Wilson did—and Wilson is so typical of the Jeffersonian mind of Southern liberals that it is almost necessary to see him from his native heath to understand him—what are we to expect when it really resumes its political authority? There is no immediate prospect of such leadership, it is true; Southern politics suffer all the deadening effects of a one-party system. But Wilson, not to forget that Southern half of Roosevelt,* as Georgia never does, proves that it is no idle dream.

What, then, distinguishes the mind of the South, and how is it changing? It is, to begin with, a provincial mind. Sectional self-consciousness, strengthened by isolation, might be regarded as one of the qualities most likely to disappear were it not that the recrudescence of the South coincides with a general revival of interest in the American past. We have all reached the age of reminiscence. Historical studies are the most popular and profitable of literary pastimes. Therefore local loyalty, mostly a feeling for the soil and sources of one's being, has the warrant and re-emphasis of fashion.

* Theodore Roosevelt's mother was Martha Bulloch, daughter of Major James S. Bulloch of Roswell, Georgia.

Feeling for the South as South, vivid in all generations, is especially significant today among the young. The schools go in for almost exclusively sectional pageantry, the universities for regional researches; the passion to preserve local customs, local culture and local memories seems to grow as the future expands and brightens. This is all to the good. Provincialism is a great quality, more than ever valuable as the million horses of the machine race about stamping out all localisms. As a specialist in this field, perhaps the South will teach the other sections how to maintain or regain their lost selves.

But provincialism has its stifling side. The province is only rich and colorful when the native stuff is a little mellowed and faded by the wear of the world. The South lacks contacts, outside competitions, the sharp catalyzer of alien bloods. The foreign observer may feel at home there, but not the immigrant, though he come no further than from the other side of the mountains. The South can always work itself into a white heat against "foreign agitators," a generic term covering labor organizers, official advisers or any interference from "outsiders." This feeling is so strong that labor legislation and new adjustments between employers and employees will probably have to wait until labor leadership develops within the ranks of Southern workers themselves. The last Presidential campaign * witnessed the clash of two powerful provincialisms, party solidarity against fear of the foreigner. With the alien enemy no longer threatening, the voter now proceeds to punish those who led him to desert the party!

Interference also runs counter to individualism, a quality deeply ingrained in the stubborn Anglo-Saxonism of this province. The Southerner admires "characters," the more flavorous the better, provided the flavor is indigenous, and

---

* The Alfred E. Smith-Herbert Hoover Campaign, 1928.

has a keen and humorous relish for personal idiosyncrasies. There is tang in his fluent talk. He wears what he pleases when he pleases. I believe the local newspapers, particularly the weeklies, have more wit and personality than any now left in America. Where there are no parties, the political battles have to be between persons; as a consequence they generate more heat and venom than if only abstract principles were involved. Here the opposition is frankly between the "outs" and the "ins" without any disguising labels.

Thus the pressure of the collective descends upon the one citizen who is even less a collectivist by nature than is the Englishman. Cooperation of any kind comes hard in the South. Business is as difficult to organize as labor. The almost hysterical opposition of manufacturers to trades unions (except the company unions which they can control) is matched by an equal resistance to team-work among themselves. It is characteristic that the campaign against the chain store originated in this section, where in several States it is a lively political issue. Sentiment is strong against the invader; special taxes are levied against him in at least three States and the volume of chain-store business has actually declined as the result of agitation.

Inconsistently enough, this individualist is also an indefatigable joiner. He joins every society in sight and invents more of his own for good measure. But this affiliation is for company rather than cooperation. He is a social being. The spirit of fellowship is as ardent in the South as that statistical emanation known as "the social conscience," offspring of the machine age, is apathetic. Another inconsistency is that this anti-collectivist society should develop the nearest thing in the United States to a collective. This is the mill village; it is our best example of the submergence of the individual in the group.

That, however, is not inconsistent. It is the product of tradition, the plantation system descending into industry through William Gregg, first cotton mill owner and pioneer in industrial welfare work in the South. Like certain modern experiments in education, it is a system designed to develop leaders, and, by the same logic, followers, the latter on a much larger scale. The ruler implies subjects. Southern individualism flourished in one class at the expense of another; the strong sense of responsibility was balanced by a sense of dependence. The factory started here in a conscious effort to build up a war-impoverished region. The early campaign for industry had something of the fervor of a religious and patriotic crusade, and so has the movement today, thereby perpetuating the tradition that employers are benefactors and employees are beneficiaries.

Tradition has great power over a mind long reduced to the traditional as an escape from present reality. Take religion: Fundamentalism is no more an exclusively Southern state of mind than is Ku Kluxism—observe Indiana, Kansas, Michigan —but the South is a more loyal defender of its traditions. It is not a matter of education; university graduates are as zealous in upholding their religious beliefs, and enacting them into laws, as are the back-country folk aroused by "preachin'." The South really believes in God and in the church as an institution. You are told that church-going is a habit, much less universal than it used to be. Of that the outsider cannot judge, but he cannot fail to see that it is the custom of the country, impressively observed. Nowhere else is anything quite like the Summer revival camp meeting on an enormous scale and with the effect of an emotional orgy. Religion enters into the industrial complex, motivates welfare work in the factories, is the strongest social force. The church represents an influence that no one ignores, and not only for prohibition and proscription; so much is heard of its fanaticism that it should be noted that labor organizers, social workers, leaders in crusades for inter-racial cooperation, promoters of peace, all those who in the South are classed as liberals, testify that their chief support comes from the churches.

One Sunday night I attended a meeting of strikers in a textile town. Since it was Sunday, the exercises were religious in character, and the strike leaders preached from biblical texts. A local lay-evangelist presided and managed to string together noble and sonorous phrases from the Scriptures that in half an hour never made a sentence or conveyed an inkling of meaning. But the old man next to me made his own interpretation. One of the phrases was "life more abundant." "I voted for it, too," remarked my neighbor. "Voted for what?" I asked. "Why, for this yere Hoover prosperity," he answered bitterly.

The young people around us sat absorbed, on their hard, backless benches; afterward they sang hymns, dozens of hymns, the "spirituals" of the poor whites. They were of a type special to the South, some with the heads of poets, boys and girls in their teens, who for two hours on a warm Spring night obviously enjoyed religion and were swayed by the power of ancient words. Rebels though they were—and let it not be forgotten that such rebels multiply in the industrial towns—they were comforted in rebellion by the strongest of their traditions. So far, the Bible Belt holds firm.

The political tradition seems equally impregnable. The South is the most political-minded section of this country. Statesmen and soldiers, orators and editors, have been its specialty. It is happy in argument and moved by eloquence. But the present system is as unreal as solidarity in the face of changing conditions is unnatural. Popular apathy at election time and a certain swaggering cynicism in public office, visible in the political farce as played in Louisiana, Mississippi and Georgia, are inevitable when all differences of opinion on other questions must be subordinated at the polls to insure unanimity on one question. "Forced to think alike politically," says Douglas Freeman of The Richmond News-Leader, "many cease to think at all."

In a section bristling with signs of economic revolution, there are no signs of political revolution, or even of the translation into political action of that sagacity and width of view on public issues, the natural gift for politics, which one meets as often in the South as in French cafés and on the Edinburgh Express. In national elections Southerners may occasionally indulge in revolt, though the secession two years ago was not from the Democratic party; but in local elections even the Republicans, whose number increases as industry develops, vote the "white" ticket, vote dry, reduce all issues to a single issue.

For seventy years the South has voted on the Negro question. The Negro is its perpetual inhibition. The revenge of the slave is to place his masters in such subjection that they can make no decision, political, social, economical or ethical, without reference to him. He made the wealth of the South, and its poverty. Due to his low economic standard, all standards are lowered and the poor whites come late and ignorant into their inheritance. Voteless, he dominates politics, since it is on his account that the South has lost its proportionate influence in national affairs and the nation has lost the full participation of the South.

Now he trickles out of the Cotton Belt and some day, perhaps, will be more evenly distributed in other States. Wherever he goes his lot is hard. The South worries over him; there he has inequality and friends. The North cares little what happens to him; there he has equality and no friends. "What a book could be written," says Dr. Alderman of the University of Virginia, "on the enormous part played by the Negro in the history of the United States."

They are building schools in every Southern State today, schools for Negroes and schools for whites.* The first preoccupation everywhere is to wipe out the illiteracy records of ten years ago. It is estimated that at least half the public revenue during the past decade has been spent on schools. You can hardly go deep enough into the backwoods to get out of the school zone or not to surprise on some new road a spreading schoolhouse built of brick with white colonnades, with a fleet of auto buses drawn up at the door to transport the children within a radius of twenty or thirty miles.

Schools on such a scale, consolidated schools and rural high schools, are made possible by the new roads. I do not know which are more civilizing, the schools or the roads, but that they are civilizing, that these buses and concrete highways and modern schools are a dramatic event on this countryside you cannot doubt after you have seen them sowing discontent and "new ideas" in the refugee cabins along the way. The schools are everywhere, but the good roads are fewer as you go further south; the States are building almost faster than they can, paying for the roads in most places out of direct taxes, on gasoline sometimes as much as 4 cents a gallon, candy, cigarettes, soft drinks, moving picture tickets and other luxuries. These States have still a long way to go, but no others are going so fast.

You get the same impression of construction and reconstruction in the universities. Probably no university has ever been built from the ground up with such splendor and completeness as the great defile of gray Gothic halls rising in the pine woods behind Durham, N. C., to house Duke University. You can see the most venerable college buildings in the

* Racial segregation in public schools was ruled unconstitutional in a unanimous decision by the nine Justices of the United States Supreme Court, May 17, 1954.

United States at Williamsburg, Va., and at Macon, Ga., the first chartered college for women in the world.* In the "sugar school" of the University of Louisiana at Baton Rouge, you find an old precedent for the complex system the Bolsheviki consider their own invention. The new stadium at Chapel Hill, sunk in a bowl of pine-clad hills, is lovelier than that of Athens, and domed by a sky as blue. If you could ever turn your eyes from the serpentined-walled gardens and the enchanted lawn of the University of Virginia, you would discover that even here new buildings multiply; harmonious buildings, in the style of Jefferson—as are most of the county schools of the new South; but the best thing to be said for them is that they leave to you the enjoyment of the old.

Virginia is the university of the high scholastic tradition of the South. North Carolina, though even older, has come to stand for a leadership along the new paths the South now enters. Virginia publishes a quarterly interpreting the intellectual life and Chapel Hill its unique Journal of Social Forces, interpreting the new economic and social trends. North Carolina pulses with activity; you can hardly open a door without interrupting somebody writing a book. It has exerted immense influence in informing and liberalizing the thought of its State, and in the recent election to the presidency of so militant a progressive as Dr. Frank Graham has given notice that it is going still further. But if North Carolina has its Institute of Social Research under Dr. Howard Odum, which has made some of the best regional surveys so far published under university auspices, Virginia also has a social research institute under Dr. Wilson Gee, in proof that the school of Jefferson is also equipped to serve the Old Dominion in this period of revolutionary readjustment.

Within the limits of this summary it is impossible even to

* College of William and Mary, Williamsburg, Va., founded in 1693; Wesleyan University, Macon, Georgia, founded in 1863.

refer to the part taken by the universities in this renaissance, or to mention the various literary, cultural and artistic movements that synchronize with the industrial expansion. If there were space, it would be obvious that the new leaven is working like a yeast in the creative mind of the South and that the creative impulse, as yet timid and young, is stimulated by the native material.

In this field, too, the Negro enters as the dominant influence. The Carolina Play-Makers, considered by many the most interesting group in the new South, dramatizes the poetry of the black man and the prose of the whites of the sand hills and the mountains. The Society for the Preservation of Spirituals, a group of Charlestonians who lived on plantations in their youth, is doing great service in transcribing and presenting, with a fidelity no one can appreciate who has not heard the spirituals on the creeks and bayous, the lost music of this primitive people. It is unnecessary to call attention to the predominance of the Negro theme in all the late literature of the South; it has deserved most of the Pulitzer prizes. Even Ellen Glasgow, who does not like industrialization, says that the one bright spot she sees in the new South is the literary and artistic revival. "What we see makes us melancholy," she says, plaintively, "and only the melancholy produce literature."

All this intellectual activity, if it could be analyzed, might suggest an answer to the question as to whether the South will preserve its identity or whether it will be literally metamorphosed and merged in the general pattern. There is not much chance for provinces or for nations in the imperial sweep of machine civilization, but I think the South has a better prospect than any other section. It is older, more set in its ways. It has had a long time to look before leaping. And now, intoxicated as it is by its new stimulant, the white lightning of power, it is in a mood of questioning and self-analysis.

That is surely the most surprising thing about this development, that it should be punctuated by thought. A business executive from New York assured me in New Orleans that the South will never change. "Why, there are merchants down here who do a business of $100,000 a year, make an income of about $10,000 and are satisfied. They say they don't want to increase their business. What progress can you expect of people like that?" The comment is typically American and the examples cited are typically Southern. They indicate a difference in standards of value a good many Southerners would like to preserve. And as long as they feel that way about it they probably will.

As to their effect on the national character the best characteristics peculiar to the South offer a valuable corrective. They are a brake on our gay dash toward economic communism. Perhaps nothing can stop us from continuing until everything we own is pooled in one gigantic combine, but if anything could it would be the conservatism of the South. Nothing can restore the former importance of the individual in a world of machines, but we need to bolster up what is left of him. We need all the provincialism we can save, as many traditions as we can afford. We need the Scriptures, however narrowly interpreted, rather than larger editions of snappy stories.

A little acceleration of the general interest in politics would not hurt us. If to these could be added the South's gentler manners, its softer voice, its lower tempo, its less earnest attitude toward success, how generous would be its contribution to the new civilization! And if, on the other hand, the South would learn from the old experience of America what follies to avoid, what a thrilling opportunity it has to build on the ruins of some of its traditions an industrial order new and distinctively Southern!

[7] 1 9 3 1 *March 8.* WASHINGTON: THE CAPITAL IN
A VACUUM. *As it grows in centralized power, it
grows apart from a nation indifferent to politics, and
yet constantly demanding more and more government at the expense of the States.*

WASHINGTON

Is Washington the only place in the United States
really interested in politics? The question intrudes as one
contrasts the conversation of the capital with that of other
American towns or, if it comes to that, of all other towns
wheresoever. It goes without saying that Washington is the
most political city on earth. It talks politics as Detroit talks
automobiles, Oklahoma City, oil; New York, stocks and styles,
for the reason that it has no alternative business to talk about.

Just three other capitals manifest a comparable absorption.
One is Athens, classic cradle of the political loud-speaker,
and there politics is a popular diversion. What really happens
when Greek meets Greek is a political argument: the amber
dust on the stones of the Acropolis must be the deposit of
centuries of golden eloquence. Another is Tirana, capital of
the incredible kingdom of King Zog of Albania. There politics
is still tribal, the incessant whispers of that whispering B. C.
village are the stealthy debates of the mountain clans, nursed
along by neighboring powers. The third, of course, is Moscow, where politics is a revelation, new as in Athens it is old,
and so exciting that this is the first proletariat that accepts
from its rulers not bread and circuses but circuses without
the bread.

Politics in Moscow includes and in Washington is supposed
to exclude all lesser interests. The American capital was
erected where it is, outside of all the States, to be a place of
detachment, of disinterestedness in the sense that it has no

local and special concerns to obscure its view of the general concerns. And what is happening to it and to us is that it is becoming a city increasingly remote from the common life of the country, more and more the camping ground of special interests.

Washington is the perfect cross-section of the United States. As a House of Representatives—and this refers to the permanent bureaucracy as much as to the successive Congresses—it reflects us all, North, South, East and West, more fairly with less dilution of foreign blood than any other city. When people say that the capital is not America they do not mean what they imply but something quite different, and more significant: they mean that it represents only the political side of America. Its "difference" grows as this political side atrophies elsewhere, as the population loses interest in public policies, as we concentrate on our own affairs and "leave politics to the politicians."

The language of Washington is not the standard language. It is keyed to one line of business, the vernacular to another. Here politics is "shop." All the bills, rulings, shake-ups, transfers, deals, perpetually discussed have a single connotation. The personalities are political, the gossip, the jokes, the hopes and fears, the standards of judgment. Successes and failures are political. The hierarchical order of politics is reflected in the social stratification. Where two-thirds of the working population is employed by the government and two-thirds of the transients want something from the government, there is nothing remarkable in that. What is worthy of remark is that our interest in politics should be so largely confined to Washington and to those whose business or whose livelihood is politics.

There is a frontier between the District of Columbia and the States of the Union. Coming or going, you feel the change in atmosphere, the difference in time, the shift in speed. On

this side is unreality, no doubt of it. It is the land of yesterday, or the day before that. But why? Is the vacuum created
by the politicians or are they merely left in it?

Within the same hour yesterday I talked to the Washington
correspondent of a Western newspaper and to an Eastern
Senator. The reporter was one of those who had followed the
tariff debate for fourteen months. He had labored to understand and explain it, to estimate the direct and indirect effect
of the various schedules on the trade of his State. At the end
of the long session he made a trip through Kansas, touching
nearly every county. "I imagined the tariff was a burning
issue in the life of this country, as it was here in Washington.
But believe it or not," he said, "I never heard a single reference to tariff all the time I was away, or to anything else, for
that matter, that I'd been sweating over here for a year."

The Senator had returned from a week-end spent in his own
State after voting for the veterans' bonus. He expected to be
taken to task by his constituents for a "raid on the treasury"
which he himself did not attempt to justify. Perhaps he was
one of the Senators who begged the President to "stand firm"
on the veto while they voted to override it. Anyway, he was
chuckling. "Here I was led to believe that the principle of
the bonus was a matter of vast public interest," he remarked.
"At home I didn't meet anybody who knew or cared a hang
how I voted."

Such experiences are reported by every representative.
Seen from Washington, the United States is populated by
people who cannot be bothered about politics, whose interest
in legislation is limited to those measures that instantane-
ously help or hurt their business, who are cheerfully acquies-
cent whatever happens, who make no sign that they are not
represented by the organized minorities, compact and vigi-
lant, that father and mother all our laws. These politically indifferent citizens are engaged in minding what they conceive

to be their private business. They are bored by debate of public issues.

The Senate, when it is near a draw, as in the last Congress, arouses in them a faint flutter of the same kind of sporting interest with which they follow the big league ball teams. "Politics!" they shrug, when the Democrats help the Republicans to pass something the Democrats consider bad for the country but useful to embarrass the Republicans in the next campaign. "More politics!" is their negligent comment when a newspaper headline calls attention to another round in the ten-year struggle for control of Muscle Shoals.*

There are many explanations for this state of mind. We are more unsettled, more delocalized than we used to be, and the citizen has not the same close connection with his immediate government. Civic spirit and civic responsibility weaken in a people whose individual orbits are larger and more variable than any swing in space and time the human atom has ever made before. The town, that tight, man-size community built and felt by men together, fades into the more impersonal city, and it is very clear that for the city and its government nobody assumes any responsibility. As a political organism it seems to be a victim of one of those disturbances which turn the normal multiplication of healthy cells into a malignant growth.

Outside of New York and Chicago the tendency of "progressive" cities is to steer away from politics altogether and hire a manager to run the municipal business; that this progress is also away from democracy is regarded by the average citizen as a point in its favor. Ownership declines; the merchant, the banker and the factory head are hired managers, too, eight times out of ten, movable and on the move.

* Norris-Morrin Resolution, urging completion of construction for Muscle Shoals for nitrate and power, suffered a pocket veto January 4, 1928. Tennessee Valley Authority, established to develop and sell electric power, was finally enacted May 18, 1933.

Political ties loosen with all other ties in this urbanized, ownerless, rootless migration. Our politics, like our proxies, are left to the discretion of little groups. In our government we exercise our own will no more than in those corporations in which, as stockholders or employees, we are all vaguely involved. We have citizenship, as we have ownership, without responsibility. Add to this the intricacy of the interlocking economic and political complex, which no man understands, and you see why the ordinary citizen falls into a mood of fatalism in respect to the flux in which he finds himself.

Partly from panic, partly from bravado, mostly from ignorance, he achieves something like that nonchalance you have seen in the attitude of frightened boys riding a particularly snarly stretch of rapids. Only he does not ride the political current; he is the nonchalant spectator. He is partisan by habit, not by passionate conviction; he laughs at the efforts of political party leaders to find an issue on which to fight. Our political indifference is so profound that there is no fear of new alignments; the fear is that we shall not be able to keep even two parties going!

But what I am here concerned with is the effect of this indifference on Washington. One of the striking results of the abdication of the citizen, the wavering of the town on the political landscape, the appalling anarchy of the cities, the general tendency of post-war America to shift the weight, is an enormous centralization of government. Washington is today a more powerful capital in relation to the States of the Union than it was ever intended to be. Not only Thomas Jefferson but Theodore Roosevelt would be shocked if they could see how little the American is now governed by the Executive of his State and how much by the Chief Executive of the nation.

Since the Roosevelt Administration the centralizing movement has been so swift that we are fast losing all local control of ourselves. Government is literally remote where once it was near and visible. As the industrial system requires for its efficient operation a world without frontiers, so it is best served by uniform laws proceeding simultaneously from one source. The national lobbies maintained by all the great businesses, the national headquarters for everything under the sun, from the academy of science to motor-bus operators, are the proof that all pressure is now brought to bear on the National Legislature; State by State work is much too slow and piecemeal for a giant whose one law is change.

I think that any one who compares the Washington of today with war-time Washington must see that it appears more powerful. Twenty years ago it was hardly more than a Colonial capital, shabby and vague and tentatively beautiful. It looked older than it does now and pleasanter, more faithful to its tradition, at home in its secondary place in an easy-going world. It has changed, changed in aspect and even more in political weight and assurance. It is fairly inflated with government; by the expansion of Federal power alone it has grown from a straggling town to a solid city of more than half a million inhabitants.

Look at the new departments—Commerce, Agriculture, Internal Revenue—and you will read in massive, unmistakable headlines how the present intentions of this capital transcend its original intentions. Five blasts of dynamite it took to shake the old Market tower the other day, but, if other traditions had not more easily been blasted away, we should not need seventy acres of new administrative buildings. The capital of the world? Not quite, but obviously a world capital, and, more obviously still, a supersovereign in what used to be a league of nations and is now, with the full consent of the governed, hardly more than a Federal system nominally divided into States.

If Washington grows in power it also grows apart. The pattern of this city is already set, and it is a pattern from which all other American cities have departed. Washington grows horizontally; it builds in masses, colossal in spread instead of height, and somehow more suggestive of power, like a man who speaks without gestures, than the pointing, nervous silhouettes we like to sketch upon the sky. New York and its continental brood of vertical towns are spectacularly American. What, then, is Washington, which keeps to another plane, chooses amplitude, wide spaces, classic form, and each year that it expands will differ more from other American cities as they expand? Without pressing the point too far, I cannot help feeling there is something dimly symbolic in this opposition.

The capital begins to show the overconcentration of government, somewhat as the lean young executive fills out and solidifies as he settles into authority. It begins to express the tired business man's idea of government: a great plant, the latest equipment, something fairly impressive to show for your money, all the help you need for the best government on earth—and leave us alone! The departments are loaded with details once handled by States and municipalities, the staffs grow more unwieldy, the law-making machinery clogs. At the same time the local administrations are not relieved; the cost of local overhead increases almost faster than Federal costs. The citizen demands more government service all the time, demands it all along the line, but lately, notably since the war, his tendency has been to demand a disproportionate share from Federal agencies.

Now if one consequence of this tendency is to make the National Government stronger at the expense of local governments, another effect, rather more important, is to weaken the connection of the ordinary citizen with any kind of government. Local elections excite nobody much any more except the party organizations and the candidates for jobs; it is a rare issue or an exceptional campaign that brings out more than 30 or 40 per cent of the vote. The popular apathy characterizing the elections also explains the steadily lowered caliber of the candidates, almost invariably picked by the organizations or by some special interest in need of "representation." And these candidates, thus casually or cynically selected, form the panel from which, eventually, all the government officers are chosen. They are, in a very real sense, our governing class.

They come to Washington to preside over this stronghold wherein we are concentrating power without precedent in our history and whence we exercise an almost fabulous influence on the destiny of the world. Named by a small, often unintelligent party group, elected by a majority of a minority, left thereafter to their own devices, or rather to the persistent pressure of other minorities, these are the men from whom is expected the technical knowledge and the statesmanship necessary to steer our course through what amounts to a social and economic revolution.

It would be nearer the truth to say that is what they have to do. For the average American, he who demands so much public service, expects very little of his representatives. They are the product of his indifference and with indifference he continues to regard them. Thrown to the lions in the sense that Washington is a jungle of prowling "legislative committees" seeking whom they may devour, any representative of the people will tell you that with "the people" as such, citizens presumably affected by changes of law or policy, he has almost no communication. Beyond the Potomac there is silence. As was earlier suggested, the politician in power is left in a vacuum; no life-giving breath of popular enthusiasm or popular indignation, no current of that famous energy that propels the American dynamo, refreshes the devitalized atmosphere of government.

So they move along in their separate worlds, the people and the politicians. If the little world revolving around Washington seems unreal, stagnant, disconnected from the main stream of American life and off on some tangent of its own, there is quite as much unreality in the world of those who imagine they can live privately, minding their own business, taking no positive stand on public policies. The conversation of the political world is certainly no duller than that of the other world. On the whole, the Washington "line" is more varied and more interesting than the "line" of New York, Chicago or Los Angeles.

The small towns today have the best talk, especially the small towns of New England and the South. All city talk is hurried and shallow, mostly remarks made in passing, but Washington's is leisurely, ranging, mellow, the discourse of men whose trade is talk. The stupidest cannot listen day after day to the worst debate without some faint perception that all things are relative, that there is nothing local, simple or wholly novel in the questions that divide and confuse us. It is a perception one misses in many who "get down to brass tacks." There are few human interests, besides, that are not in some aspect political. That is why, between the view that elections are the important issues and the view that elections have no importance, it is difficult to decide which is narrow or further from reality. Certainly the two states of mind together create a division absurd and artificial; they make two words out of political economy and no sense out of either.

The architecture and plan of Washington were not designed to differentiate the national capital from other American cities. It is not horizontal because they are vertical; it simply grows in the ample mold in which it was conceived.

Yet it is not without suggestiveness that the political metropolis has gone one way and the commercial and industrial metropolises another; nor, as the capital gathers to itself more of the government other towns are too busy or too bored to administer, that it should assume features and manners distinct from theirs.

But it must be strange to the older Washington to mark how much more than formal is its difference from the rest of America; to see itself increasing in size and power at the expense of the idea it was built to perpetuate. For if democracies die, it will be because of the progressive lessening of popular interest in government; like other religions they begin to die when the form is more impressive than the fact.

[8]   1 9 3 1   *August 16.* AMERICA IN A MID-AUGUST MOOD. *A nation which sees the depression blacker than it is, which now doubts the faith it has always proclaimed and is painfully aware of the world.*

NEW YORK

Is America growing old? Have we—the young adventurers, the Innocents Abroad, the pioneers, the buccaneers, the racketeers—slumped into that sad maturity which submits to events, accepts the universe? At any crossroads of the continent this Summer the mood of mid-August is heavy on the land. Mid-August, mid-afternoon, middle-age—only these torpid tenses describe our state of mind. The great American nation is to be discovered in an attitude as elderly and unenterprising as that of Mr. Micawber. Our inertia, if it is that, is no more physical than his; never were we more in motion, but aimlessly, going around in circles. It is not even mental; we think in circles, too, grow wrinkles trying to figure out the lost quantity in equations that yesterday seemed so simple. The lull is suspense. Un-American as it sounds, we are all waiting, waiting for something to turn up. We look a little like that fat comedian in the movies who sits in heavy contemplation after he gets tangled up in his own gear.

Part of the heaviness is wheat. Upon the midland plains the yellow harvests lie like a curse of abundance, the bread that has become literally a stone. Part of it is coal. There are whole regions whose populations go hungry and sullen in the shadow of immovable mountains of anthracite. Much of it is gold, dead and buried in the mortuary vaults of Manhattan. And some of the aimless motion is nothing-to-do, uneasy loafing and the ranging hunt for work. With un-American patience skilled workmen hang around or mill around day after day hoping for odd jobs. With un-American meekness they accept the dwindling weekly hand-out of the Community Chest.

Other portents appear. Everywhere you meet salesmen, the biggest parade of salesmen in history, and half of them are questioning their own sales talk; how much of the present sales resistance is reaction from that golden policy of mass-seduction, the deferred-payment plan? From the lips of the most orthodox issue doubts of what so short a time ago was unquestionable orthodoxy: Were we demonstrating a "new economics" or only a brain storm? The New York multimillionaire stuffing his safety-deposit box full of government bonds displays the same un-American timidity as the occasional queue of small depositors in Middletown withdrawing their savings to tuck them away in the old bureau drawer.

We embark on an un-American foreign policy. With a sudden jolt we go into reverse in regard to official participation in European affairs, make a complete right-about-face respecting the relation of war debts to reparations. For a dozen years we have been told by politicians of both parties that such a policy runs counter to the collective will of the

American people and would prove fatal to any statesman who initiates it. Does a ripple of protest stir the sluggish air? If there is any sound it is the sound of cheers. Whether the Hoover Plan saves Germany or not, it is a life-saver for Mr. Hoover, the most popular act of his administration.

Less than two years of depression,* scoffed at by our elders as nothing compared to the panics they have weathered, and we have this spectacle of a headlong people afraid of the next step, a people prodigal in spending the millions they hadn't, afraid to spend the hundreds they have, a people whose audacity is a legend afraid to take a chance. A people, moreover, so abnormally subdued in spirit, manifesting so little boldness of initiative in the highest ranks, and so little tendency to rebellion in the lowest, that if Mr. Hoover had announced the cancellation of war debts instead of a year's moratorium, if he had annulled the latest tariff, recognized Russia, given one good feed to China with all our surplus wheat, set up a supreme economic council, done half a dozen things he cannot be imagined doing, public acquiescence in these revolutionary changes (supposing Congress still out of session) would probably still be as unanimous, and as passive.

Now the American is not dazed by the contrast between the mood of 1929 and that of 1931. He is accustomed to our ups and downs, our exaggerated heat and cold, our forward rushes and our unqualified retreats. We are far more volatile than the French, who below their manner are rather too solid for this erratic earth. But we bewilder the foreigner who sees us in the depths. There is something almost comic in the dismay of a visiting delegation of German grocers. Fresh from a country whose S O S was inevitably shouted in our direction, a bit jealous of their priority as the world's chief mourners, they are introduced to a Midas as poor-mouthed as themselves. "Chained grocers, free grocers?" puzzled one per-

* Stock Market Crash occurred October 29, 1929.

spiring burgher in a mid-West town. "And nothing but grief for both? I did not expect this in America. You Americans feel your little troubles very much."

The Britisher, on the contrary, does not minimize our troubles. He is never surprised or unwilling to admit that we are worse off than England. Either he takes the view of a writer in The Contemporary Review, the calm English view: "In our generation, with the exception of Germany and Russia, no nation has undergone a reverse so catastrophic" as the United States. For he assumes the we-like-our-dole attitude of an English friend in transit, who thinks all we need is hunger reverses. "Wait until hard times are chronic, as they are with us," he boasts, "and you'll get used to them. What paralyzes you now is the fear that you are involved in the common misery of mankind, not episodically, as in wars, not politically, as in alliances and leagues of nations, but all the time and down to your last cent. That's the great American tragedy—to suspect that you can't go as far as you can, can't forge too far ahead of the procession. It is the anti-climax of every national climax."

One way or the other, it is easy to exaggerate what has happened to America in the past two years. Easier still is to look out upon this groaning continent—groaning under plenty —and decide there is nothing in our circumstances to justify the chute from the mad optimism of two summers ago to the profound pessimism of today. What we want, says James Truslow Adams, is perspective, the long view instead of the close-up, the weight of history to balance the plunging scale. But perhaps this is perspective: this new outlook upon the encroaching world, this first glance into the jungle of the future, this pause of doubt upon a road whereon we have met all sorts of hazards, but never before the question whether it was the right road going in the one desirable direction.

Previous depressions have been marked by more bank fail-

ures, riots, sharper falls of commodity prices, longer bread-
lines, a less massive background of national wealth and government solvency. Today's adversity, seen superficially, is
hardly more than a petrified prosperity. But that is the newly
disturbing factor in the situation. People see something irra-
tional in this prostration under surpluses, the reductio ad
absurdum of our economic system. Other factors, too, are
without precedent in our experience. For one thing, there is
the height from which we crashed. A fall from the twentieth
story causes a bigger bump than a descent from the fourth or
fifth. In this sense our reverse is as catastrophic as the Englishman reports.

Then there is the impartiality with which this depression
affects all localities and all classes. It brings the manufacturing areas down to the level of the agricultural States, already
eight years in the hole, and hits the cities as hard as the small
towns. The very spread of industrial prosperity, the extraordinary sweep of corporate ownership, diffuses the gloom of
unpaid dividends among millions who never before owned
a share of stock. But though the prosperity was spread far it
was spread thin. The biggest jolt we receive is the revelation
that the economic philosophy that made us a nation of owners made us also a nation of debtors. After we had abolished
the Rainy Day from our calendar as confidently as the Russians abolished Sunday, suddenly the skies opened and the
torrents fell.

At the end of a decade of the highest wages in history, the
average American worker is only a month or so away from
the breadline if he loses his job. Social agents who have
served through other crises are agreed that this one is the
worst in the extent to which it has caught people unprepared.
It strikes a higher level; executives, clerks, professional people, tradesmen, skilled workers, are now obliged to accept

help. A good deal of our high-stepping, in fact, seems to have been done on stilts.

Added to all that is the enveloping fog of world depression. This is not a tumble which we have taken alone and out of which we can rise by our own power. Not only do we see our strength threatened by the weakness of other nations, the solvent at the mercy of the insolvent. We begin to despair that any country is powerful enough to make the upgrade by itself. We cannot help perceiving that the international economic system is out of control, and since in this system the highest stake is ours, everything we count on, our principles and our interest, is threatened by its breakdown.

The outlook is further clouded by the first appearance in the world of an alternative system. In the valleys of despond we have struggled through heretofore no Communist empire loomed on the horizon. Now Russia is on the mind of all the nations. The persistence of the Soviet experiment acts like a universal enchantment. The intense interest and curiosity with which it is regarded, whether inspired by hope or fear, is almost pathological. In this country Russia is today the best known of all foreign countries to the average citizen.

People who have no concern about the operation of the political system under which they live, who know nothing about the budget, the taxation or the labor code of their own country, are enormously excited by the Five-Year Plan. Its well-dramatized progress, almost exactly coinciding with the progress of capitalist depression, has given us a new basis and new terms of comparison. What business slump before was casually referred to as "a crisis of capitalism"? Since when have we all been so conscious of our "unplanned economy"? Contrast the American anxiety over Germany's present peril with our detachment in the crisis of 1923. The new element in the picture is Russia, changed from a vague shadow east of the Reich to a powerful Red Army marching over Europe.

Perspective? Once, in the quiet little museum of Perugia, the eager old custode arranged a procession of masterpieces to teach me the development of perspective in painting. I saw the great, gold-encrusted, hieratic figures of the Primitives emerging from the flat, stepping out gradually, awkwardly, from the canvas until at last—after how many droll, tentative attitudes!—they stood free in the air and sky. And as they became figures in the crowd, or in the gentle Franciscan landscapes of Umbria, of course even the central saints became smaller, spaced to fit into a design instead of being the whole picture themselves. They became sadder, too, I thought. The solitary, lily-like Madonna of Bonfigli was in Perugino the queen of a distracting court, half in heaven and half on earth.

So America emerges heavily from the flat into the round, arrives at the stage where the world impinges not on this side or that, but on every side. It is a painful process, the development of perspective, painful and slow. Nations do not make these evolutions willingly or overnight. We are not "isolated" and independent on June 19 and on June 20 converted to an entirely different attitude, just because Mr. Hoover sponsors an international debt moratorium and orders the ranking members of his Cabinet into such a conference with the statesmen of Europe as we have not engaged in since Versailles. Rather, the President's action recognizes an existing reality and corresponds to a change already made in the national mind.

The proof of this is evident to any one who listens at the crossroads this Summer. Although the rest of the country is never so concerned in international affairs as the East, and is not now, one hears more talk about Europe in the Middle West today than at any time since the war. There is nothing

altruistic in this interest, nothing of the lofty argument pro
and con the League of Nations. We were not ready to interfere in Europe so long as it was simply a question of saving
Europe, but if we must interfere in order to save ourselves,
we submit to the sacrifice. Although the step taken is not
very audacious and the results up to date are disappointing,
the fact that the state of Europe actually supersedes prohibition as a topic of conversation in the United States is a
striking sign of change.

Even more than the state of Europe, the state of America
displaces the wet and dry issue as the major theme of American social intercourse. Now, when we refer to the liquor question, it is in terms of revenue only. Why should not the government collect reparations in our private wars, desperate in
our cities as those of mediaeval Italy; why not have the boot-
legger's income instead of his income tax? But generally we
discuss subjects of more immediate importance. And if the
thought of the country is disclosed in the discussions heard at
dinner tables, noontide clubs, gas stations, Pullman smokers,
labor locals, even beauty parlors, then we are experiencing
a change of values as well as a change of emphasis.

If this was ever a complacent land, it is not complacent
now. If we are intoxicated by bigness—and we must have
peaks, even in panics!—we are sobered by new doubts of the
superlative. There is a good deal of nebulous but earnest
questioning of what we have learned to call "the industrial
pattern"; you discover that in industrial America as well as
in industrial Germany there is a tendency among the young
to revolt against the civilization developed by industry.
Americans everywhere are talking about simpler standards
of life. They are interested in the French system of national
economy. Russia suggests something new and terrifying, to
many in this country the logical climax of our own system.
France, with its small units, its conservative balance between

agriculture and industry, coupled with its preeminent solidity in the present flux and its successful enactment of our old role in the recent conferences, begins to symbolize everything old and safe.

The strange patience of the unemployed means that they, too, share the common uncertainty. They do not know which way to turn. If the economic planner has found in Russia a standard by which to measure the failures of our anarchic system, the worker also, it must be remembered, finds there an actual instead of an oratorical basis of comparison. He sees the dream of the soap-box orator in process of fulfillment. And so far he does not like "the working man's paradise." It is the intellectual and the economist who are enthusiastic about the Five-Year Plan. The American proletarian is not. He has besides his own hangover: "The next time I get $10 a day I won't be in the Line when it stops," likewise, the strong sympathy of the community, which feels as never before that unemployment is as much a charge on industry as taxes or dividends, and that there is a common responsibility for the muddle in which we find ourselves.

Faith in the American formula of prosperity is wavering. The same economists who two years ago were the prophets of a new economic doctrine, seeing in high wages, mass production and scientific management the infallible combination that would keep us going at the same pace forever, are now busy explaining the depression as the result of unforeseen world events. But the ordinary citizen at last suspects that we bid too long on an all-trump hand. The combination on which we profiteered for ten golden years was a unique and transitory set of circumstances, not of our making; it can happen again only if we are a going concern when the rest of the world is not.

But the most striking effect of two years of waiting for something to happen, the sum of all these doubts and fears,

is the general feeling of insecurity. Money is timid. At a time
when all the emphasis is on long-term planning, nobody
dares to plan for next year. If you are looking for courage and
confidence you will find more among small business men
than in Big Business as such. The heroes of this crisis are not
the captains of industry, the great Tycoons who are supposed
to lose fortunes as nonchalantly as they make them. They
are the small tradesmen and little manufacturers hanging on,
carrying their customers, expanding as far as they can, and
not those whose hoarded wealth enables them to see the storm
through without great personal inconvenience. All the grand
gestures are made on a miniature scale. Of spectacular daring, the celebrated American nerve and bold initiative, the
examples are few.

Political leaders exhibit the same timidity and poverty of
ideas, which explains why the popular attitude toward political solutions remains as apathetic as usual. The only positive idea crystallizing in the country is the demand for some
form of unemployment insurance and provision for old age.
This measure of defense against industrial insecurity neither
political party will be able to dodge. Otherwise, nobody
seems to have any constructive suggestions to offer. With an
election around the corner, and a people yearning to be led
almost anywhere, as the response to the Hoover Plan demonstrates, the "outs" cannot think up a relief program different
enough from that of the "ins" to rouse any real hope or enthusiasm in the electorate.

If any nation was ever justified in a panic of the spirit, it
is this country facing the problems pressing for solution today. Here we are, the new decisive power in the world at
one of the turning points of history. It is the characteristic of
this crisis that it piles up the questions that have been evaded
since the beginning of the industrial revolution a hundred
years ago, and demands all the answers at once. The United

States stands as a symbol of most of the ideas now under critical examination. Is democracy the final form of government, efficient and flexible enough to keep pace with the movement of events? Can democracies look ahead, secure authority to plan? Ask the greatest and oldest democracy. Is capitalism a more workable economic system than communism, or, to put the query in the only practical form in which it will ever be asked, can private capitalism compete with State capitalism? Inquire at the general headquarters of capitalism where wealth has been accumulated and distributed on a scale elsewhere unknown. Can industrialism create a satisfactory and liberating civilization? Look to the country which has set the pace for the mechanization of the world.

Faced by responsibilities like these, no wonder our psychological depression is deeper than the facts warrant. But why this paralysis of the intellect? Where are the big American brains to deal with unemployment, with group planning, with the ghastly cost of competition, with that hoary old wheeze that supply balances demand, with the control of industry, with a modern credit system? Or are we to go on waiting for something to happen until it does?

[9] 1 9 3 2 *January 3.* THE AVERAGE AMERICAN EMERGES. *If there is a hero of this hour, it is he—all over the country one feels the stirrings of that rising spirit which signalizes the recognition of a great national emergency.*

WASHINGTON

Perhaps this is no time for cheers or trumpetings on any theme. Certainly, brass has never sounded brassier than when some wheezy drum major tries to galvanize the political bandwagon with the march tunes of 1928. At the beginning of 1932 the firecracker patriot has about the same effect on the audience as static on the air, as none should know better than the members of Congress exiled in their constituencies for the best part of the last year. The same is true of the professional business optimist; the cheer-leaders and gloom-chasers flatly fail to whoop us up. Indubitable as are the uses of adversity, they are generally celebrated only by those who still have jobs. To all such rhetoric the popular answer is, "Oh, yeah?" The phrase sweeps the country as if it were coined to express the present mood of America.

Still the eager victims of ballyhoo, we have grown up to the point where we can bite and at the same time chortle at ourselves for biting. What most foreign and domestic critics fail to grasp is that we like our superlatives more than we believe in them. If you doubt it, listen to the rude jests on hard times exchanged on park benches in the cold, across the lunch counter in the drug store, on the interurban buses. Witness the new crop of local weeklies from New York to Houston and Minneapolis, and points between and beyond, that flourish on nothing but satire of the home town. Even the radio has its "cuckoo hour" to make fun of radio programs.

America has not lost that capacity to enjoy its own extravagances which constitute the national sense of humor. In fact, the country echoes today with dry, wry and wholly heroic laughter. And as one who in the third Winter of the Great Depression has traveled from coast to coast and caught glimpses of the Northwest, the Southwest and the Middle West as those great kingdoms see themselves, it seems to me that it is time to pin a sprig of mistletoe on the shiny lapel of the American who is never heard on the air or on the Hill, who is neither summoned to big business conferences nor commissioned to write treatises on economic planning, but who pays most of the taxes that are paid, supports all the relief drives, sits tight as he can on that slippery level called the American standard of living, and meanwhile manages to crack a hardy joke or two at his own predicament.

I refer, of course, not to the prominent citizen but to the little fellow—the small manufacturer, the independent merchant, the farmer, the country doctor, the school teacher in a bankrupt city, the mechanic, the corner grocer, the mother keeping the children in school on next to nothing. Maybe this American is not the brains of the country, wherever they are. He understands little of the world-wrecking transfer system of international bankers or the spreading spider web of big holding companies. His ideas on planned economy are desperately personal. But he is just as confused as if he were an expert in these intricate matters. He has the haziest notions of the epoch-making changes in which he is involved. For the most part he is looking backward rather than forward. You'd be surprised to know how many millions in this progressive nation are homesick for the past.

If there is a hero of this hour, however, it is this average American. If the country weathers crises, it is because he keeps his head and holds on. For two years he waited, hoped, temporized, refused to believe that conditions would not better themselves. He was like a passenger in a ship keeled over by a big wave who holds his breath until another big wave restores the balance. Now for the first time he realizes that he belongs to the crew. All over the country you feel the stirrings of that rising spirit which means the recognition of an emergency.

Thoroughly frightened, the average American always whistles; by his wise-cracking you know that he knows he is up against it. He cannot be expected to have more wisdom and foresight than his business and political leaders, but he perceives that something has to be done and, as far as he can, he is doing it. He is the force behind the "drives" which seem funny to the satirist, stupid to the Socialist, and to every clear-eyed observer inadequate, whether the sum collected is $18,000,000 in New York or $10,000 in a county seat in Dakota.

But if these campaigns are not the sound method of coping with hunger and unemployment, they are, up to date, the only method. They represent a communal effort unequaled even during the war, when patriotism was at fever pitch and all the factories were running full-speed. "Nobody is going to starve in this town this Winter," the truculent boast of every town, implies a good deal more strain and sacrifice than the meatless, wheatless days when we maintained a fighting army much smaller than the present army of the unemployed.

No traveler can cross the continent without a renewed sense of the physical magnificence of America. As he traverses the still plains and the grave mountains in these slow-pulsing times, he is more than ever conscious of the power in the land itself. Up to now this land has seemed more an empire than a country, by which I mean that it has been more possessed than possessive; has reflected the movements of a restless and volatile people but has not been marked by the character of that people. You cannot say of it what the first glimpse enables you to say of older, smaller and more homogeneous countries: This is France, this is England. The American soil has not been cherished enough for that instant identification; as a people we have only "worked" the ground we camp on as a means to push on to something else, to somewhere else.

But now, perhaps because the traveler of today, wherever he goes, must be more preoccupied with the human than with the natural scenery, he notes signs of a new relation between the American and his local environment. One looks at the people more than the landscape and discovers that as a nation we are commencing to settle down. Oh, not as any race before has planted itself in one place and acquired roots and ancestral acres. The transcontinental highways are full of us in motion, and never in our history was the sentiment for land ownership so weak. But we have gone as far west as we can and the countryside between the coasts at last shows marks of permanent habitation. The flimsy frontier towns are changing from wood to brick and concrete. Gone are most of the bleak, isolated villages of yesterday. The further west you go the brighter are the towns, each with its flashing signs, and you realize that what most distinguishes this country from all others is the lavish use of light and power.

This is a land beginning to be loved for its own sake and not merely as a splendid idea, a land beginning to be enjoyed. More, it is a land beginning to impress itself upon the inhabitants, or they upon it, so that in the newest States local types and local patriotism are becoming as definite as in the oldest. That is an observation impossible to make without stopping at most of the way-stations, and if you do that, now that every community is facing hard facts, and the ordinary citizen is acting as he can act in a crisis, you are likely to come back shouting, not over the landscape, which subdues everybody by its scale and splendor, but over the spirit of the people.

There are times when the complacency, the rugged selfishness and the greed for hokum of one's compatriots are hard to bear. This is not one of those times. At the bottom of the market we are much nicer than we are at the top. Main Street in a depression is the most neighborly street in the world. It is a very patient thoroughfare, patient with its debtors, patient in its faith that the American Government is the most intelligent government on earth, though temporarily out of ideas. It is enlivened by a kind of humor that is about the most American thing in America; Will Rogers expresses it better than anybody else.

In the years when we used to shove the French off the Grands Boulevards, some American in Paris wrote a poem which was very popular at the time in the American colony. It was called "I Hate Americans." In Paris that is too possible; also in New York in the flatulent years when the ticker is the pulse of life or in Presidential campaigns when the opposing gangs start hitting below the belt. But visiting the home front in the zero hour how often you are impelled to say: "I like Americans!"

The reason for this warmth is the plugging, everyday citizen. He is more visible in slumps than in booms. The pattern of prosperity is made by the big money-makers and the big spenders; as in every society, Russian, French, Hollywood, the whole canvas takes its color from the most conspicuous figures. Now the millions in the background take the center of the stage. And as the background American moves into the foreground, he draws attention to certain other features of the contemporary picture, which appear often and far apart enough to have value for purposes of generalization. If one were asked to characterize the high points in what has been called the new America, a land sobered and reshaped by world-wide depression, one would have to say that most of them are reactions, temporary perhaps, but none the less retrogressive; the Bolsheviki would call them counter-revolutionary.

The first is that the darkest gloom centers are just those centers of wealth and population to which there has been a stampede during the last ten years. Now, the characteristic of this depression is that it has no "areas"; no locality nor any class of citizens has escaped. But outside of conditions in the mining regions, which affect thousands instead of millions, the worst spots are the big industrial cities, particularly in the Great Lakes district—Detroit, Chicago, Cleveland, Pittsburgh.

The atmosphere lightens perceptibly as one goes west. The wheat and corn belts, so bitter in 1924 and 1928 that I expected to find them now on the verge of revolution, actually complain less loudly than before. The South with the price of cotton at the vanishing point and the Middle West, mortgaged beyond the limit, could hardly be in worse plight, but one section has the habit of poverty and the other enjoys the cold comfort of no longer suffering alone. The farmers are not now a caste singled out for punishment in a general opulence; they see business and industry where agriculture has been for ten years. The difference between the attitude of the bankrupt farmer today and that of the unemployed mechanic or salesman is the immeasurable difference between knowing and not knowing where your next meal is coming from.

As to the Pacific Coast, and in particular that great State whose sufferings are so eloquently described in the Senate by Senator Johnson,* it is a zone of light and cheer compared to the East. One reason is that the accustomed and valorous West takes its troubles lightly. The other, more suggestive, is that, while the needy flock to cities in quest of relief, the urban organism proves less adjustable than the rural and does not stand up so well under economic strain. The poorer sections of the country are today more buoyant and definitely better off than the rich.

That is one anomaly. The second is that this is actually the day of the small business man. True, he has been conspicuous among the casualties, but considering that his doom has been written by all the economic prophets he exhibits a surprising sturdiness under attacks that have proved too much for many big corporations. The little plant, frugally managed, with a

* Senator Hiram W. Johnson (R), California.

personal relationship between employer and employees, can
be adjusted to keep going without profit as the great corpo-
rate-owned, dividend-paying enterprises cannot. In instance
after instance the small business is run at a loss to provide
work and keep the personnel together. "Tiding over" is one
of the best things the small proprietor does. After seeing him
in the process, I think he deserves the palm for courage and
resourcefulness in a crisis. If big business were as bold in attempting the impossible the country would be humming.

In Kansas and other prairie States one hears that the small
farmer bears up better than the big corporation farms under
ruinous wheat prices. The explanation is the same. The factory farm has to carry a factory overhead; when it fails to
earn wages and profits the loss is swamping, while the small
farmer can make some sort of living and hold on for years, as
he does, with no profit at all. A similar story is told by the
independent merchant, and that means the fittest who has
survived chain-store competition. With careful buying, small
margins of profit and sleepless attention to details, he can
enjoy even now a modest prosperity. This is true of small department stores, mills, hotels, even theaters, and it is especially true of newspapers, which of all enterprises seem the
least decimated by the depression.

That, too, is an anomaly—that the small concern tough
enough to hold on emerges in a stronger and more assured
position in respect to chains and mergers than it had occupied for years.

This may or may not be a step backward, a score of the
old, inefficient system against the hard corporate efficiency.
There can be no doubt about the reactionary character of
two other expedients now resorted to in many States. One,
the substitution of manual labor for machines on the roads
and on various county jobs in order to give work to the re-
cipients of unemployment funds, is a public emergency meas-

ure, of no significance save as an ironic comment on a civilization that displaces skilled men by machines and then compensates by giving them the unskilled jobs of other machines.

But the return to barter is a private enterprise, and one of the striking phenomena of the present chaos. The direct exchange of goods for goods is now a common practice of small producers tied up by the shortage of money and credit. In many Western towns are improvised "exchanges" in which commodities are the currency. I observed the movement chiefly in the Southwest, in Southern California, Arizona, New Mexico, Western Texas, but it grows in a score of other States. A truckload of oranges travels as far as 200 miles and comes back a truckload of apples. A calf is bartered for a load of beans. There is something joyous about these transactions; trading without money is an entirely different temper from ordinary buying and selling. You see multiplied proofs these days of how gladly people turn to the primitive, but none more convincing than the lively zest of this new-old commerce at the crossroads.

Neighborhood meetings of all kinds are more frequent than usual. Local political apathy is still pretty profound, as the sunken state of municipal government everywhere bears witness, but there appears something like a general resurrection of that long-atrophied impulse called community spirit. This is partly the effect of the civic drives for relief funds, conducted with a wartime fervor, and partly the welding heat of a common protest.

Main street is patient, and on its own initiative—without campaign oratory, that is—is not inclined to load its grievances on a political scapegoat. Its mood is one of trouble and dark uncertainty rather than of bitterness, but in its panic it is easily swayed by any argument. Its first instinct is to turn out anybody in office in favor of almost any outsider. It yearns above all for action, audacity, which explains the enormous popularity throughout the West of direct tactics like those of Governor Bill Murray of Oklahoma. At this moment, though there is a distinct hardening of heart toward Europe, a general stiffening of nationalistic sentiment, it would be easy to persuade America either to cancel all the war debts or to insist on the last farthing. We want nothing so much as to be told, with enough assurance, which way to turn.

Lacking any such leadership, the ordinary citizen just protests on general principles. His rebellions are amazingly orderly, but in one respect, at least, they mean business. Wherever you go you run into mass meetings called to protest against taxes. That is nothing new, of course, but opposition has seldom been so spontaneous, so universal, so determined. The nearest thing to a political revolution in the country is the tax revolt. For the first time in a generation taxpayers are wrought up to the point of willingness to give up public services. "We'll do without county agents," they say. "We'll give up the public health service. We can no longer pay the cost of government." In many district taxes are practically noncollectible. Moving among the embattled rebels, one wonders how deficits are to be met if any branch of the government tries to increase the levies of these merchants, farmers, small property owners, who in their numbers furnish the bulk of State and national revenues.

What the community spirit really thrives on, however, are not emergency campaigns or tax revolts. These only bring into relief a widespread national movement which might be described as a separatist movement, except that it does not tend to regionalism or subordination, but only to a strong, more or less self-conscious localism. Everywhere there is a new stress on local color, local customs, local foods, local history. The observer who finds these United States standardized observes them very superficially. We have the most stereotyped equipment of any nation in the world—gas stations, store windows, plumbing fixtures, Cellophane wrappings—and the widest distribution of identical mass-produced articles. These trappings may tend to give us the monotonous appearance of an army in uniform, but that's as far as it goes. Underneath you find a people almost as variegated as the hodge-podge on the European Continent. We have as many racial memories, geographic types, natural frontiers.

To the tenderfoot, all the Stetson hats of the West look alike; if you think they are alike, try to palm off the Wyoming type on a Texas cow-puncher, and you will soon learn that a different brim, a different band and a different crown is made for every locality. Americans are like that, only more so. Between the Kansan and the Missourian there is nearly as much difference, for example, as between the German and the Frenchman. Southern California is almost exclusively populated by people less than ten years away from the Middle West, and already the climate and the country, as alien to their own as Morocco to Russia, is making them over into a strange new breed.

Perhaps the new localism is a reaction against surface standardization, the instinctive resistance of the first fully industrialized race against becoming itself a machine product. Perhaps it is the effect of the settling down I have spoken of, the land putting its seal upon the inhabitants. At any rate, we are becoming more, rather than less, local-minded. The tendency manifests itself in various ways, sometimes in the buy-at-home campaigns which even in these States echo the futile slogans of European nations aiming at self-sufficiency; sometimes in a passion for markers, monuments, revival of local traditions; oftenest in a review and revival of the local story, with special emphasis on its points of difference from the story of the neighboring settlement.

Oregon is as passionate about a 60-year-old past as Virginia is about Jamestown. Not all States can rebuild to as definite a local pattern as does New Mexico, but the ambition of all, the newer more than the old, is to preserve and create something distinctive. "That is old Nevada," you are told in Carson City, or "This is a typical Nebraska landscape," as you gaze out upon a scene that only its intimates can distinguish from Kansas or Dakota. Yet there are differences; the States of this Union would be, in many respects, as separate as nations if they had not had 150 years of Federal Government.

After a hundred years of trying to be alike, surely nothing in the new America is more interesting than the general desire to revive and reemphasize local differences, even to create distinctions where none exist. Every State, in so far as it can, is producing a local literature; the West especially, that young, unconquered land, bursts with reminiscences.

There is a good deal of local pride in the desperate push behind the relief drives. And local feeling, the need for community, is one of the elements in the new social consciousness of the average citizen. In a crisis he feels part of his community as he did not in prosperity, and his sense of participation today has little in common with the shouting, pumped-up, better-business buncombe of a decade ago. It is deeper, full of fear, of premonitions of loss and change, the search of a lonely man for support in a strange world.

It has frequently been remarked that in no previous depression was there a common recognition that unemployment is the fault of the community and the system and that those who earn owe a living to those whom they have in a sense displaced. That is true, as it is also true that the social consciousness of today is in reality the instinct to defend the existing social order. The average American is profoundly conservative, more so today than ever. You see by the signs I have been suggesting that in his present confusion and dismay he is trying to retreat. He has experimented with new ways, new speeds, new conceptions, and he is fumbling back to find out if there is any possible adjustment with the old.

The little fellow holding on by the skin of his teeth is a heroic conservative. He believes there is something worth saving in the American system and he is doing more than politicians, bankers or big business men to save it. He keeps his courage up by whistling, making sarcastic remarks—"Oh, yeah?"—and celebrating the pioneers of the simpler past. He is conservative, but it would be unwise to bank too heavily upon his conservatism. In his present perplexity he could be led in almost any direction. "If this keeps on—" he threatens, darkly. And then he laughs. "Say, did you hear that one about the Indiana family that collected enough to spend the Winter in San Diego because every time they stopped some town paid 'em to move on?"

[10]   1 9 3 2 *February 28.* MAIN STREET REAPPRAISES WALL STREET. *A report upon the country's changed attitude toward the financial canyon which it explored for gold.*

WASHINGTON

In spite of literary whispers to the contrary, to Europe, and especially to official Europe, New York seems still, seems now more than ever, in fact, the real capital of the United States. The diplomats in Washington have the habit of assuming that they should be stationed in New York to get the true view of this country, and the foreign newspapers are so sure of the location of the American center of gravity that their correspondents, with very few exceptions, turn their backs upon the national capital and report America from the watch-towers of Manhattan Island.

The basis of this assumption is not that the metropolis contains more real Americans than any other city, as visibly and audibly it doesn't, or, more reasonably, that its half-assimilated mixture of races best represents this gargantuan mongrel among the nations. It isn't that as the national broadcasting station, center of print and publicity, New York is the great factory of American opinion; nor even that the place hits the old world in the eye, so to speak, sticking out there in front like an enormously extended and distended Colossus of Rhodes.

These reasons are valid enough, but of course it is as the seat of financial power that New York rivets the attention of mankind. It is assumed to express us because where our treasure is, there the heart, soul and mind of America are supposed to be. Observers from countries where the financial and political capital is a single city, with a single policy, when forced here to choose between two capitals, not unnaturally decide for Wall Street as against Capitol Hill. From the international point of view, Washington was never so overshadowed as it is today, when New York has become not only the national money center but the money center and therefore the nerve center of the world.

From the American point of view, however, the story is different. Americans in the hinterland never admitted that New York, above all financial New York, was representative of the country at large. And today they are less than ever willing to admit it. It happens that while the outer world hangs anxiously on the policies of American financial leaders, in the domestic circle there is a strong reaction against these policies. In a country which suffered more than 2,000 bank failures last year and has lately listened to revelations of the extravagant competition for foreign loans, the tendency is to blame the bankers for almost everything that has happened at home and abroad. Among the revulsions character-

istic of the depression, and they are many and profound, not
the least is the popular swing-back to the traditional view
of Wall Street. Not in a generation, at least, has the feeling
against money barons been so bitter as it is among the flat
and deflected multitudes who yesterday were on the way to
becoming money barons themselves.

For a brief and tropic period lower Manhattan was the
most representative place in the country. Only a little while
ago Wall Street was hardly distinguishable from Main Street.
It was the thoroughfare on which we all did business. Not a
crossroad in the land but was dealing in New York bank issues
and trading joyously in the New York Stock Exchange. The
"vested interests," whatever they may mean, apparently loosened up. The bogey-land they are wont to inhabit turned into
a kind of Aladdin's Cave in which every dollar thrown in
came out multiplied ten, fifty, a hundred-fold. This magic
multiplication we associated with the New Economics, an
American patent process which we protected with raised tariffs and on which we issued large mortgages. It was a time
when such thoughts as we had and many dollars that we
had not all traveled in one direction. Certainly the American
mind was to be found concentrated on one spot during that
carnival—and that spot was not Washington.

Now, as I say, we are in a mood of reaction. Whoever
would read the unsettled mind and interpret the wavering
policies of the United States at the present juncture would
better turn from the Hudson and take his stand on the banks
of the Potomac. Between the financial and political capitals
of this country there is a historic line of cleavage. All Americans recognize this line, but it has been so exaggerated in
political oratory and is often so vague that they sometimes
forget that it is real.

In separating the two cities geographically, the fathers of
the Republic succeeded in setting them apart spiritually, so

that even to this day they are never quite at home in company. Seldom do they see alike or pull together; even when they try to cooperate, as in recent years they have aimed to do in the matter of international loans, they do so awkwardly, uncertainly, with an air of furtiveness. Notwithstanding the gibes about dollar diplomacy, the average American, likewise the average officer of this government, feels none of the nonchalance of the expert in the use of finance as an instrument of national policy.

Now to speak of "Washington" and "Wall Street" as symbols of politics and finance as if one term did not include the other, is as meaningless as to refer to national and international policies as if in the present world, or any world, indeed, they could be independent one of the other. Yet it would be foolish not to recognize differences between the two. Washington does represent the translation into politics of the sentiments of the American majority. The translation is often free and always slow, so that changes in the public mind usually occur long before they are reported in Congress, as on the subjects of tariff and prohibition, for instance; but it is as faithful a rendering as it is possible to obtain of the thought and the mood of the nation. And, like it or not, as I listen to Washington today after hearing the same conservative opinions, the same revival of old slogans, in nearly every State in the Union, it seems to me that Washington has seldom rendered so literally the general state of mind.

In Washington, then, and at this moment more clearly than usual, you hear the voice of Main Street and there can be no manner of doubt that Main Street is in sharp disagreement with Wall Street. In the highest quarters here you may hear New York described as "a stink in the nostrils of the country." Political prophets debate seriously whether New York—not Tammany, mind you, not the inordinate, many-millioned town toward which the whole country gravitates, but New York the financial capital—is not too great a handicap for a candidate to carry into a Presidential campaign. Governor Alfalfa Bill Murray gets a handsome hand from a representative Washington audience when he excommunicates "the island in the Hudson River which is detached from America and attached to Europe."

All this is in a familiar strain. In the political fairy tale it is always assumed that the people are on one side and the capitalists on the other. But America has long since ceased to believe that. There has been too wide a spread of corporate wealth, linking the big and the little stockholder in a common greed for dividends. The lusty, avaricious breath that blew to the bursting point the great bubble of 1929 was the flatulence of a whole people more than any inflation in history. We are a nation with a capitalist psychology. Money-makers and bankers are the people we respect and follow.

Hence the present indictment of financial leadership and the dull groping for political leadership, so long despised, indicate a disillusionment that means more than a mere reaction, a return to pre-war slogans and pre-boom bombast. It means, in reality, the death of a dogma in which we believed, in which the Communists believe even more religiously: that money is itself omnipotent, so great a power that those who control the world's wealth can do almost anything. We somehow took for granted that great financial institutions, magnificently wicked though they might be, were also magnificently wise in pursuing their own ends.

Now it appears to many Americans that the bankers (with, of course, many notable exceptions) were as lacking in foresight and wisdom as were the politicians. This discovery has done something to Americans. It has shaken the faith of a people whose cathedrals are banks, as conspicuous on all the downtown corners of America as churches were in old Moscow and old Rome. The average citizen always suspected the morals of the financial hierarchy, but now his distrust goes deeper; he doubts its intelligence.

Thus the present divergence between Wall Street and Main Street does not follow the old line. Even in Congress there is little talk just now of "predatory interests," and the forlorn shade of "the bloated bondholder" disarms even the Ways and Means Committee, which is terribly hard put to it to find anybody worth taxing in the nice round sums. Two new elements change the picture. The first is that in a sense unknown in the America of yesterday the great bankers involve us in the fortunes of the world: Wall Street entangles us in foreign affairs more than the League of Nations ever could. The second is that in drawing the whole country into a movement of wild inflation it identified Main Street with itself, so that the difference between the "bust" and the other is mostly a difference in scale.

On the domestic side, the case against Wall Street, as heard on Main Street and echoed in Washington runs something like this: "In the boom years the bankers had a lending complex. They cut down their reserves to the danger point in order to pour out money. When the margins of security were small and values and prices sky-high, loans were large and easy to borrowers, who as often as not were speculators. Legitimate business was active, so the banks did not have excessive amounts to lend, yet the stock-market adventurer could get all he wanted. Now the very opposite condition exists. Regular business has contracted, there are huge reserves of idle money, yet the man with ample security, able to pay interest, cannot borrow for legitimate enterprises from banks which have surplus money and need the income. The business of the country is therefore in the power of bankers who once lent recklessly and now as recklessly withhold.

"Granted," says Main Street, "that we went along. We were all swept along by Wall Street ideas into the Wall

Street 'system.' We believed that the big fellows on the big-
time knew their stuff. Sometimes they did, at that. The thing
to do was to recapitalize: independent concerns went into
mergers, personal businesses were incorporated, old corporations were recapitalized, millions who never did so before
were enticed by the daily hullabaloo to buy stocks on margins. Like flies we got stuck in 'investment trusts'; on all these
operations profits compounded for banks and brokers. But
in the main the sword-fish had no more premonition of the
deluge than the sardines. That's what gets us—that there are
no big-time brains for these big times! Another of their new
eras and there won't be even a creak left in the old Board
of Trade."

Turn now to the popular reaction to the story of our adventures in international banking. Up to about a year ago,
when the first big cracks began to appear in the dangerously
patched financial edifice of Europe, the average American
was only vaguely concerned in the intricate operations of
world finance. Then he began to worry in earnest. Not only
were the repercussions of every bank crisis in Mittel-Europa
felt in Mid-America, but our banking casualties were more
numerous than theirs. In June came the Hoover moratorium;
you recall the nation-wide response to that gesture. It seemed
like doing something, something nobly American, toward our
own recovery and that of the world. When the stimulant
proved as inadequate as near-beer, enthusiasm cooled, but
we were still ready to follow any bold initiative, wherever
it led—to a longer moratorium, to reduction of war debts,
even to conditional or unconditional cancellation.

Now the mood of the country has changed, and the reason
for that change is the widespread belief that the movement
for cancellation is inspired by the international bankers in
an effort to salvage private debts at the expense of public
or what they term political debts. Other influences enter in:

the wide circulation of plausible evidence that Germany squandered her borrowed substance and brought on her own bankruptcy; tales of French "sabotage" of all plans for readjustment; the sight of iron rings around Europe and what might be called expensive hate affairs among our debtors. But primarily the hardening of the American heart against Europe is due to the bankers. As soon as they took one side of the question Main Street took the other!

In Washington this reaction can be seen crystallizing into a policy. It modifies the attitude of the administration and strengthens the "home-front" movement. It pushes to the surface in the committee hearings on the thorny subject of taxation. Not since the war has so much nationalistic bluster blown freely through the halls of Congress. Against the 10 per cent internationalism of Wall Street, Main Street is 100 per cent American.

Recently the ambassadors of these two governments, the political and the financial, met in a Senate committee room. It was a long-drawn-out interview, lasting several weeks, but continuously interesting and dramatic and producing a total effect so clear and impressive that I think it has done more than anything else to define the issue I am trying to describe. This was the investigation by the Senate Finance Committee of the foreign loans made by New York bankers and the manner in which they were passed on to the public by the flotation of bonds. In the course of the hearing, most of the heads of the great banking houses appeared before the committee and were exhaustively cross-examined as to their investments, their profits, their methods and their banking ethics.

Day after day there was spread out in that room in the Senate office building a fair sample of the world's bookkeeping. The room was always full of smoke, full of intent people and full of solemnity; it had something of the atmosphere of a coroner's inquest. The representatives of the people reclined in leather chairs around a long mahogany table: Senator Smoot drooping at the head; Senator Shortridge * with his Byzantine gestures; Senator Walsh of Massachusetts, bland and calm; Senator King, walking up and down scattering greetings. Other members of the committee passed in and out, Reed, La Follette, Couzens,* Harrison,* Connally,* Gore. They participated, but Senator Hiram Johnson prosecuted, sitting forward in his chair, sharp-faced, quiet-voiced, prodding, pouncing.

The representatives of Wall Street sat upright, too, as one by one they took the chair directly facing the chief inquisitor. They brought their balance sheets, their chief clerks, read long prefaces, answered questions with apparent frankness, sometimes with a confessional air, as if they yearned to unload their burdens and their mistakes on the government. They were of two distinct types. They were the bankers of the old school, who spoke slowly, with a German accent, and suggested rich old counting rooms in Frankfort, and long lines of solid, mellow money-lenders with a taste for art. Of these were Otto Kahn, Frederick Strauss, James Speyer, F. J. Lisman, Henry Breck. The other type were crisp, younger on the average, self-assured rather than resting on a tradition, men of the American "executive" pattern like Charles E. Mitchell, Clarence Dillon, W. W. Aldrich, J. R. Swan, Thomas W. Lamont.

As the hearing proceeded millions and billions fluttered lightly about us like the paper figures that they are. But the world was close and intrusive. We saw paved roads through Peruvian deserts, garden suburbs in German cities, electric light plants in Tokyo, railroads in Hungary, national budgets

---

* Senator Samuel M. Shortridge (R), California; Senator James Couzens (R), Michigan; Senator Pat Harrison (D), Mississippi; Senator James J. Connally (R), Pennsylvania.

everywhere and mendicant presidents we had never heard of. The American dollar knows geography; it goes where nobody else goes; too often it fails to come home. A great many of the bond issues we learned about were in default, particularly in South and Central America; others, in Europe were described as at a "stand-still."

It was plain from the evidence that the bankers were, as they described themselves, "merchants" in these transactions. They bought to sell, and to this end encouraged borrowing on the one hand and buying on the other. So overstimulated was the demand for foreign securities from 1925 to 1929 that there was the fiercest competition to lend money to governments, municipalities and private enterprises all over the world. Huge commissions and bonuses, such as the $415,000 to Juan Leguia, son of the former President of Peru, were paid for the privilege of placing loans. High-pressure salesmanship was then employed to market the issues. Through a succession of syndicates, each adding a little to the price, the bonds were passed on to the eager investor; large blocks were sold to small banks.

The government itself had a hand in the business. The State Department censored such loans as were made to governments, at least to the extent of affirming that there was "no objection to the proposed financing," and in the case of Colombia intervened to urge the bankers to complete a loan contingent on the balancing of the Colombian budget.

The sums involved were marginal, the bankers testified, compared to the national wealth, compared to the amounts invested in domestic securities. All told, exclusive of government debts owed to the United States Treasury, our foreign investments total something over $17,000,000,000, of which about $8,000,000,000 are involved in the bonds and securities under scrutiny in the Senate investigation. And in fact not only do American investments in foreign bonds represent a

mere fraction of our investments in domestic issues, but many
of the former have depreciated less than American stocks and
securities.

They are weighty sums, nevertheless, in the world economy, weighty enough to deepen the gloom of the money
merchants in Threadneedle Street, who are convinced, anyway, that the deplorable state of the world is due to the
passing of financial leadership into the hands of the irre-
sponsible and the inexperienced. They are weighty sums in
Main Street. The story of our first grand plunge into international finance was spread over the front pages of every newspaper in the country. As one of the most complete and illuminating stories ever widely published of the processes of
world banking, it was everywhere read and discussed. To
Main Street it threw light on the local credit situation. It
profoundly affected the general attitude in respect to international debts.

So if again, as of old, the hinterland inclines to gaze sourly
and sadly on the financial capital, it is because the little
canyon down by the Battery is no longer the glory-hole of
the latest gold rush; rather it has become a mean cavity which
gives the nation a toothache. Look what you lured us into,
accuses Main Street. Look how you stampeded to get here,
retorts Wall Street. And there you have the new point in the
controversy as old as America, older than the oldest fable of
the money lender and his prey.

Never before have all the Main Streets of a nation gone
pouring into one narrow byway, choking it up, blowing it
up, and seeing at last what a sterile and overrated street it is
compared to the broad highways that tap the fields, the
forges and the production centers of the country. If Main
Street had not itself gone Wall Street, down all its length, it
would not so bitterly know the worst!

[11]   1 9 3 2   *June 26*. THE NEW ORDEAL OF DEMOC-
RACY. *The country is showing itself increasingly
distrustful of politics, while the politicians everywhere are beset by confusion and uncertainty.*

WASHINGTON

This is a story in two parts. The first is written in the
Middle West, home address of America, and generalizes the
talk to be heard almost anywhere in the United States during this highly conversational, politically heated and finan-
cially frigid campaign year of 1932. The second is written in
Washington, the only place in the country whose business is
in full production, and reports the outlook there in a time
constantly spoken of but not yet recognized on Capitol Hill
as an hour of national emergency. Thus it glances at the
same picture from two angles, both pretty obtuse, one that
of the representatives of the people, the other that of the
people represented.

Together the two views form a commentary on the whole
scheme of representative government, in principle so simple,
in operation grown so complex that many begin to think it
is unworkable in a crisis. At any rate the principle is now at
test throughout the world. It is not too much to say that its
vindication, not to say its survival, peculiarly depends on the
decisions to be made in this country in the next few years,
perhaps in the next few months.

We are the oldest existing democracy. No nation has enjoyed universal manhood suffrage so long as ours. None has
been so free to develop without outside interference, to shape
its own environment, to create a system of government under
the uniquely favoring circumstances of geographic security,
economic independence and modern political ancestry. We
have not been circumscribed by poverty of natural resources,

by encroaching neighbors, by the fibroid traditions of old societies, by the compromises required of nations living in a crowd, like the nations of Europe. We have not been circumscribed at all. We voided the past by beginning late, with a century which gave birth to a new kind of civilization. We laid our own patterns in fresh soil. Industry is our contemporary and lent us speeds unknown before in exploiting the wealth of a rich continent. To this point, in a word, we have governed ourselves, arrived where we are in our own way and under our own power. Our progress has been automotive, almost automatic, and loudly touted as the progress of democracy.

Now the question is: Where are we? Nobody seems quite sure, least of all the masters of our political fate currently engaged in nominating the contending candidates for the Presidency of the Republic and building platforms designed to be indistinguishable one from the other and to contain no plank not broad enough for every voter to stand on. This year's conventions are like all conventions, splurges on the grand scale of competitive salesmanship, yet they are held in one of the real crises in human history, a crisis not only economic but political.

For ten years and more we have been hearing about the crisis of democracy. Until a few months ago, however, that particular crisis did not hit the mass mind of America. Our democracy has been rather like one of our automatic devices, as much a part of our regular equipment as the telephone, taken for granted as available whether used or not. But lately, from the grass roots to the glass towers, the attention of the country has been focused on government. Everything has piled up together—taxes, tariffs, the crushing cost and corruption of local machines, congealed credit in State and Federal banks, unemployment, snow-balling relief budgets, hunger and thirst, rackets and panic—to fill the valley of depression with a mountainous exhibit of our dependence on politics.

At last we discover that government manages our lives; we wonder if what we suffer is not first of all a crisis of democracy. If it is not a failure of productive or consumptive power, of supply or demand, as obviously it is not, then it must be a failure of the democratic intelligence embodied in political institutions. To point to the simultaneous break-down of other governments or systems of government is no comfort or no answer to the rudely awakened American. He insists that democracy fostered our famous spread of prosperity and that it must be proved equal or unequal to the stresses of adversity.

To a country beginning to face that radical fact, the Congress now adjourning seems feeble and frivolous. The conventions seem frivolous. The whole political bag of tricks looks as cheap and useless as a deposit box stuffed with stock certificates or a counter piled with goods reduced for clearance. During this strange interlude when the national slogan is "No business as usual," repeated everywhere with a certain grim gayety, the nation's business is government. For the first time to anything like the present extent, the eyes of all the States are glued on their political representatives. Under the unflickering gaze of this new and once indifferent gallery, the political show appears something like a costume party, quaint, pre-war, full of Spencerian flourishes, of eternal gestures, of nimble sidestepping, the "à la main de" left and right of the old quadrille. "Actually they are behaving as they always behave!" gasps the audience—embittered because it cannot do the same!

The multitude does not blame the politicians for the depression. The guilt for that has been firmly fastened on the bankers. What is resented in the men of politics, and resented with a unanimity that may unseat them all, is their solemn levity, pussyfooting, resourcelessness, the unbreakable habit of "playing politics." Observe how the slump has multiplied ballyhoo magazines; watch what people read on trains and buses, in the long Summer evenings on the porches of the suburbs and the small towns. Then you will understand why 7,770 Texans telegraphed Congress to adjourn and why Iowa expressed a violent preference for a "chicken-stew" candidate as against "the same old boloney" of Senator Brookhart. *

On the most metropolitan main streets today people stop to talk. One of the strange signs of the times is the little groups on the downtown sidewalks exchanging rumors, views, echoes of views, on the state of the nation. There is a lot of echo; for once the talk is the same in industrial city and country town; for once both have plenty of time to talk. There is also an air of leisure long absent from the American scene. Turned colloquial, the urban streets become village-like and friendly, and the colloquies themselves bring back the lost flavor of the cracker-box, a ghostly cracker-box overwhelmed by motor traffic but essentially the same old mourner's bench of the country store.

Ten to one the talk goes straight to the new question of America: "What's the government going to do?" The tone is not tragic. It runs around in circles, as in a labyrinth without an exit, but the habit of optimism is strong in us; it never stops in despair. It is not revolutionary. The contemporary models of revolution are mentioned often enough, but as bogeys rather than as beacons. "I'd as soon be in Russia as here." "If Congress keeps on fiddling we'll be saddled with a Mussolini yet." These are common remarks, but delivered in the accent of Little Orphan Annie referring to the goblins.

Nobody yet believes in such alternatives, and none would be more surprised than the few who seriously predict communism or fascism if their words were to come true. Such

* Senator Smith W. Brookhart (R), Iowa.

prophets of doom as there are speak without conviction. America would be more reckless if it had any real fear of doom; now it presents the novel paradox of a people saving not for a rainy but for a sunny day. The talk is seldom without humor, wisecracks and sallies of heavy sarcasm. As often as not the huddles break up in a laugh, sour but hearty.

The general tone, however, is one of exasperation, directed particularly against the politicians. Wherever two or three citizens gather together, there is a political convention. In these private conventions, however, the keynoter has no encomiums for any candidate or either party. Four years ago the manoeuvres at Kansas City and Houston were followed with a mild sporting interest mixed with shrugging cynicism, the usual attitude of prosperous America toward politics; such heat as developed in the 1928 campaign was kindled from fires going deeper than politics. In normal times we are spectator citizens as well as spectator sportsmen. Now the interest is intense to the point of anger, not a dynamic anger driving toward action but a vague irritation, mostly against hokum and cowardice, which may spend itself in turning out most of the present officeholders and replacing them with names drawn from the same hopper, by the same methods, and promising no change except a greater inexperience.

The elector does not rationalize this resentment. He is not consistent. He curses Congressmen in general for logrolling, for obstructing and delaying national measures in favor of local interests, in the same breath in which he demands from his own Congressman nothing but local representation. If there are no national representatives, neither are there any national citizens.

From the beginning the country has looked to the economy program as the real test of the sincerity of its official representatives. Here, too, it is unreasonable, since the establishment it now rebels against was built to the specifications of the voters, always calling for more government service. Nevertheless, the failure to slash costs is viewed with something like despair, as the final proof of political stupidity.

Can democracy function in an emergency? More and more this question worries the congresses of the street. It is a question I have heard many times, but not in crowds, and not in this temper, except during those fumbling preludes which in other countries lead to dictatorship.

But America is not like other countries. The reporter who has made the international round feels that strongly as he circulates among his protesting and bewildered countrymen. Something destructive has happened to us in the past few years, the same thing that happens to people under dictatorships. Here it is the combined effect of government increasingly concentrated, of mergers and chains and corporate ownership, of ownership without effort, of easy money and paper profits and losses. We were fast becoming a nation of clerks, deputies, high-priced hired men. The sense of responsibility atrophied, the sense of values was corrupted; after the gaudy 1920s we were flabby and a little the worse for synthetic gin and synthetic prosperity.

That shows up now just as Congress shows up now. This session has been better than most, anxious, laborious, less partisan than usual, more cooperative. When one turns at last from the represented to the representatives, it is only to meet in Washington a group of tired, harassed and baffled men, up against problems too big for them and unhappily aware of it. Was Congress aware that it was under scrutiny more close and critical than ever before, that the public was sick and tired of old stratagems, of stale campaign speeches, of flag-raising on top of a volcano?

Washington remains strangely secluded on its smokeless river, an Olympus hiding in clouds of talk, but I have never seen it so exposed to the harsh weather outside. It is fully cognizant of the mood of the country. Every Representative and Senator I questioned made these three points: first, that Congressional mail was never so heavy as in this session, nor so peremptory; second, that newspapers everywhere now publish daily the record of the local representatives on each roll call and increasing pressure is brought to bear to make them mere delegates for their constituencies; third, that for two months there has been a concerted campaign of propaganda against Congress, in behalf of the business and banking interests seeking to hasten adjournment, in behalf of the administration seeking to gain prestige at the expense of the legislative body, or in behalf of both. That they are victims of a planned attack of ridicule and misrepresentation is firmly believed by both houses and members of both parties. In this session the persecution complex, so called, has moved from the White House to the Hill.

"Why should we be the scapegoat?" asked a distinguished member of the Senate. "If we had rejected some inspired plan for national recovery, any plan, in fact, we might reasonably be damned. But not a single group in the country, business men, industrialists, bankers, labor leaders, not a single individual, from the President down, has yet come before us with a real program, a constructive suggestion. No, the country pretends it expects nothing of Congress and now condemns us for not doing what nobody can do. We are blamed if we act and if we don't act. Having led us to ruin, the great business brains of the country can think of nothing but to berate this contemptible body for not pulling them out."

For years all honest Congressmen have lamented that there is no counterweight against the pressure of lobbies representing special interests; the people as such, they say, are never heard from. In this session the people have been heard from again and again, but in such confusion of counsel and de-

mand and protest that they have but added another element
to the general bewilderment. The truth is, of course, that
democracies cannot act as democracies when there is vital
need for quick and disinterested decisions. Representative
government gives satisfaction but not efficiency. One reason
for the St. Vitus dance of Congress is that it is too representative, pulled by too many strings.

Emergency shows us up, shows up our system of government, and shows up with complete clearness certain processes that have been going on for a long time without much
remark. One is that for twenty years we have been electing
our public officials on the prohibition issue, making a candidate's sentiments on the liquor question practically the sole
test of his fitness to deal with the most intricate problems
ever put up to legislators. Another is that our great popular
reforms, such as the direct primary and the referendum, as
worked out by a heretofore wholly indifferent electorate,
have weakened party responsibility without giving us better
officers or fairer laws. A third is progressive centralization of
power and function in Washington that has neither relieved
nor simplified State establishments, but has radically disturbed the original balance between the executive and legislative branches of the Federal Government and turned every
session of Congress into a struggle of the waning against the
crescent power.

Most important is what has happened to the party system.
Under our rigid two-party system, with power and responsibility in the hands of the majority, there is no provision for
those legislative sessions, like the last, in which no working
majority exists. Usually such sessions are sterile or stormy.
But aside from that, it is perfectly evident that the two parties have long since ceased to have any sustaining principles
or vital points of difference. Every tariff and taxation bill
proves that we are divided not into parties but into economic

sections, so that the parties themselves have degenerated into little more than rival machines for electing a President and controlling Federal patronage. For effective government under our charter, the parties have to function as such, strongly led and unified. Much of our present confusion and impotence arise from the fact that we are organized under one system and operating, or trying to operate, under another; nominally we have two-party rule, but actually we have rule by group, bloc, section, lobby; we have an unorganized economic parliament without the legal machinery to regulate it.

America is not like other countries. It has not even so much logic as England, which hates formulas but moves pretty steadily in one direction without them, while we love formulas, and with them manage to proceed in any direction. Thus you cannot predict of America what you might of really rational countries that follow premises to conclusions; you cannot say that because we are in a mood to welcome it that there is the least likelihood of a dictatorship.

Our government is not like other governments. It may be doubted if any other could ride along with so many wheels within two wheels. That feat supports the hope that even democracy might work in a modern State if it were tried. Representative government breaks down in times of stress mainly because it has never been adjusted to the facts.

This is a time of great decisions. Among the greatest questions, because it involves the future of the democratic principle in government, is whether we can revitalize the parties to make them mean something, by giving them fighting programs, new names, new aims, modern machinery, and then whether we have intelligence and courage enough to build up another and more honest system of representation, strengthened by some sort of economic council, appointive, non-partisan, non-local, of such intellectual caliber and practical experience that it can function as a brain for the body politic.

No ordinary political campaign is this on which we now embark. It may be our last chance to prove that there is initiative enough left in democracy to make it worth saving and spirit enough left in Americans to turn this abstract, sentimental, agitated but unfocused Americanism into positive and adventurous citizenship. It is our representatives, after all, who personify and indict us. "I consider myself a poor Congressman," one of the wisest said to me, "abdicating most of the time my own fairly informed judgment. But you know why, don't you? I am a poor Congressman because I want to continue to be a Congressman."

[12]   1 9 3 2   *September 4.* A NEW AMERICANISM. *Amid political uncertainties, one discerns a slow uprising of the spirit and a firm purpose to make a fresh start.*

WASHINGTON

The contemporary American is not primarily a citizen. Since the beginning of the century he has been a man in a hurry, so diverted and distracted by new things, new speeds, fabulous opportunities for personal expansion, that he has lost his early zest for citizenship. Not that he has ever ceased to regard himself as something pretty choice and privileged in the way of a citizen. "Civis Americanus sum" expresses quite as much pride of status as the boast of the cockiest old Roman who looked down on the world from the first Capitol Hill. In point of fact, it expresses much the same sense of prestige and civic superiority. You have only to glance at the clean-shaven, strong-jawed, thoroughly self-satisfied civitans preserved in marble in the Capitoline Mu-

seum to be reminded of a meeting of the New York Bankers'
Club or the United States Senate in one of its keener moments. All alike are unmistakably aware of their role as leading citizens in a dominant State.

Probably the Roman professed his citizenship more than
he practiced it. Certainly, for the American, the term denotes
status rather than state of mind or habit of life. You can't
think of the typical inhabitant of these States as first of all a
citizen: he has too many prior interests. You don't think of
him as political-minded in the same way that the Englishman,
the Irishman or the Frenchman is political-minded, not to
speak of the Pole, the Greek or the new and violently civic
Teuton.

We talk politics almost as much as any of them. We are
deluged with political news and immersed in civic movements more than any people on earth. For the past year we
have followed the policies of our government and the actions
of our representatives with an almost painful intentness. But
that is an unnatural and unwilling concentration. We are
exasperated when forced to recognize that political decisions
are momentous and exigent, a vital factor in our private lives.

One reason for the present unpopularity of politicians is
that they have become too important. Ordinarily we don't
take them seriously. Our interest in public affairs is never intellectual or absorbing. Occasionally it is emotional, often
it is personal, mostly it is conversational. Listen to the talk
of America in normal times, and you cannot escape the conclusion that politics is just another subject, like the weather,
prohibition or the baseball score, handy for making casual
conversation among a friendly and gregarious people.

Perhaps man is not naturally a political being. Perhaps the
freeman of an electrical age, adventuring in new dimensions
of time and space, is already, if we knew it, outside the realm
wherein the political authorities vainly reiterate the tradi-

tional traffic rules. It may not be entirely due to indifference or reaction that the first fine rapture for self-government, hallmark of the nineteenth century, seems to be petering out in the technical excitements of the twentieth.

If there is any clear tendency in the confusion of our time, it is revulsion against the burdens and obligations of self-government. Nobody, least of all we who claim to be the tutelary deities of democracy, will take the trouble to try to renew it for new times. But all over the world are impassioned millions in black shirts, brown shirts, red shirts, khaki shirts —if it were only white shirts they'd solve the unemployment problem!—shouting for their favorite shade of despotism. The old revolutionists took off their shirts to fight for freedom; the present uprisers, whether Communist, Fascist, Hitlerite, or any other brand, must have shirts to signify their desperate resolve to let Joe or Benito or Adolf do the whole job of citizenship.*

During the demonstrations following the nominating speeches at the Democratic Convention in Chicago, I happened to sit next to a visiting correspondent of The Manchester Guardian. Behind us, Will Rogers and H. L. Mencken kept up a rapid fire of ribald comment on the circus features of our great political folk festival: the doves wheeling in the tropic glare, the girls in kilts, the bands in fur shakos parading impartially for every candidate, the radio singers whooping it up on top of the chairman's desk. But the Englishman was fascinated, as well he might be, by a spectacle unique in the world. As spectacle it was immense—"like a Doré rendering of hell," he said—with cinematic effects of mass and color, of grotesque shadows thrown against a human horizon, beyond the imagination of Hollywood. As exhibit, however, it was something else again. When some one asked the visitor

---

* Joseph Stalin, Premier, Union of Soviet Socialist Republics; Benito Mussolini, Premier of Italy; Adolf Hitler, President of Germany.

how American politics, thus illustrated, compared with English, he looked surprised. "Politics?" he repeated. "Politics? How should I know? So far I have seen everything here except politics."

He meant, no doubt, that in such an atmosphere it is impossible for responsible party organizations to think out or seriously debate the policies they have to present to the choice of the nation. But is not the national convention only a concentrated sample of the political atmosphere of the United States? To how many Americans "politics" is just what Chicago exhibited: parade, ballyhoo, dickering for place on a ticket, trades between candidates, tongue-in-the-cheek oratory. Who expects the party conclaves to be other than get-together meetings of business organizations pepping up the sales force to compete for the biggest of all contracts? This year the organizations seemed more antiquated than usual, the gestures feebler, so that some observers imagined they were seeing the last of the convention in its present form. "It is a relic," they said. "It cannot survive the radio. As an institution it is already as dead as a chicken flopping around after its head is cut off."

Such observers are too optimistic. Conventions will flourish as circuses and sales gatherings as long as the typical American attitude toward politics remains that of the spectator at a professional game in which he has a large stake and no place. The English "stand" for office and Americans "run," but the words do not indicate the comparative pace of the candidate; they describe the kind of interest manifested by the gallery. Our eyes are on the race. As a nation we have the spectator habit. Nearly 30,000,000 of us, it is estimated, four or five million more than in 1928, are stockholders in 200 big corporations. The role of passive assistance we play in these corporations, a new role of ownership without voice or responsibility, has done something to the national character and cannot but affect our conduct as stockholders in the United States.

Even now the typical citizen is not talking like a citizen. Harken to the dialogues echoing on the Summer air—and how they echo, everywhere the same!—and you must be struck by something oddly detached in the general tone of the comment. Wherever he expresses himself—and that means wherever he is: at gas station, country club, chamber of commerce, produce exchange or park bench—the average commentator speaks as an anxious, critical, almost fatalistic non-participant. He discusses present conditions as they affect himself and his neighborhood. He gossips about the candidates, or rather about two candidates, since his interest seldom extends beyond Hoover and Roosevelt. He may have something vague to say about dictatorships, revolutions, alternative systems of government. Invariably the villain in his piece is the banker, local money-god, or bankers in general. Almost never does he speak as a citizen obligated or impelled to do anything about the issues he endlessly debates.

Even now, I repeat, because that is the point. For if at the beginning of the active season of a Presidential campaign waged in the deepest depression the country has ever known, Americans in general evince no positive interest in politics and only curiosity about the outcome of the election, what does it mean? What does excite us? Here is a crisis involving the whole population and every sort of business. We face national decisions heralded by all parties as crucial in resolving that crisis. Why are signs of political animation confined to the candidates? Has the "Civis Americanus" become a museum piece, like the busts of the Roman elders, as passive as the ear at the end of the radio, the mind of the movie audience, the millionth shareholder in the modern holding company?

The answer is a contradiction. If it were possible to draw

conclusions from the unreported talk of the United States at this moment, the honest analyst would have to answer in the words of the candidate for Governor in one of the rowdy political farces that begin to appear in the movie houses. To every query he makes the stock political reply: "Yes, and then again, No." What else could you say of the fact that wherever you go people are talking politics, or at least complaining at the entanglement of all their affairs in politics, and at the same time taking no real or active interest in candidates or issues?

What else except that for some reason these people feel helpless, feel caught in a web too intricate to untangle, feel especially, and in spite of the purely emotional relief of making a stab for or against a party or a candidate, that there is not much to be gained or lost however they vote? In other words, the citizen is not so much dead as dazed.

And not so much dazed as painfully coming to life. Politics in America is mostly conversation, but in that conversation one senses, nay, one hears, deep as the undertone of an incoming tide, some slow uprising of the spirit. This voice of the people that seems so garrulous and aimless, talking in circles, everywhere alike, is not really aimless. It is fumbling, and fumbling en masse—never before has a mass been as shrewdly loquacious and aware as this—toward definitions. Something is happening during this year of talk and waiting; something is revealed in this slowed-up, backed-up picture of America in depression; uncertainly but inexorably it is finding its "line."

This hardening of the mold even the politicians notice, and they seldom notice anything until the movement has gone so far that they have to run to catch up. They call it nationalism, but in that they are mistaken. It is what might be named Americanism, but only because it expresses a new synthesis of all those forces, ideas, race strains, mechanized folkways, social patterns, international relations, that have shaped this post-war, post-boom, post-millennial America. Up to now Americanism has been a method, a pioneering process, an industrial technique, what the Russians mean when they "Americanize," what Europe thinks of when it speaks of Americanization. We have had no conscious ideology, no settled tradition, a spectacular surface but no known depth; no gauge, that is to say, of the extent to which our technique was a method of the mind, the instrument of a civilization deep-rooted and precious enough to be defended.

There are negative signs in plenty. At the meeting in Columbus, Ohio, at which Governor Roosevelt fired the opening gun of his campaign, the audience numbered 25,000 or 30,-000. The Governor made a fighting speech, full of the kind of punch and thrust that stirs an audience. During the last campaign attacks less telling set the listeners roaring. But this speech drew little applause. There was no suggestion here of the pumped-up delirium of Chicago or of the spurious excitement of old-time political rallies. The crowd listened quietly and as quietly dispersed. Afterward I spoke of the temper of the audience to a farmer from a troubled southern county, one of thousands in that apparently passive throng who had come from a radius of 200 miles to hear and see the Democratic candidate. "I guess we were too busy listenin' to applaud," he said. "Down our way we're not cheerin' much these days. The farmers haven't much to do but change their minds. That's slow business and you don't shout about it."

Here are two small manufacturers in a mid-Western town. They are typical of thousands of their kind all over the country who are performing miracles of endurance and ingenuity just to hold on. One is working himself at a casting machine at a subsistence wage hardly more than the community chest doles out to the unemployed. The other is driving around in his car picking up small and profitless orders, anything to keep his skeleton force together. Because they show loss in current operating costs, though perfectly solvent, neither can get any credit from the local banks, whose gospel is to keep liquid though everything else in town dries up. Both know of huge orders for tool-making and die-casting ready to go out at the first sign of loosened credit. Both meantime are marking time. "Nothing to do but wait," they sigh. "Nothing anybody can do but wait."

And here is a little park in the middle of Detroit. It used to be covered with grass, but now it is bare as a board, rubbed bald by the recumbent bodies of the unemployed. All day and all night they lie there, in the shadow of a big hotel, as they lie along the lake front of Chicago, in the plaza of Los Angeles, in all the central spaces of all the cities. In Detroit the other day they filled the little square when a storm blew up. The sky grew black and they did not move. The clouds opened and rain fell in sheets and still they did not move. Across the street the passers-by ran into the open door of the hotel and found shelter in the empty lobby. Not one man among those homeless hundreds but pulled his hat over his eyes and took a drenching. Something in that submissiveness was disturbing.

When you speak of the passivity or the patience or the fortitude of this country you are thinking of the unemployed. They are a nation within a nation, almost a nation apart, as big as a Balkan State and twice as docile. If they vote, they might vote as a nation. In their millions they are the balance of political power, yet aside from the hapless bonus marchers and Father Cox's army it has not occurred to any of them that they could form a majority party.

Look now at the other side of the picture, the positive side. These unemployed are meeting in the fairgrounds of a comfortable manufacturing city in Indiana. The foreigner, espe-

cially if he came from Nizhnif Novgorod, would be astonished to see the parking space around the grandstand filled
with automobiles. But the American is accustomed to think of
the motor car as part of the necessary equipment of life; he is
not surprised that the unemployed drive to their meeting.
What interests him is that the purpose of this gathering is to
formulate a plan for self-help.

These men and women out of work are establishing a labor
exchange, one of those new communities springing up in
dozens of cities, from Portland, Ore., to Rochester, N. Y., communities like pioneer settlements, where the carpenter builds
a porch for a suit of clothes and the cobbler mends shoes for
a crate of garden truck. These, too, are cities within cities.
Like the produce exchanges set up by farmers throughout
the West, like the housewives' canneries, preserving surplus
fruit and vegetables in almost every town, they form part of
the great movement of barter, of trade without money, sweeping over the land this Summer to an extent unrealized by
those whose observations of contemporary phenomena are
confined to one State or one city.

The headquarters of these moneyless cooperatives are
usually cheerful, even jolly. You learn there that Americans
can be happy in the most precarious circumstances, can be
happy without cash. You see that 50 per cent of the heaviness of the depression is the heaviness of inaction. And that
is one clue to the general indifference toward politics. Wherever Americans can do anything, can see anything definite
to do, they are optimistic and resourceful. Their political inertia, due in the first place to absorption in selfish, more congenial affairs, is now the helplessness of those who feel that
the power to act has passed out of their hands. Incredible as
it sounds, the average American looks upon government as a
closed corporation, the monopoly of a class which, under
one name or another, seeks only to perpetuate itself.

We are in the tentative stage of a revolt against inaction. Taken singly, the various self-starter movements do not amount to much. The farmers' strike in Iowa, the rehabilitation of abandoned shacks along the roadside for subsistence farms, the dilapidated cross-roads store reanimated as a place for barter, the enlivening of the village and the small town as the young folk drift back from the cities, the commodity and labor exchanges appearing on conspicuous downtown corners, the new one-man and family businesses: all these enterprises, small in themselves, when seen everywhere are no longer local and accidental. They have the significance of a spontaneous national movement.

In truth they are not so much a movement as movement, the slow stirring of a nation to action. On its face this action resembles reaction, a shift into reverse, the retreat from the too-big, the too-impersonal, that is characteristic of the times. More truly interpreted, it is the sign of awakening from a dream. The New Economic Era was mirage. Not an American but admits today that he has lived through an epoch of illusion. But now—and this is the new thought germinating in the mass mind—it is dawning on the country that this illusion, like the mirage of the desert, was the false shadow of something real, a potential city, a possible State. What we saw in the skies during the last decade was one side of an edifice. It represented the productive capacity of a technically emancipated people. It fell because there was no social or political structure to support it. But it can rise again, whole; we are the first nation challenged to solve the problems of superabundance.

If people do not talk about depression as they did a year ago, six months ago, it is because the panic phase has passed. We have experienced a change of mind more than a change of basic facts. Anxieties are multiplied with time; unemployment does not decrease and strain to the breaking point the last resources of every community; unpaid taxes, 40 and 50 per cent uncollectable, create civic problems which no one yet fully faces. But the central fear is gone. Already there has been enough lift to convince the most pessimistic that America is not sunk for good, that the system under which we live is not near collapse; above all, that there still exists in this continent, whether considered as a material or a moral empire, an incalculable reserve of power for reconstruction and new construction.

There is less talk of prohibition than there has been for a decade. That obsessing argument is on the wane. Now it would be secondary to more vital topics, even if it were not generally believed that nothing is left of the Eighteenth Amendment save some question as to the date and manner of its interment. The engrossing subjects today are near and immediate: a hundred men added to the factory payroll, the curtailment of the school year, taxes, the cost of local government, the price of hogs and grain. We have more dark doubts of tariff policy, even in the protectionist strongholds of the mid-West, than Mr. Hoover would believe. A nation of worried debtors, we are more sympathetic to the cancellation of all war debts than any political leader except Senator Borah has yet sensed. "A clean slate" has become a kind of symbol of that new beginning, that deliverance from the consequences of our mistakes, for which all Americans yearn. As a campaign slogan it would be more popular than any so far invented.

Campaign slogans, campaign issues, campaign promises, interest us little. Never were we more aware, however, that all these near and immediate problems are political issues. Never were we more aware of America. Out of this anomaly grows the consciousness, still hardly more than a subconsciousness, that we have in our hands the magnificent makings of a new society, a really new economic era. It waits only for the liquidation of our biggest frozen asset, the active and responsible citizen. Revolution? America has gone through not one but a series since 1900. It's all over but the official and social recognition!

[13]   1 9 3 2   *September 11.* ROOSEVELT'S VIEW OF THE BIG JOB. *The Presidency is "a superb opportunity for applying the simple rules of human conduct," says the Democratic candidate.*

WASHINGTON

The first impression produced by the Democratic candidate for the Presidency is that of the fortunate man who is doing what he most likes to do, a man who enjoys his present office, is eagerly on his way to one he will like better, and in all circumstances maintains a "smilin' through" philosophy and a singular zest for the adventure of life. In those good old days when he nominated the Happy Warrior, he was, like the painter who suggests his own characteristics in his portraits of others, extolling the political temperament he has successfully cultivated in himself.

When I first saw Franklin D. Roosevelt, at the Cox notification * ceremonies in Dayton in 1920, he was a handsome and radiant figure, faring forth on a hopeless campaign with a smile of gay good humor. Twelve years later he swooped down from the skies to accept his own nomination from the Chicago convention. In the interval he had suffered one political defeat mostly vicarious, and a physical disaster so valorously surmounted and lightly borne that it has become almost an asset. Otherwise his luck has held; the luck of being a well-born and comfortably circumstance American,

---

* James M. Cox nominated for President, Franklin D. Roosevelt for Vice-President, on the Democratic ticket. Republican Warren G. Harding was elected with Vice-President Calvin Coolidge, 1920.

happily following a chosen career, mounting with rapid steps
the political pyramid until at fifty he stands at the apex,
leader of his party in a year when the winds blow in his direction.

Back in 1900 Governor Roosevelt, then a candidate for the
State Senate, made the first automobile campaign. He made
another precedent when he flew to Chicago, and by that
characteristic touch of drama, plus the same smile, now more
fixed and deepened, like his voice, he succeeded in dissipat-
ing the glumness of an assembly that toward the end had
gone heavy and more than a little sour. His campaign
speeches have a similarly inspiriting effect. He is not a
speaker to raise the echoes and the temperature, like Governor Smith, but he does raise the hopes of the Democrats,
and their eyes to the Promised Land.

It is in Albany, however, on the job and eating it up, that
his gusto is most impressive. There you see him stimulated
by the stir and movement, the light and spotlight, of the
public tournament. He enjoys attacking the problems of administration. He relishes the stratagems and surprises of the
election fight. Above all he loves the crowding contacts with
all sorts of people. He has something of the indiscriminate
enthusiasm, the "dee-light" of the first Roosevelt. His first
interest, he says, is in the theory and practice of government;
his second is in people. When he speaks of "humanizing
government," a favorite phrase, he means bringing the two
more closely together. If called upon to move in, he would
"humanize the White House," too, and at Albany you can
imagine what effect that might have on the pleasant, piti-
lessly public but austere domicile of the Presidents.

Stodgy and heavily Victorian in outward aspect, the Executive Mansion of New York State under the present régime
is probably the most informal official residence in the country. This is also a house without privacy, but nobody seems to

mind. It is a house full of life and laughter. The Governor's ready laugh rings out from nearly any room, the members of the family have a lot of fun among themselves; even the visitors are cheerful. It is a house of wide-open doors and few secrets. The Governor's study is immediately to the left of the front door and he is not only visible but apparently accessible to any one who enters. People seem to wander in and out, glancing at the telegrams on the hall table, eavesdropping if they will, examining the books piled up on the tables in all the rooms, in variety like a circulating library of current publications. The day I was there a reporter picked up a copy of Stuart Chase's "A New Deal," * and discovered fifty new one-dollar bills between the pages, so sent as a campaign contribution.

This was an off day. The Walker hearings were suspended and the Governor did not go to the Capitol.† He took advantage of the first lull in three weeks to catch up with his correspondence, dispose of accumulated routine business of the State and map out the series of speeches for his Western trip. As if this were not enough, with an interview or two thrown in, in the afternoon there were hearings on the cases of two prisoners condemned to death in Sing Sing; a two-hour conference with representatives of the railway workers' unions, invited by the Governor to give their views on a perplexing public question; a discussion with two State Commissioners on new power houses; a review with counsel of Judge Staley's decision on the Walker appeal; ‡ the daily

* Stuart Chase: "A New Deal" (New York: The Macmillan Company; 1932). This book furnished the Democratic Party and Franklin D. Roosevelt with their triumphant political slogan in 1932–3.

† James J. Walker, Mayor of New York City, resigned September 1, 1932. This ended the hearings into corruption in his office by a state legislative committee when Franklin D. Roosevelt was Governor of New York.

‡ Decision by Justice Staley, New York State Supreme Court, on case of Donnelly vs. Roosevelt, when effort was made to have court prohibit Roosevelt from hearing the charges against James J. Walker or making determination. Justice Staley denied the application.

press conference. There were besides a stream of other callers, letters to sign, a dozen calls over the long-distance telephone.

All the motion and commotion, the flow of people and talk, naturally revolved around Governor Roosevelt. He moved from room to room, everywhere interrupted, but always unhurried, unworried, good-humored interested in everything and everybody, thoroughly enjoying himself; in his element. Between-times, at odd intervals, I asked questions which he answered with great facility. Not only is he quick-minded, but so pat and fluent, speaking in paragraphs and never hesitating for a word, that he might have written out his answers. My last interval was at half past 10 at night, and when I left, some time after 11, to catch a train, he was still untired and smiling starting in to draft a radio speech.

An interview under such circumstances is not wholly satisfactory, but the glimpse it affords into the mind and methods of a possible President is revealing. To an onlooker, the "off day" seemed unorganized and overcrowded. At the end, however, you saw that Governor Roosevelt in his casual way had tossed off a vast volume of work and had exerted his well-known charm on a considerable number of people. The railway union men, for example. At first they sat in a stiff circle, reserved and quiet. In no time they were in a close huddle, all smoking, shooting questions and answers as fast as they could. The charm is interest, in Roosevelt real and inexhaustible.

Anyway, systematic or not, that is the way he works. He likes to know something about everything. He is a great "skimmer" of books, he says; books on history, biography, economics; as a hobby, books on naval affairs, of which he has the largest collection outside the Navy Department; as a diversion, detective stories and children's books, particularly the latter, in which he finds huge delight and also texts about Alice in Wonderland and the Delphic Oracle to illustrate policies of his political opponents. He admires the encyclopedic, the versatile mind. To him the four most interesting men in American history are those most distinguished for their many-sidedness, men of sufficient range and curiosity, as he puts it, to take in the whole sweep of civilization. They are Jefferson, Franklin, Count Rumford, that early New England genius, scientist, sociologist and political philosopher who spent most of his time illuminating the courts of Europe, and Theodore Roosevelt.

One guesses that "T. R.," to whom he constantly refers and whose career his own parallels in so many particulars, is the north star in Franklin Roosevelt's firmament. All the Roosevelts were Democrats until the Civil War, when they became what was known as Lincoln Democrats. Most of the clan returned to the fold in Tilden's time, but James Roosevelt, Theodore's father, remained an independent. Whether or not his progressivism derives from T. R., the example of his distant and distinguished kinsman fired the imagination of Franklin from his earliest years and probably set the course of his life. After a family caucus he voted for Theodore in 1904, "because he was a Roosevelt," but not in 1912; by that time Wilson had emerged and "T. R. had no chance of election." T. R. gave away his niece on the day of her marriage to her sixth cousin, of all Franklin's lucky days the luckiest, as every one agrees who knows the part played by Mrs. Roosevelt in her husband's life. "Let's keep the name in the family," chuckled the first Roosevelt on that occasion.

It is a potent name, easily the most potent influence in the destiny of Franklin Roosevelt. Yet, though the Governor's versatile interests and unconventional methods are Rooseveltian, they do represent, nevertheless, his own conception of the personal and human relationship that should exist between the Executive and his State and, by extension, be-

tween the Chief Executive and the nation. He thinks that
the President should personify government to the citizen,
should express the ideas germinating, ready for realization,
in the popular mind.

"The Presidency," he says, "is not merely an administrative
office. That's the least of it. It is more than an engineering
job, efficient or inefficient. It is preeminently a place of
moral leadership. All our great Presidents were leaders of
thought at times when certain historic ideas in the life of the
nation had to be clarified. Washington personified the idea of
federal union. Jefferson practically originated the party system as we know it by opposing the democratic theory to the
republicanism of Hamilton. This theory was reaffirmed by
Jackson. Two great principles of our government were forever put beyond question by Lincoln. Cleveland, coming into
office following an era of great political corruption, typified
rugged honesty. T. R. and Wilson were both moral leaders,
each in his own way and for his own time, who used the
Presidency as a pulpit.

"Isn't that what the office is—a superb opportunity for re-
applying, applying in new conditions, the simple rules of
human conduct we always go back to? I stress the modern
application, because we are always moving on; the technical
and economic environment changes, and never so quickly as
now. Without leadership alert and sensitive to change, we
are bogged up or lose our way, as we have lost it in the past
decade."

"And you?" I asked. "Is that the reason you want to be
President? What particular affirmation or reaffirmation is
required of the national leader of today?"

The Governor laughed. "Months before the nomination I
told you I didn't know why any man should want to be
President. I repeat that I didn't grow up burning to go to
the White House, like the American boy of legend rather

than of fact. I have read history and known Presidents; its a terrible job. But somebody has to do it. I suppose I was picked out because the majority of the party thought I was the best vote-getter. Now that I am picked out, naturally I want to be President. I want to win." He laughed again, then went on gravely:

"The objective now, as I see it, is to put at the head of the nation some one whose interests are not special but general, some one who can understand and treat with the country as a whole. For as much as anything it needs to be reaffirmed at this juncture that the United States is one organic entity, that no interest, no class no section, is either separate or supreme above the interests of all or divorced from the interests of all. We hear a good deal about the interdependence of the nations of the world. In the pit of universal calamity, with every country smothered by its own narrow policies and the narrow policies of other countries—and that goes for us, too—everyone sees that connection. But there is a nearer truth, often forgotten or ignored, and that is the interdependence of every part of our own country.

"No valid economic sectionalism exists in these States. There are opposed economic interests within every section, town against country, suburb against city, but as a nation we are all mixed up, fluid. All the States are in some degree like New York, a blend of agriculture and industry. The rural South is changing, the Western prairies are planted with factory towns. East and West, as we use the terms, are mostly states of mind, not localized but everywhere. What we need is a common mind, and, even more, common sense to realize that if we are not acting for the interest of the whole country we are acting against the interests of every section."

Perhaps this is Governor Roosevelt's answer to the charge that he is trying to be all things to all sections, conservative in the East, radical in the West; he simply denies that there

are sections in that sense. He classifies himself as a liberal. I
asked what he meant by that elastic term, how he defined
the difference between the outlooks vaguely called conservative and progressive, or between his program and that of the
opposing party.

"Let's put it this way," he explained. "Every few years,
say every half generation, the general problems of civilization change in such a way that new difficulties of adjustment are presented to government. The forms have to catch
up with the facts. The radical, in order to meet these difficulties, jumps, jumps in groups, because he doesn't count
unless he's part of a group. One group usually differs from
another in its program, but they are all equally definite and
dogmatic about it. They lay down categorical terms—'my
plan or none.' Their characteristic is hard-and-fast processes,
cut-and-dried methods, uncompromising formulas. The conservative says: 'No, we're not ready for change. It's dangerous. Let's wait and see what happens.' Half way in between
is the liberal, who recognizes the need of new machinery
for new needs but who works to control the processes of
change, to the end that the break with the old pattern may
not be too violent.

"Or say that civilization is a tree which, as it grows, con-
tinually produces rot and dead wood. The radical says: 'Cut
it down.' The conservative says: 'Don't touch it.' The liberal
compromises: 'Let's prune, so that we lose neither the old
trunk nor the new branches.' This campaign is waged to
teach the country to move upon its appointed course, the way
of change, in an orderly march, avoiding alike the revolution
of radicalism and the revolution of conservatism."

In this credo of the liberal is nothing new but rather the
echo of something very old, the voice of the country gentleman in politics. The voice was dominant in the early history
of the Republic. It is familiar still in England. And in fact

it expresses what is most deeply rooted in Franklin Roosevelt. He differs from T. R. in being country-bred instead of town-bred; fundamentally he is up-State and not New York City. He farms, plants, is himself planted in what is, for America, the ancient, coercive soil of Dutchess County. When he speaks of understanding the country as a whole, he is identifying himself, consciously or unconsciously, with those who have settled this continent and who now, across the plains, are bewildered to see it passing out of their control.

Like Henry Ford, the repentant mass producer, Roosevelt goes back to the soil for his solutions. Like Ford, he believes in decentralization of industry, sees the same loss of balance between the country and the town. Pressed for definite specifics which he would offer, or order, were he in power, as remedies for our present economic ills, he always contends that you have to begin at the base. You cannot build a healthy industrial civilization, he says, until you restore the solvency and purchasing power of the farm.

"I agree," he declares, "that our main problem is to get people back to work. All programs that fail to do that do precisely nothing. Until unemployment is cured, we're sick, and will get sicker. Unemployment insurance is necessary, but it's the second step, not the first. It cannot meet the present emergency. I believe we could spend $2,000,000,000 in construction work, partly self-liquidating without bankrupting the country. With effective economy in government, it would hardly increase taxes. But that's not enough, either. Unemployment was increasing long before the depression. It's inevitable when half the population had lost its purchasing power. That's the fellow you've got to start building up, the farmer."

Governor Roosevelt will develop his farm relief proposals in his speech at Topeka. They include a sharp reduction in rural taxes and reforestation of marginal lands, a national program based on what he has accomplished in New York, where since 1929 the State has purchased at nominal rates and reforested more than 102,000, acres, giving employment to something like 10,000 men in each planting season. The main remedy, however is a measure no longer called the equalization fee, a debenture plan or any of the old names, but described simply as the extension of the benefits of the tariff to the growers of the great export crops—wheat, cotton, &c.—"temporarily," he qualifies, and "on that part of the crop consumed in this country."

If that brings up the whole vexed question of tariffs, on which the Democratic record is no longer clear, it at least puts the farmer in the vicious circle along with the rest of us. Unlike President Hoover, Governor Roosevelt believes that tariff is a foreign policy. He goes a bit further, or at least further than the party platform, in proposing to call at once an international conference to discuss export and import duties. "The entire question is now reduced to such absurdity," he says, "that all nations are ready for a new deal. They all know, even while they keep on adding new spikes to the wall, that there can be no world recovery without a flow of world trade. Trade is exchange; you can't argue away that fact. We'll have to go back to some form of reciprocal barter, and we'll have to do it soon."

The way of the liberal is the middle way, the way of compromise. Compromise is the essential tool of the fine art of politics. "To accomplish anything worth while," Governor Roosevelt once wrote, "it is necessary to compromise between the ideal and the practical." He himself is an adroit politician. He has the great political gift of playing the game with spirit but without rancor. He can fight hard with good temper; all that happened before his nomination he has already forgotten.

The way of the campaigner is the way of attack, and Governor Roosevelt is a good campaigner, ready, friendly, vigorous, sharp to seize every advantage of the offensive and to hold it. He may be expected to give a good show of fight wherever he goes and to find all the weak places in the enemy position. When all is said, the Lochinvar who rides out of the East will ride on his personality, on his zest and gusto and confidence, on his eighteen-carat American background, on the blind desire to punish and to change, which is the mood of crisis.

[14] 1 9 3 2 *October 9.* As WALL STREET SEES A CHANGING WORLD. *Deflated and chastened, the financial kingdom realizes, as it never has before, the force of public opinion.*

NEW YORK

This is the account of a visit to a unique and fascinating village which has the distinction of being a very small kingdom and a very great power. It is ruled by modest men, now also meek, who, unlike political rulers, dislike to be quoted and refuse to admit their authority. It contains the greatest of all markets, though it never sees the things it buys and sells. Nobody lives there, yet it is the most populous spot in one of the most congested centers in the world. It is more international than Geneva and more insular and homogeneous than Emporia, Kan. It is as independent as the government of the Stock Exchange and as sensitive to every rumor of news and every whisper of public opinion as the oscillograph in a radio transmitting station. If this sounds like a conundrum, many will agree that a conundrum is what it is. The name, of course, is Wall Street.

Wall Street was always a symbol. The oldest inhabitant

cannot remember a Presidential campaign in which it was not an issue. Today it is more than a financial capital or a political dividing line between rich and poor, little fellow and big, East and West. During the past two administrations, even since the last election, the relationship of Wall Street to the rest of the country has completely changed. What we meant by the "unprecedented diffusion of prosperity" under Coolidge was that a full fifth of the population had surplus money enough to invest in stocks and bonds. The same phenomenon explains the unparalleled spread of depression under Hoover.

Never in history did so many people stand to gain or lose by the rise and fall of a market of which they have no knowledge or control. Wall Street is no longer the treasury and trading place of the big investor. It is everybody's bargain counter. What transpires there is the personal business of nearly thirty million shareholders. More, the depositors of every country bank, where it is a survivor or a casualty of the storm, have learned from sad experience that the thin streams of credit trickle from a single source. They are now directly instead of indirectly implicated; from critical observers they have become nervous or aggrieved participants in high finance.

It is easy enough to see the effect of this participation on the country at large. Not only is it by far the most interesting economic and social development of recent years, but it is a continuing development. The number of small investors has strikingly multiplied since the market crash. The biggest corporations, like United States Steel and Standard Oil, have watched their ten-share stockholders increase by 25 per cent in the past two years.

But what is the effect of the enormous spread of corporate ownership on Wall Street itself? Has the multiplication of small investors influenced the management of big corporations? Does it affect the Stock Exchange? That question suggests others. What and how much have the financial leaders learned from the depression? What adjustments are they making to changed times? Has the experience of the crisis raised doubts among its sponsors as to the durability of the economic structure? In other words, what is Wall Street thinking after three years of loss, deflation, Congressional investigation, of general attack on the whole system of speculation, banking and credit control?

These queries, easier to ask than to answer, I kept putting to all the citizens I could buttonhole during my wanderings in the powerful village extending from Fulton Street to the Battery. One goes from tower to tower, for these principalities, like the dynastic families of the Middle Ages, have their separate pinnacles and take counsel in board rooms looking out, not upon the city behind or the continent beyond, but upon the international highway of the sea. One goes from number to number "26" or "71," "33" or "115," for this is an arithmetical universe of which these towers are so obviously the creations that they might almost be described as columns of figures. The newest has the effect of a long, ruled balance sheet in black and white. It is one of the few domestic examples of the style beginning to be known in Berlin as the "Wall Street period," in graceful recognition of the substantial impetus given to the new architecture of Europe by the Medicis of lower Manhattan.

Some of the villagers I questioned bore names that everybody knows. Others were more obscure. The replies were neither complete nor conclusive. Wall Street is not so fluent as Washington; it has not so many ready answers for stock questions. But everybody tried to answer; it was evident that the interviewer repeated inquiries that the executives had already mulled over. One need only circulate among the lobbies of this capital on a day of 1932 to perceive how chastened and rueful it is, how doubtful of its own opinions, how cautious in its predictions, how changed in its attitude toward the public.

If this power was once arrogant, it is arrogant no longer. The representatives of Wall Street were humble before the Senate investigating committee last Spring; at home this Fall they are still humble. A political reporter is used to hearing statesmen and candidates claiming inside knowledge, but here were magnates making a boast of their ignorance.

Listen to an official of the Stock Exchange regretting that he advised a financial writer to buy a stock that immediately collapsed: "But at least it convinced him that I knew no more about the market than he did." To a great banker commenting on the tragic course of recent financial history: "What it means is that we suddenly became world bankers and that we simply had neither the experience nor the capacity to handle the business." To the head of a big corporation, asked if he did not find the general outlook a little brighter: "Ask any one but me," to which he appended a typical answer of the Wall Street of 1932: "Not brighter, shall we say, but less dark?" To the successor of a famous dynasty explaining a hysteria that in his grave and solid presence seems more incredible than it did in 1929:

"That's what happens when Wall Street goes literate, reads too much. It was the reign of the economists, and we bet with the college professors on the New Economic Era. Everything went wild, art, architecture, human conduct, and, yes, I admit it—money went wildest of all."

Wall Street has suffered, no doubt of it. It has suffered in its morale, in its prestige, in its pocketbook, in its personnel. The slaughter of the vice presidents alone has made a big hole in the population. When you mourn for the forgotten man, spare a tear for the discarded ornaments of this kingdom, its diplomatic corps, decimated by the sweeping axe of efficiency and economy. For Wall Street has learned from the depression what business everywhere has learned, that it was supporting an army of supernumeraries.

Nowhere is the proportion of unemployment greater than here; from the president down this is an organization of employees, high-powered, highly paid, but employees none the less, and nowhere are employees under such pressure to produce and to prove their value.

"My customers are cut by two-thirds," reports the proprietor of a popular lunch counter near the Exchange. "I miss the bright young brokers, the flocks of customers' men, actors, football stars, prize-fighters, bridge players. I read stories of what has happened to Vienna and Berlin to Broadway and some burg in the Middle West where the factories are closed down. But what about Wall Street? I'll bet not a spot on earth is as deflated as this."

Recent events have changed the temper, the attitude, the mood, the self-assurance of Wall Street, but the interviewer is left wondering if a succession of terrific shocks has really changed its mind. It is a curious mind, flexible and inflexible, open on one side and closed on the other, at the same time audacious and traditional. Characteristic of this village is that it was the first section of Manhattan to erect skyscrapers in clusters and is the last to retain the atmosphere of old New York, of early America. The financial mentality exhibits the conservatism of an ancient dynasty and the recklessness of the speculator, whether he plays with poker chips, astronomical hypotheses, decimals on a ticker tape, or any other token not quite real. Here is the same queer blend of caution in theory and boldness in practice which makes America so radical in technique and so stand-pat in policy.

The piquant discovery one makes in Wall Street is that it differs only in scale and degree from any little financial center in the country. This is no remote Olympus, inhabited

by supermen, either sinister or superb. Like it or not, this is
the sublimation of the intelligence, the vision and the general
moral standard of American business. In common with the
rest of us, it lacks leadership, it has few incandescent brains,
it has no clear sense of direction.

Take the question of the effect on management of the
spread of ownership. Three executives of corporations thus
owned agreed that the effect so far was nil. Myron C. Taylor
of United States Steel said it increased his sense of personal
responsibility but that you worked as hard to make profits or
prevent loss whether you represented 100 or 100,000 owners.
Walter C. Teagle of Standard Oil pointed out that an increase in the number of stockholders increases bookkeeping,
correspondence and office overhead, but does not otherwise
affect either the conduct of the business or the attitude of
the executive. The third declared that stockholders had not
now and never had any voice in the management, but—and
this is the point—that the ten-share owner is more anxious
for profits at any cost than is the 1,000-share owner.

"Three or four years ago," he explained, "our mail was
heavy with letters from small stockholders protesting against
our policy of accumulating surplus for a rainy day. They said
it was dishonest, that we were bound to distribute every cent
of profit every year in stock dividends. For two years now,
like most corporations, we have been in the red, but so far
we have been able to pay dividends out of that dishonest
reserve without protest from anybody. Furthermore, this
company aims to take care of its own slack; we consider a
certain percentage of unemployment relief a legitimate
charge on the industry. But the small stockholder disap-
proves. He wants dividends! My opinion is that if the little
fellow has any effect it will be to increase the pressure to cut
costs and increase profits."

Nevertheless, Wall Street is not quite at ease on this point.

It repeats what it likes to believe, what every one repeats, that the steadiness and conservatism of the American people under stress are largely due to this diffusion of ownership, which makes every stock owner not only a potential but an aggressive capitalist. My own impression is that such ownership develops the collective rather than the capitalist psychology and that title without responsibility, the decline of individual business, paper gains and losses, tend to create apathy, a general mood of unreality.

Wall Street agrees with that suggestion, too, when it is mentioned. If it could be worried by any but pressing affairs, it would be disturbed by the possible development of the corporate democracy it has created. So far this share-holding body is practically voiceless. It works, in fact, to give the directors more exclusive control, since they are able to vote huge blocks of stock by proxy for absent owners.

"But this will not last," asserts an executive more forward-looking than most, one of the "radicals" of the Street. "The small shareholder is still new, the whole development is still new. We are in the first stage of evolution in ownership and management. I foresee that we shall have popular parliaments in business, large committees representing perhaps half a million owners of a corporation which may itself include all the branches of an entire industry.

"The productive system may be divided into a dozen of such corporations, recognized and regulated monopolies, democratically owned rather than State-owned, but also democratically governed—and, of course, autocratically managed, perhaps on the city-manager plan, which seems to me the ultimate solution of the democratic muddle. The twelve committees, in their turn, could assemble on occasion for discussion of inter-related problems and policies, forming something like that economic parliament talked of but impossible of achievement under any existing system."

A few in Wall Street are not afraid of change. Mr. Teagle, devoting all his time to the President's share-the-work movement, conceived as an emergency plan for the spread of employment, is of the opinion that we shall never go back to the old working hours. This crisis, he believes, marks the end of the former norm, perhaps of any norm, for the work-day and the work-week. The workers see this; they are more willing to divide work than the employers are to revise schedules. The next problem, he says, is to find a balance between wages and shorter hours in order to build up buying power from another base.

The more open minds in Wall Street see that the whole system is in flux, that as a matter of fact the spread of ownership has an important bearing on the current problems of industry and finance. But this is often the industrial mind in contradistinction to the financial mind. You soon learn that there are two lobes in this brain, and they do not synchronize. The forward movements come from one, the pull-backs from the other.

In general, Wall Street resists change. By nature it is conservative, so we say, and then we think of 1929. Actually, what is more reckless than money? What political adventures in our history have compared with the wild plunges of finance in the last decade?

The truth is that Wall Street does change, is changing rapidly at this very moment. It has been the fulcrum in enormous shifts in our economic relations with the world, in this revolutionary investment movement which involves us all in a new kind of ownership, a communistic capitalism that means the end of "private possession" in the old sense. No one can pass through this besieged and shaken kingdom without feeling the ferment underneath, the shock of impacts from the outside. Slowly, under the pressure of public opinion, it has been obliged to recognize the necessity of some sort of regulation of the banking system and the machinery of speculation. That point in the path of reform is passed. Now the fight is for the privilege of self-regulation.

The Stock Exchange, for instance, organized like an exclusive and expensive club of 1,175 members, is publicly committed to a policy of rigorous self-discipline. Under its president, Richard Whitney, one of the newer leaders in the Street, and the governing committee, a body which looks and acts like a Senate and Supreme Court combined, it proposes a drastic reform of the abuses revealed under the time-exposure of the past four years; strict enforcement of rules regarding publicity of accounts and operations of "insiders"; scrutiny of the activities of "customers' men"—reform at so many points, indeed, that you begin to realize that the "evil practices" denounced in Senate probes can be more numerous and complicated than even Senators dream of.

In fact, the outsider comes away from a composite interview in a state of considerable confusion. But if it were possible to draw conclusions from the contradictory observations, at least three would be definite. To this extent the questions you took to Wall Street are answered.

First, the widening of the field of investment to take in the millions has had as yet no actual effect on the conduct of big business, but already it has an immense psychological effect. Already it is the subconsciousness of all the great corporate bodies. Wall Street is perfectly aware that it portends changes in the whole economic structure. "You say that the small town has changed because its leading citizens are no longer owners but managers," said one executive. "But observe that down here, also, there are no more owners. Everything is now too big for anybody to own. All the big men of Wall Street are just high-salaried managers."

Second, Wall Street has learned from the depression neither more nor less than business men everywhere. It has learned to curtail, to cut out waste, to examine itself from the operating point of view. Hard times have performed the task of an efficiency expert. Public opinion focused on it during these days of deflation, the terrific blasts of popular indignation let loose on the bankers and investment houses, have had more effect than the panic itself. More subdued than anyone remembers it, Wall Street has learned that it is far more dependent on public confidence than is any political government. It has not learned to doubt the system under which it operates. If anything—and this holds true for America in general—it believes in it more than ever.

"Suppose we had had a complete crash," suggested a magnate in the field of public utilities. "Suppose we had gone practically bankrupt, like Germany or a dozen small countries I could name. Suppose everything you think of as Wall Street had collapsed. When you consider that picture you realize by what vast margins we have escaped the worst. But even if the worst had happened, as it will not happen now, I haven't a doubt in the world that this country would carry on not only under the same form of government but under reorganizations of the same economic institutions. Nothing yet has fully tested the reserve forces of this country or our profound attachment to our own ways and our own habits."

Third, Wall Street is a capital in the same sense that Washington is. We have long recognized that we have an economic government. It draws unofficial ambassadors from every country in the world. The press agencies and the newspapers maintain important bureaus in Wall Street; many are larger than the Washington bureaus, and some journals, notably the European, station correspondents there instead of in the political capital. But I mean capital not as a center of news or government but as a place representative of a country or an interest, as the head and nerve center of a great body.

Observing Wall Street on the spot, talking to those who speak its language, it is impossible to think of it as a separate phenomenon. If you look at this capital in the light of America it may trouble you more but it will interest you more, because here you can study the characteristics of the American mind, acquisitive, vague, hopeful, curious, young and still deeply uncertain of itself, rushed to conclusions by the swirl of events, the kind of mind which builds a city like New York, the greatest of cities, without a plan or a thought.

Wall Street is terribly American. The corporation is American, the mass production of securities, the Stock Exchange, solemn in structure, hyper-sensitive, as unrestrained under excitement as a football rush. It is remarkably American in its makeup and leadership. Ask anyone who knows to name the twelve most important men in the Street and invariably they are representatives of the oldest native stock. Few are New Yorkers; they come from all parts of the country, "the top of the cream," and they prove, as a roll-call of the leaders in industry, politics and commerce everywhere proves, that the original American stock is still on top.

You may go to Detroit to study motor-making, to Washington to study law-making, to Wall Street to study money-making—or losing!—but wherever you go you are studying a manifestation of America. Inflated or deflated, towering or cowering Wall Street is the ten-share stockholder grown to colossal size and power, and more impressive, too impressive, only because he is big.

[15]   1 9 3 3   *January 15.* PREPARING FOR "THE NEW
DEAL." *How Roosevelt is getting ready to tackle as
difficult a job as any President has ever faced.*

NEW YORK

The center of political pressure in the United States
has shifted from Washington to New York. The swiftly moving finger of the spotlight already points away from the retiring President and blazes on his successor. Mr. Hoover has
to thunder at Congress to make himself heard—and would
have to use more thunder than he generates to make himself
heeded. For the first time in more than four years he traveled South in the comparative obscurity of the inside pages
of the newspapers and was able to fish as he likes to fish—in
a publicity so muted and perfunctory that to one accustomed
to the glare of the White House it must have seemed like
utter privacy.

The eyes and ears of the nation are now turned on the
President-to-be. The bombardment of big guns and little
guns, the pull and pressure, the swarms of people, asking,
offering, selling, buying, collecting political debts, advising,
informing, recommending—all the clamor and encampment
attending the rise of a new power has begun.

Ever since he turned over the Governorship to Mr. Leh-
man and returned to New York, for two months a nominal
private citizen, Mr. Roosevelt has been like a man besieged
in his own house. For two weeks now he has been seeing
callers at the rate of forty or fifty a day. Most of these five
and ten-minute appointments were made weeks ago, and,
except for a few delegations and his conference with the
Democratic leaders of Congress, the interviews are with individuals, gathering from everywhere to squeeze a word in
before the Presidential slate is completely covered.

The conversations will continue without interruption during the fortnight Mr. Roosevelt will spend at Warm Springs, but there they will be more leisurely and only with those summoned for consultation. In February he will board a boat and escape for ten days, unaccompanied by a politician, a reporter or a typewriter. For ten days he will be alone, "to rest and think," he says, but practically every moment of this two months of intensive preparation for the hardest job in the world will be passed in conferences.

Add to this pressure the weight and urgency of the problems into which the new President must plunge on the very day he assumes office, the expectations and anxieties of millions of citizens, converging on him as palpably as visible crowds. He has been swept into power in the depths of an unprecedented, almost insoluble, crisis. He inherits a government deeply in debt, deeply involved in about all the difficulties governments are heir to. He assumes leadership of the greatest democracy at the moment of severest strain and test of the democratic system. He steps out upon the world stage in a magnificent stellar role, but at the zero hour when all the scenery is being shifted and all the actors are improvising new lines or mumbling old ones in an obvious effort to keep the performance going while they look around wildly for a prompter and a cue.

Of the thirty-one Presidents who have preceded the second Roosevelt, probably only three have had to meet problems comparable with his. Under Washington the nation was created, under Lincoln it was held together at heavy cost, under Wilson it was transformed into a world power. But these choices, fateful as they were, were clear and simple compared with the decisions required of the American President in 1933.

Even while we rode the crest of the wave four years ago we had a dim apprehension that the tasks of government had

become too confusing and complex for the old political laissez-faire. We elected an engineer to devise a new order, to organize a prosperity we felt to be perpetual but a little out of
plumb, like the Tower of Pisa. Then it did not matter much,
however; the nation had no such desperate concern in the
Hoover policies as it exhibits now in Roosevelt's. The interest
in the new administration is not civic only, but personal. In
the suspense with which the country waits for the outlines of
the "new deal" you perceive how helpless the average citizen
feels himself in the modern world. With something of a
shock you realize how, even in America—perhaps most of
all in America—dependence on government has become universal.

Not only is the President-elect the first Democrat in the
White House for twelve years, and, therefore, a symbol of
change to millions yearning for any kind of change, but he is
actually the biggest potential employer at a time when jobs
are fiercely competed for and safe government jobs are at a
high premium. To some he represents the last hope of democracy, to others the prelude to socialism, but he embodies
some form of relief to all—the hungry and the thirsty, those
in business and those out of employment, the mortgaged and
the mortgage-holders, the farmer and the factory worker,
debtors abroad and debtors at home; and that means everybody in a population fed on credit and sheltered, equipped
and transported on the deferred-payment plan.

Of all this Mr. Roosevelt is perfectly aware. He sees clearly
the overwhelming magnitude and complexity of the tasks
ahead. More, he recognizes that time presses, that the Executive in an emergency has to move quickly. In his view, a diagnosis of the national situation indicates the necessity of immediate and drastic remedies. He has not announced his
program and probably will not announce it before his in-

auguration. In his conference with the Congressional leaders
he acted in his capacity as head of the party rather than as
President-elect, approving and discussing interim measures,
but not presiding or dictating.

He is pledged to balancing the Federal budget, including
rigorous cuts in the veterans' appropriations. He counts on a
large revenue from a beer tax, strongly opposes the sales tax,
prefers but does not sponsor an increase and wider spread of
the income tax. Beyond that he has not declared himself, but
when he does his program may contain surprises for those
who interpreted "a new deal" as no more than a good campaign slogan.

Yet at the center of pressure, in the shadow of the mountains closing in, the next President shows no sign of strain or
fear. The prospect before him might well daunt the hardiest
spirit, but Mr. Roosevelt faces it calmly. He is cheerful and
confident as ever, looks better today than he did at the end
of the campaign, and every one who sees him is impressed by
his serenity and poise.

This equanimity is a matter of temperament. Mr. Roosevelt
is not the worrying kind. He does not lie awake at night mul-
ling over his problems, as Mr. Hoover often does; he boasts
that nothing keeps him awake except strong coffee. He does
not agonize over decisions. His "yes" and "no" are swift and
positive. He proceeds on the theory that the percentage of
mistakes in quick decisions is no greater than in long-drawn-
out vacillations, and that the effect of decisiveness itself
"makes things go," creates confidence.

To him the Presidency is not a superhuman eminence, but
just another and bigger job, which the incumbent must stand
up to with all his capacity, but in which he is not alone. In
his philosophy the Chief Executive is neither a miracle man
nor a ruler shut behind walls of unbreakable glass. He draws

strength from the people and expresses as best he can their "common sense," the ideas which at any given time rise to the surface and somehow become personified.

Moreover, to a man who thrives on personal contacts, this crowded and staccato prelude to the Presidency is rather stimulating than exhausting. To one watching him in action, it is interesting to see how easily he communicates his own cheerfulness. Many of the visitors who fill the reception room in the narrow house in East Sixty-fifth Street are nervous as they wait. They study the prints of old ships which line the walls and rehearse what they have to crowd into a five-minute audience. But almost invariably they come downstairs satisfied and smiling.

Yet it is safe to assume that the satisfaction arises from their reception and not from any assurances they have received. Mr. Roosevelt gives audience comfortably, in a smoke-filled library, mellow with well-used books and well-worn chairs. He is a sympathetic listener, very friendly and responsive. But he went through a campaign for election without making promises and he is not promising anything now. He has a gift, a great political gift, of saying nothing graciously and "no" so reasonably that the refusal seems almost a mark of confidence. I have no doubt it is true, as he has more than once reiterated, that, out of the hundred or more names he has under consideration, he has not yet definitely selected a single member of his Cabinet or decided upon the men who will occupy the high posts in his administration.

Mr. Roosevelt has great faith in the man-to-man approach to any problem. He learns by the conversational method. When he wishes to be informed on a subject, he is likely to send for any one he has heard of who specializes in that subject. If he wants an issue reviewed or a lot of factual material summarized and predigested, he asks some authority to do it for him, not in writing but in talk, so that he can put questions as he goes along. He likes to collect different points of view, and usually summons the "antis" when he has heard the "pros."

He has political and economic advisers, whose advice he values and often takes. Like Mr. Hoover, he enjoys contacts with younger men, professors such as Moley, Tugwell, Berle and others, whom he uses to collect information and assist in the preparation of his speeches. The "brain trust," however, is only a pleasant myth, laughed at by Roosevelt himself and by those reputed to belong to this group of industrious cerebrators.

In point of fact, during the past few months he has consulted not a few but hundreds of persons on the questions he considers most urgent—unemployment relief, restoration of the purchasing power of the farm, government economy and taxation, farm and home mortgages, railroads, money and the credit structure, foreign debts and tariffs. He has listened to a vast variety of opinions and modified some of his own. But, expansive though he is, it is characteristic that he does not often express his own views at these discussions. He consults without confiding in the consultants.

As President, undoubtedly, he will continue this practice of consultation. Congress, even the special session he hopes to avoid holds no terrors for him, for the reason that he counts heavily on winning its cooperation by keeping in close personal touch with members of both houses. On the thorny issue of war debts, his natural impulse would be to talk things over, face to face, with representatives of the governments involved. The request for a conference with Secretary Stimson, whether or not the result of the diplomacy of Norman Davis, is an indication of what Roosevelt would have done in the first place if the initiative on the debt discussions had been his.

A public dialogue by telegraph is not the new President's idea of a conference. He always prefers informal pourparlers. He opposes a commission on the war debts because he knows that formal conferences usually become forums for making speeches for home consumption instead of meetings sincerely working for compromise and agreement. He was an observer at the historic peace negotiations in Paris and as a political realist he knows that open covenants cannot be openly arrived at any more than the work of Congress can be done on the floor instead of in the tedious give-and-take of committee rooms.

Most men who attain the Presidency have a sense of themselves as men of destiny, propelled by fate. The first Roosevelt had a strong faith in his star; Wilson believed himself ordained for a great mission in the world; Hoover felt a "call" to public service. It would not be surprising if the latest President, with his brilliant luck, his potent charm, his keen and happy "hunches," looked back upon his life from the threshold of the White House and saw all his experiences as a long-range preparation for a foreordained event. A Democrat is always justified in regarding himself as the elect of destiny: in the natural course he is never elected at all!

Of course, Mr. Roosevelt does believe in his destiny. Consciously or unconsciously, he sees his career as a process of education for the Presidency. A student of history and government from his youth, member of a political family, he turned to politics in his early manhood as naturally as the poet lisps in numbers. He was always fascinated by the lives and State papers of the Presidents, especially the early Presidents, who pioneered in the job and in a pastoral colony drew the framework of a continental republic. There is a good deal of the early American in Roosevelt, the sense of "the tradition," the nostalgia for the good life, free and simple, of our rural past. That is the explanation of his sympathy for the

Progressives, Norris, Johnson, La Follette, even Borah. All the Western radicals are early Americans, searching for a kind of liberty forever lost.

The President-to-be studied law, the textbook of government, and practiced it long enough to acquire fluency in argument and precision in the use of words, but not long enough to grow stiff-minded and legalistic.

Life in Washington is not strange to him. For eight years, as Assistant Secretary of the Navy under Wilson, he was part of the Federal Government. He knows how the machine operates, how the bureaucratic mind works. The Washington of today is not the Washington of Wilson and the young Roosevelts. It is a capital more monumental in its aspect and in its mind, but its rarified and stratified atmosphere changes little. To go green to Washington, with no experience of its peculiar insulation, is as great a disadvantage to a President as it is to go too well seasoned direct from Congress or one of the departments.

For four years Governor Roosevelt presided over the administrative unit next in size and importance to the Federal Government, all of the time against the opposition of a hostile Legislature, all of the time holding the uncertain balance between an East and West of his own, a jealous countryside against the most powerful of cities.

He has not the wide foreign experience of Mr. Hoover or the international spirit of Mr. Wilson. Yet his equipment for handling foreign affairs is much broader than that of most Presidents. Few have traveled as much as Mr. Roosevelt, from his childhood on, and few have enjoyed his social contact with the leaders of political and economic thought in other countries. He spent much time in Europe during the war and the peace conference. He is a constant reader of foreign newspapers and reviews. Thus he is able to understand, if not always to sympathize with, the point of view of other nations.

Back in November he said to a distinguished Frenchman visiting in this country: "If France defaults, it will be the fault of the French press, because the French people have never been told the facts regarding the debt to America by their own newspapers." The Frenchman agreed. "You are absolutely right," he said, "but I wonder that you have time to inform yourself on the molding of French opinion."

But these are not the experiences which Mr. Roosevelt himself values most highly as he reviews the record. If you should ask him what best qualifies him for the place he is soon to occupy, he would probably mention two things the onlooker would not think to emphasize. The first is that he lives in the North and in the South and he has campaigned across the country in two national elections.

That is to say that he has experienced America. He has felt the unity and variety, the immensity and power of the land he is called upon to govern. He has seen how the social pattern changed almost beyond recognition between 1920 and 1932. He has met people in all sections. The States are real to him, living places and not political divisions good for so many electoral votes. He remembers how the farmers of Iowa live, the cotton pickers of Georgia, the fruit growers in the Santa Clara Valley. To know the country so that you can never forget it in Washington is his conception of the elementary course in the education of a President.

Next to that schooling he places the terms he served as a legislator. He used to say in Albany that what best prepared him for the executive office was the fact that he knew and could sympathize with the legislative point of view. There is a natural difference in emphasis between the representative who is out to serve his constituency and the representative who has to defend the whole people from the claims of any constituency; to have served in both capacities should be required of all legislators if that were possible, in

Mr. Roosevelt's view; at least it should be compulsory for
executives.

It is because he feels for Congress that he believes, perhaps
too blithely, that there will be peace between the two powers
during his administration. He goes far to establish peace by
his shrewd suggestion to the Congressional leaders that since
it is almost impossible for the representatives of a specific
district representing special interests to put economies into
effect, in their own interests they would be wise to give him a
temporary grant of broad powers so that the sole onus of
locally unpopular measures should fall on him.

President Roosevelt will be in a position to assume broad
executive powers. In the next Congress, as distinct from the
present assembly, which he is always careful to explain is not
his, he will have majorities in both chambers and a host of
new members carried into office by his landslide. He will
announce at once, it is predicted, a comprehensive emergency
program which will have strong Congressional backing
whether the Legislature is in session or not. Even President
Hoover, whose relations with Congress were strained from
the beginning, had no difficulty in putting through emergency measures; no legislator would be brave enough, in the
present temper of the country, to stand against any experiment that held out a promise of recovery.

As he approaches his inauguration, Mr. Roosevelt inclines
more and more to lead his party and more and more to lean
on the support of his party. When he says "we" today he does
not mean his personal advisers but the party councils. If he
should put a Progressive in his Cabinet, for which the prime
qualifications are "intelligence and loyalty," it would be because he is extending the party boundaries to take in all the
liberals, not because he does not count heavily on Democratic
solidarity.

He will need to count on all the assets he can muster, and

he knows it. Optimism is a magnificent quality in the President in a crisis, like the courage of a great captain riding into a storm, but among admirers as well as critics are some who regard Mr. Roosevelt's confident poise a little uneasily. They wonder if difficulties will be as easy to negotiate and people as amenable to reason and persuasion as he seems to imagine. In his presence solutions seem simple enough. He has a way of reducing the most intricate problems to elementary sums which any one could work out. There is danger in this oversimplification, but perhaps there is also design.

Mr. Roosevelt believes that one of the elements in the present confusion of the world is the departure from elementary principles and a fuzzy-minded tendency to make things more complex than they really are. People despair when things tangle up on them, he says, and they are lost in a maze. His conception of the function of statesmanship is to simplify government and give the citizen a clear sense of direction, well-marked political and social thoroughfares, so that he knows where he is going when he makes a turn.

As an instance of the tendency to needless complication he points out the number of agencies dealing independently, often at cross-purposes, with the same problem. Eight different Federal agencies, for example, are empowered to extend credit to farmers. No two have the same policy and some pull in opposite directions. The result is confusion, aggravation of an already dangerous situation.

The first task of an efficient government should be to consolidate these eight agencies into one, or at most two, in some central place, and then and there to survey the whole system of farm mortgages as a basis for deciding whether or not there is need for more comprehensive legislation on the subject. Most public questions are treated in the same manner, phase by phase, sporadically, instead of whole, so that the picture we see is an unassembled jigsaw puzzle, which is complex only because it has been laboriously snipped into unrelated bits; put together, usually it is a very simple and familiar scene.

Surveys imply commissions, and the Roosevelt administration, like that of Mr. Hoover, though perhaps on a more modest scale, will have its quota of commissions. The new President, however, does not believe in commissions unless they result in definite recommendations for action, or in appointing them unless the recommendations are put into effect. And the more immediate problems cannot wait for commissions. "We must," he says, "be ready to go!"

Whatever lies behind Mr. Roosevelt's durable smile, be sure it is not political naïveté. He simplifies, but his personality is as complex as that of his predecessor's, and much more adroit. For we are witnessing the return to power of the political mind. Mr. Roosevelt has been trained for the Presidency by a career predominantly political. All his life he has dealt with political facts, which are people, human reactions. He goes to the very door of the White House finding out what people think, what they know, what they want. The approach to the "new deal," in a word, is by way of one of the oldest avenues of democracy.

[16]   1 9 3 3   *February 5.* HOOVER LOOKS BACK—AND AHEAD. *With political philosophy unshaken and holding no regrets for the past, he is confident that the American system, though still facing great difficulties, will triumph.*

WASHINGTON

Despite the precedent set by George Washington in his Farewell Address, the President delivers an inaugural but never a valedictory. It is a pity, because if there is one time

more than another when the Chief Executive might utter
words it would profit his countrymen to hear, it is at the end
of his Administration. Then he has nothing to promise but
much to impart. Of his policies there remain only his convictions presumably broadened and modified by experience.
Four years in the White House have given him a unique perspective on the Presidential office, on the operations of government, on the national problems. At the moment when he
lays down his great office, almost more solemn and searching
than the moment of assuming it, he stands detached and disinterested as he cannot be while in power and eminent as he
can hardly be again as a private citizen.

President Hoover has been the pivot of the dizziest turn
of the wheel in this permanent revolution called America. He
has been at the center of catastrophe. More than any one else,
he has been on the "inside" of those decisions and events
which have crowded his administration and the fifteen years
before. He has been a leading figure in an epoch that puts
the width of a century between the business world he left in
1914 and the business world he returns to in 1933.

He is not the man to underestimate either the historic crisis
he has lived through or the momentous part he has played in
it. He has a strong sense of history. The truck load of papers
he recently removed from the White House will be filed away
with others in his personal archives to complete the record
of a thoroughly documented career. This record has high
historic value, and it is significant of Mr. Hoover's love of
order and sequence, of the importance he attaches to his
administration and of his desire to clarify and justify his official acts.

Nevertheless, Mr. Hoover has no "last words" to pronounce
as he prepares to turn the government over to his successor.
The air is already full of his words, he says with a smile, and
adds that in a month they will all be forgotten. Washington

buzzes with rumor that the campaign for a "come-back" is already begun, but nothing in the President's own attitude, or in his present temper, supports the view that he plans to be a candidate again. Nor does he manifest any sympathy with the suggestion frequently heard throughout the country that in an emergency the new administration "use Hoover" and his experience, say in the Reconstruction Finance Corporation or in some such coordination of all kinds of relief in the United States as he once organized in Europe.

He believes in cooperation when necessary, but not in coalition governments in any form. Rather, he is convinced that the safety valve of democracies lies in the fact that they offer an alternative. The people can always throw out one administration and put another in. When they have done that, the retiring President should get out of the picture. For a time, at least, Mr. Hoover will be a very private citizen. He does not intend even to write, though the careful compilation of voluminous source material suggests that it will soon be turned into the text of history.

Up on the Hill the lame ducks talk themselves to death, but the President works away at his desk, less interrupted than usual but no less industrious. He does not adopt for himself the short day and the short week he believes inevitable for all workers in the future. To the end he maintains the record he has established for the longest hours, day in and day out, Winter and Summer, in the annals of the Executive office.

The White House is quiet. In the lull of this strange interlude between the election and the inauguration, the last interregnum of its kind, it has the air of suspended animation common to all houses when the tenants are moving out. The routine goes on, but it is dead routine, like that of a government department. One morning there is a stir of life, the familiar crowd of reporters, photographers, casual spectators.

The President-elect is arriving for a conference. Next day the waiting rooms are almost empty again.

Presidents must be philosophical, but to the outsider it is saddening to be so sharply reminded that the only visitors to the seats of power are those who want something. "Gimme! Gimme! is the word you'll hear oftenest in the next four years," said a friend the other day to Governor Roosevelt. Well, now the "Gimmies" are no longer here; they are pounding and hounding the new potentate.

Mr. Hoover is philosophical. He approaches the end of his term in a mellowed mood, partly relief, partly resignation, partly, it may be, quizzical anticipation of "the new deal." There is a glint of humor in his speculations on the careers open to ex-Presidents in a time of unemployment; he does not mean to compete for the present, he intimates, not until he has sailed the Pacific and savored to the full the sense of lightness and release old Atlas might have felt if the earth had ever rolled off his back.

He looks back without regret. There can be no regret for actions that had to be taken, and in Mr. Hoover's view most of the time he had no choices: after his first few months in office his hand was forced by the pressure of events. For him the White House has been a place of many sleepless nights, of hours in the dark haunted by phantasmagoric shapes, of dawns that might bring any bad news—and always brought calisthenics.

He seems to regard that early-morning medicine ball as symbolic. Characteristically, he never flunked it, any more than he flunked the mental gymnastics with which he associates it. Probably he enjoyed that hour, and the company it assembled, more than any in the long Presidential day. Yet as he looks forward, apparently he anticipates as much as anything the luxury of sleep that does not always end in calisthenics, mental or physical.

The man who goes out of the White House is never the same man that went in. The sheer weight and power of the office, a hundred times magnified in recent years, the sound of his words echoing around the world, isolate him in an official personality which is either a blur or an exaggeration of his own character. Mr. Hoover's blurred from the first, and that made his task harder when he so soon turned into a depression President; a man engrossed in outlines, definite plans, he could not outline himself.

But the years have helped to define him, particularly the past year. He is probably better understood, better liked in defeat than he ever was in power. Office has both hardened and softened him, made him at once more direct and more flexible. It steeled him finally to strike instead of beating about the bush and to take punishment without wincing. Whatever defeat cost him, a sensitive die-hard who had never met it before, he slept late the day after election and rose to plan a new future.

Now he is philosophic. Old stand-bys around the White House, the regulars who watch Presidents come and go, note that he is happier since the November verdict, more relaxed. He is mellow, with a mellowness that extends even to Congress. This is not merely a parting gesture, a forgive-and-forget attitude when the fight is over. Mr. Hoover has often pointed with pride to his successful relations with the Legislature, and the record, surprisingly, bears him out. Most of the measures he wanted to put through have been enacted, and that is true even of the last session, when his party was in the majority. Now he concludes that it is not difficult to work with Congress, and that the balance of power between the two branches of the government is salutary for both.

Mr. Hoover has the temperament that worries desperately before the event, but never after. He is inclined to struggle with the universe, up to the last ditch, but in the end he

accepts it. When I saw him just before the election he was in
the last ditch, refusing to surrender, but cheerful in his rather
wintry way. In the retrospect, indeed, it seems to me that he
has cheered up and warmed up in inverse ratio to the steady
lowering of the political barometer.

In the honeymoon period of the administration, so bright,
so brief, he was weighed down by an impossible mandate to
put some sort of scientific controls on a machine already out
of gear and running away. A few weeks after the inauguration I talked to him about his foreign policy and was impressed then, as on other occasions since, by his clear picture,
definite as a map, of an intricate situation. He expounded his
ideas point by point seriatim, as is his habit. In the mental
haze of Washington, to which I was then unaccustomed, this
clarity stood out like the Washington Monument in a fog.

Whatever he had not, Mr. Hoover always had a program.
He is responsible for bringing the point program into practical politics—we all do it now! The economic planners would
be the last to admit it, but his is the type of mind, the method
of approach, they want on the Supreme Board.

But the new President was ill at ease. The atmosphere was
already a bit sultry. By the Spring of 1930 the sky was dark,
though not yet appalling. Mr. Hoover has been much criticized for his early optimism, for delay in facing the realities
of the depression. At that time, however, when neither he
nor many others foresaw the panic ahead, I recall being
struck by the pessimism of his attitude. Naturally, one
guesses, he is inclined to pessimism rather than optimism.
That is one of the striking contrasts between him and his successor.

The next year Mr. Hoover was in the thick of his first real
battle with Congress. The Republican House, docile up to
then under strict party discipline, had bolted and joined the

untrammeled Senate in open revolt. The President was fighting mad as the news came to his office that the legislature had overridden his veto on the bonus bill. "Beware of the anger of the mild man," says the proverb, and I had a glimpse of the blaze banked under the ashes. He was level-voiced, patiently expository, but pretty grim.

By 1932 Mr. Hoover had lost his working majority in Congress. Financial panic was piled on top of unemployment and economic crisis. He had been forced to grant a moratorium on war debts which the Capitol had sustained unwillingly, with loud threats. The fortunes of the nation and the rating of the administration had sunk to a new low. And then, when things seemed about as bad as they could be, the President was cheerful. He was genial, for the first time at home in office. In the hour of deepest gloom, in fact, he was at last optimistic. The explanation of the paradox is that now everybody recognized that the situation was desperate, and the Executive was working as he works best, alone, putting through his emergency measures with practically no political interference.

What happened is that year by year President Hoover has become more himself. The new surface is the more natural surface. Underneath, his essential characteristics and fundamental ideas have not changed a bit. His self-confidence is not dented by strain and defeat; neither is his confidence in his program for recovery; he believed then, he believes now, that it is sound.

He thinks it was proved effective, that it worked. By last October the machine had been pumped up by confidence and credit to the point where it began to go, timidly, tentatively, but surely. Recovery had actually started, he believes, and when the movement was arrested it was by political rather than by real factors—the uncertainty incident to the election, governmental impotence in what amounts to a hiatus between administrations, the disturbance caused by the debt question. In other words, in his view, the mechanical part of the job is done, but the mechanism is like a millwheel grinding no wheat because no water pours through— the flow of confidence is lacking.

The Hoover view, naturally, is that uncertainty would end and the upward movement would resume if the Democratic administration announced that in principle if not in method it would follow his policies. And not those alone; others now have to be added to measures already in operation, since the time element is so vital that delay for any reason causes new weaknesses—adds to the weight that has to be lifted.

In the Hoover philosophy, likewise, there is no change. Nothing that has occurred shakes his faith that the phenomenon named America is the synonym for individualism and that to save one is to preserve the other. Either the United States drew its vitality from that idea or it did not; either it grew and expanded to a shape different from other nations because of certain principles planted in a favorable environment or it did not. Mr. Hoover's story is that it did, and he sticks to it. If the old formula conquered one frontier, he is sure it can conquer another. In a profound sense he is a political and economic Quaker.

You may object that never has the American Government deviated so far from that line as in the present administration. Beyond any other Executive Mr. Hoover has put government credit and supervision behind all kinds of business and multiplied the interventions of government in the social and economic life of individuals. His answer is that these are strictly emergency measures and carry within themselves the provision for their own annulment. Agencies like the Reconstruction Finance Corporation are as temporary as the War Industries Board. They are stimulants justified only by necessity, as poisons may be used as medicines to cure disease, safe because administered by those whose purpose is not to weaken the system but to support it.

Whether these measures are called conservative or radical is of little interest to Mr. Hoover. To him these are vague and meaningless terms. He would be the first to insist that he is for change—of methods, speeds, techniques—but always within the system. It is plain that he sees himself as an innovator. When he speaks of technocracy as "a lot of bunk," he does not refer to the fact of the energy survey, or even to the rush of the surveyors to make a great annunciation out of a few computations, but rather to the tendency to theorize on that basis and construct a whole new hierarchy on a multiplication table.

Those who supported Mr. Hoover solely because he is an engineer should hear his opinion of "theoretic engineers"— they are as bad as "legalistic lawyers," and that, apparently, is about as bad as possible.

Mr. Hoover is a large-scale surveyor himself, initiator of the two most illuminating factual studies of the modern American revolution: "Recent Economic Changes" and the newly published "Survey of Social Trends"; but to his mind such researches represent not conclusions but reports, not programs for action but raw material for informed judgment. "You have to know what a situation is before you are in a position even to disagree as to the way to handle it."

Thus he does not agree with all the deductions of his Committee on Social Trends. In his philosophy social insurance, for instance, is not a function of the State. He believes we must find a way of giving security in old age and stabilizing employment, but "an American way," as distinct from the government schemes tried elsewhere.

Insurance is almost an American monopoly, he points out. The people of this country, up to a certain point, have solved the insurance problem for themselves better than it has been solved by any government. Out of their surplus they have built up a reserve against death, fire, accident, disability amounting to nearly three-fourths of all the private insurance in force in the world. Believing that this individual effort pointed the way to a general solution, in the early days of his administration Mr. Hoover consulted with actuaries, economists, employers, &c., with the idea of working out an old-age insurance scheme that would be compulsory but privately supported like workmen's compensation acts.

It is interesting to speculate on how far along that road Mr. Hoover would have gone if circumstances had not forced him down another. If he had not been the administrator of a crisis, what kind of a President would he have been? Still more interesting, what would have happened if the Ship of State had run into storm under another type of captain, one who believed in either more or less government intervention? It is itself a sign of change that while no Executive in peacetime has assumed so much direction of business, none has ever been so generally blamed for not doing more.

Mr. Hoover is himself a sign of change. Few men have participated more actively in a process of world transformation. His public career, from his emergence in London at the outbreak of the war to his defeat at the polls, is an illustration of a movement in which he, like most of the governors of his time, has been in a sense both high priest and victim. The contradictions in his struggle to keep to the old course while tacking with the winds, to reconcile a Jeffersonian philosophy with finance corporations, Federal farm boards and railroad regulation, is typical of the inner conflict of America.

It is not without meaning that the new President and old unite in preaching a return to first principles, in invoking the oldest American ideals as a touchstone for present policies. The familiar phrases are no longer mere political patter.

They echo now the cry welling up from the troubled deeps of the nation. The American mood is that of the prodigal son, waking up in a strange city with a terrible headache and longing to get back to the old home, the house of the fathers.

Mr. Hoover belongs to his time. More clearly than ever, perhaps, as he turns the job over to the next superintendent, he sees the structural weaknesses of the present system and the points which have to be strengthened. Every President goes on building the never-finished bridge between the past and the future; his span, as he sees it, revealed a dangerous strain due to too much one-way traffic, with all the weight on one side. If one could summarize his view of what has happened, it would be something like this:

By 1928, the last normal year, the United States had solved the first and most difficult phase of the economic problem of mankind. It had learned how to produce enough for everybody. That solution was a triumph of individual enterprise and initiative; no other force or impulse had ever driven a people so far in so short a time. We had attained the highest general standard of living the world had ever seen. The spread of services and commodities had reached a new level and given us a surface uniformity, a "standardization" which represented the highest human plateau so far attained. We had mobility, jazz, leisure, ascending curves on all the graphs.

The mechanical side of distribution was on a par with production. Communication was up to the level of living. But when we turned to the social side of distribution there were great discrepancies—peaks too high, layers too low, loafers at the top, loafers at the bottom; even with a high median, millions of producers were, so to speak, distributed against. The trouble with standardization, in fact, was not that it was universal but that it was not.

Here was the great question mark. The American system worked better than any other, but that it worked far from perfectly was never more visible than at the peak of prosperity. Then came 1929, with the maldistributed earnings of the system going into speculation on a mammoth scale and stocks and sales and values sky-rocketing until they hit the ceiling and exploded.

Evidently the system was out of balance and had inadequate safeguards. The crisis showed up many cracks, but demonstrated above all that the fatal flaw in distribution was in the flow of money and credit. The financial structure had not kept up with the production structure; it belonged to a period long outgrown and had not improved in fifty years. It did not balance, did not synchronize. What should be merely the lubricant of the economic machine had become the master in control, a master behind the times and without wisdom to match his power, since all the other banking systems in the world withstood the same shocks as ours, and worse, without anything like our percentage of failures.

It follows that the next great step in the development of America is to invent machinery of distribution to match that of production. Mr. Hoover's conviction is that what we have done before we can do again under the same system, but recognizing that the spread of wealth itself is a reason for a reorganization and reform of the financial establishment. The danger in the obvious lack of balance is that it suggests unbalanced remedies.

No one needs to be informed on the retiring President's views on inflation. He believes we are now at the fork in the road. In one direction runs the broad highway which no nation has ever taken without final disaster. A few months, a few years, the illusion of improvement may last, but the end is always the same. The post-war world is full of tragic examples of the speedy unmanageability of "managed currency."

The other road is to go boldly into a world conference which shall have for its first objective the stabilization of money. It is now clear to the blindest that the disparity between currency values, like the disparity between debtor and creditor, has become a problem of the utmost urgency. When producers with debased currencies undersell us in the few foreign markets left and slide under the tariff walls to undersell us at home, it becomes obvious even to Mr. Hoover, who never acknowledged before that tariff is a foreign policy, that it might be a subject for international discussion.

The hope for such an effort lies in two facts: one is that all nations have what Mr. Hoover calls "the ache in the bones," the same structural ache; the other is that everybody knows that even an intention to stabilize money would cause an immediate rise in world prices. People are so eager to go ahead that "if a man sees daylight anywhere," says Mr. Hoover, "he will run toward the light."

This is the hard road. A workable and acceptable plan would be difficult to find. Such a conference would be a kind of blacksmith's shop in which the conferees would have to hammer away at one plan after another until they struck something that rang like true metal. They would have to be so desperately resolved that they would not leave until they found it. Mr. Hoover's experience is that there are no easy international negotiations.

Seven months of thorny preparation led up to the Mac-Donald visit * and the famous conversation on the Rapidan, and eight months more were required before the general

---

* J. Ramsay MacDonald, Prime Minister of England, visited the United States in October 1929, to meet informally with President Hoover at his fishing camp on the Rapidan, Virginia. The conversation revolved around the rearmament of Europe. The outcome was an invitation to the five naval powers to meet in London to control competition in the building of war vessels.

agreement reached there was ratified. And that was on the comparatively simple subject of naval armaments, which governments themselves control. One wonders what will happen when conferences start to tackle problems as complicated and touching so many interests as world trade and war debts.

The President begins to look at the Presidency as a private citizen might, the one citizen left who has looked at the citizen from the Presidency. He speaks of its few personal satisfactions, but of how easily one adjusts the mind and habits to its routine. I suspect that Mr. Hoover enjoys the routine, that to wade into a pile of the toughest problems would be what he might do for amusement. He speaks of the rewards, putting policies through, the tremendous interest of the job, the response of the people. He intimates with a grin that as a political casualty he was willing to stand up against the wall and take the final shots for such unpopular measures as cutting costs and raising taxes, or reorganizing the government departments, but that supreme sacrifice was not required of him.

The last-named reform has been contemplated for twenty-five years, since the Taft administration. Under Harding a commission was appointed of which Mr. Hoover was the head. It was one of the achievements expected of this administration. Why it has not been done up to now is explained by one of the favorite Hoover formulas—that it is impossible to get authority to do anything in a representative system until it is almost too late.

Yet the representative system as it fumbles in America, as he has seen it fumble at close range for four hard years, is the one thing for which Mr. Hoover would fight, bleed and die. It is the system which favors the individual and rewards enterprise, the system under which little boys from West Branch can work up to be Presidents. He is comforted by the thought that, while the system lasts, thanks to the restrictions of the Constitution and the limits to the borrowing power of the government, no subsequent administration can go much further than his in putting the government into business. He makes no prophecies as to what is going to happen, but he knows that whatever happens the nation will survive it.

[17] 1 9 3 3 *March 19.* THE NATION RENEWS ITS FAITH. *Out of the swift succession of events that has marked two weeks of the New Deal, the confidence of the people in government has been re-established.*

WASHINGTON

After two weeks of the New Deal it is hardly an exaggeration to say that it is about the biggest surprise Washington ever had. The capital is in a state of exclamation.

The seventy-two-word message on the beer bill seemed to clinch it. Not because it was about beer, forgotten now in the flow of other stimulants, but because it was the perfect antithesis to years and tons of talk. Because it capped other messages in tone and brevity unlike any Congress had been in the habit of receiving. Because it followed a radio talk, the first of its kind of the President to the people, explaining very simply the government banking policy. Because day by day executive acts had been issuing from the White House like a series of special extras.

"We have a President!" they were exclaiming in the Senate galleries. On the steps of the Capitol I met one of the oldest and most skeptical political observers, and he was exclaiming, too, as he gazed at the men knocking down the inaugural grandstands. "Can it be that it is only a little more than a week since all this began?" he asked. "The New Deal in person? Evidently what this country needed was a master's voice, Government."

And, indeed, the popular response to the first acts of the new administration is like the rising of a nation. When we can pause long enough in the rush of events to get a perspective on the historic transition now in progress we may see that the crisis we are passing through is as much governmental as financial.

Perhaps it is more than coincidence that the advent of Roosevelt is marked by two tremendous if temporary abdications, that of Wall Street and that of Congress. During the emergency, at least, both the financial and political capitals have moved into the White House.

Today we have a concentration of powers in the President we never knew in war. Roosevelt is the successor of Wilson in that in far different circumstances—in what another world! —he restates in part the political philosophy of Wilson. He is quite as much the heir of Hoover, in the sense that under Hoover the scope of Federal administration and authority was immensely expanded.

Most of all, perhaps, he is an instrument of history. What happened on March 4 was more than a transfer of authority from one party to another. It was more than a shift in temperature and temperament. It was a real transposition of power, so that instinctively people refer to the event as a change in government instead of a change of administration. How far that change will go no one knows. At present it gives us a tempo and temper in government that seem to win the unanimous consent of the governed.

The more precedents he breaks, the more authority he assumes, the more applause the new Executive receives from his admiring audience. The yearning of America is for action, almost any kind of action. Roosevelt makes a flying start by satisfying that long-balked appetite. One suspects that he expresses the kind of revolution that fires the American mind, a 100 per cent American revolution, whose manifesto is the Constitution.

All this was implicit in the inaugural. So much has happened in the interval that already it seems a long time since the new President, grave and pale, stood up beside his grim-visaged predecessor to take the oath of office. Ranged behind the two, on that day, we saw the government: Senators, Justices, Governors of States, Cabinets coming and going— the "public faces" that represent the ruling personnel of both parties. Somberly, a little stunned, they looked down upon the faces of the people, a great field of upturned faces, dazed, too, and wistful, the composite face of America. In all the faces, above and below, was reflected the tension of the country. We felt it more than the chilly air blowing through the grandstands. Nobody was quite certain what the inaugural was inaugurating; nobody was certain of anything.

Only the dome of the Capitol seemed solid and familiar. Poised between a shaken earth and the restless clouds in a gray sky, the old cupola never looked more like cast iron. And cast iron never looked more beautiful. A kind of ultimate safe deposit vault, so at last it appeared, in which had been hoarded for a long time a lot of forgotten securities. The quiet crowds jeered a little on hearing their "excitement" described by the radio reporters. If they could have been broadcast, they would have been heard talking anxiously about government, wishing for decisive policies in Washington. "Everything else seems to be falling," commented a doubtful Democrat from Michigan at the end of the inaugural address, "but maybe the government still lives."

This is the fact that overshadows all other facts in Washington today: Once more there is a government. The capital is experiencing more government in less time than it has ever known before. Always a chameleon city, changing its color with every President, it is now as tense, excited, sleepless and driven as a little while ago it was heavy and inactive. There is an element of fantasy in the contrast between the frantic hurry of today and the torpor on the Hill, the isolation of the President, during the comatose months of the interregnum.

Silence has been succeeded by a deluge of proclamations, executive orders, conferences at all hours, grants of power of a kind governments seldom make except by force. White House and Treasury are in operation night and day, like factories filling rush orders. In a single week Congress pushed through more legislation than in the entire preceding session, and these hastily passed enactments propose to change the financial, economic and administrative structure of the United States more drastically than it has been changed by legislation in fifty years.

In a dizzy fortnight, with hardly a murmur, Washington has become the seat of an executive dictatorship. While no single one of the grants of extraordinary powers is without precedent, in sum they constitute a centralization of authority and responsibility unique in our history.

Most of this authority the President requested, but some of it he is implored to assume; if the tendency to unload on the Executive continues, he will soon be swamped under mandates to take charge of everything. For the present, at least, it seems that he cannot be too absolute to suit the people. This is partly because the sense of emergency grips the land, partly because Congress has shown so little conception of the urgency of the popular mood. One reason for the present meekness of both houses is that every member is practically buried under avalanches of telegrams and letters from constituents. These messages come to Democrats and Republicans alike. Sometimes profane, always imperative, they are mostly variations of a single order: Support the President; give him anything he wants.

No comparison can be made between these powers and wartime powers. In the first place, the emergencies are not comparable. The present crisis means more to more people, devastates a wider front, than any war ever did. It recognizes no age limits, no neutrals, no safety zones. In the second place, the problems of military mobilization are simple beside the complex and radical relief measures acquired in an economic breakdown. In the third, no wartime President could have the popular support given to Roosevelt in his first offensive on the home front.

Spectators noted a resemblance between the last preceding Democratic President and the new Executive as he appeared at the inauguration, jaw thrust forward, cheeks deeply furrowed, a man newly stiffened and hardened, apparently, by the shock of events. There may be some similarities besides that occasional superficial likeness. If so, they are yet to be revealed, though it begins to look as if under the warmer manner and greater flexibility of Roosevelt lie the Wilson will and the Wilson courage. But Roosevelt has already more power than Wilson had. In a more challenging epoch, he presides over a greater crisis.

The remarkable thing is that this supreme command is exercised so openly and informally, as part of the day's work —"nothing personal about it!" is the laughing explanation— that the atmosphere of Washington today is freer and more relaxed than it has been for many years. The capital is in a state of reanimation. I have never seen it so much like a real town, at last annexed to the United States, sharing the common lot of the country.

The full brunt of the depression did not strike here until the banks closed. By that time the capital was also hit by the

Roosevelt administration, and the double blow has had a curiously tonic effect. Washington is poorer and more uncertain than it has been for many administrations, terribly worried about the inevitable cuts in government bureaus. In the vast reaches of the Department of Commerce, doomed to deflation, it is said, with other of the pet projects of Mr. Hoover, the clerks sit lost in space and sad speculation. The head of a fashionable rental agency exhibits his best locations in vain. "Democrats never have any money," he complains. A hotel manager puzzles over the name of a new bureau chief. "I don't know Democratic names," she sighs.

Under all the strain, however, the place is unwontedly gay. Even when out of office Democrats are more cheerful than Republicans. I don't know why. They have less money but more fun. Perhaps it is the South in them, used to making the best of things. Perhaps it is the twinkling Celt. These accents cross and blend wherever the Democracy digs in. In the present concentration they are diluted by the pleasant twang of the West and the humorous slang of New York.

Mostly, however, the good humor radiates from the White House. The Roosevelts had hardly moved into that haunted mansion, so impressive and so hard to impress, when it became as "unofficial" as the Governor's house in Albany during their occupancy. The President and the First Lady will never be official personages; under all circumstances they are themselves. When they spoke long ago of "humanizing" the White House, it sounded as if they might work at it, with an effect somewhat dreary, like a child forced to smile. But already the old house, treated like any nice house, smiles naturally. It is not open indiscriminately, but it has the effect of being open all day long. People dash in and out, as everybody dashes in Washington nowadays. The President hangs his ship prints in his room and his Hudson River pictures in the Executive office. Mrs. Roosevelt has her old chintzes and her rows of family photographs on the walls of her sitting room.

Everything is simplified, even the meals and the service. Everything is informal. Washington was startled the other midnight when it heard the reporters, waiting for the end of a conference, singing glees on the porch of the White House, led by one of the President's secretaries. It was startled to see Mrs. Roosevelt, hatless, sitting knitting in the gallery at the opening of Congress. It is surprised by the ease and freedom and fun of the President's press conferences.

That is the tone of the administration, and it is interesting to see how the whole orchestra takes the same key. The atmosphere of Washington is now the Roosevelt atmosphere as two weeks ago it was Hoover's. The whole pattern is different. All the doors seem open. All the talk sounds candid, whether it is or not. It starts out by being a very accessible administration.

What strikes one most, in the terrific pressure of these early days, is that it is a conspicuously polite administration. The secretariat, reduced in number compared to Hoover's and greatly overworked, reflects the unhurried, unflurried good temper of Mr. Roosevelt himself. He can be grim; he kept saying "No" to Mr. Hoover until eight hours before the inauguration; but in the thick of conflict, climbing out of chaos, he remains the most buoyant and confident person in Washington.

The members of the Cabinet were not selected for their good manners, but they might have been. Secretary Hull * is a gentleman of the old school, deliberate and deferential. Secretary Woodin,* with his Viking name and his Pucklike

* Secretary of State Cordell Hull (D), Tennessee; Secretary of the Treasury William H. Woodin (D), New York City.

face and figure, speaks with almost exaggerated courtesy. Secretary Wallace * is shy and soft-voiced, Attorney General Cummings * courtly and judicial. Miss Perkins * has plenty of charm and a gorgeous sense of humor. Mr. Dern *—lest you'd suspect that his West is very tame—wears a coat made out of an Indian blanket. Mr. Morgenthau * will, as a competent aide, do a popular job in interring the Farm Board and co-ordinating all the farm credit agencies, and Mr. Douglas * will perform with skill a major operation on the budget. Like all the members of the administration family I have seen, including the three Columbia professors, Moley, Tugwell and Berle, they are quiet, friendly people, eager to oblige.

The President's official advisers are mostly his friends. He has been blamed for making his selections on the basis of loyalty, from among those only who supported him for the nomination. By some elements of his party he is criticized for his generous recognition of the Progressives. But behind Mr. Roosevelt's choice of little-known liberals for his Cabinet is a definite idea. He has his own concepts of political economy and he deliberately seeks to introduce a new mind into government. He wants to make a Liberal party out of the Democrats and the "great" men of the party, the obvious Cabinet material, are set in party lines, set against change.

Perhaps he wishes to be boss on this adventure. Perhaps his appointments are in settlement of political debts, as such appointments usually are. At least they represent the direction of his own mind and convictions. They fit into the pattern he is making, help to define what he is after. After you look at the administration family as a whole, allowing for the exceptions, you begin to perceive that it expresses something

* Secretary of Agriculture Henry A. Wallace (D), Iowa; Attorney General Homer S. Cummings (D), Connecticut; Secretary of Labor Frances Perkins (D), New York City; Secretary of War George H. Dern (D), Utah; Acting Secretary of the Treasury Henry A. Morgenthau (D), New York City; Director of the Bureau of the Budget Lewis W. Douglas.

important to interpret if you would understand the Roosevelt objectives.

Already it is perfectly clear that it is a Roosevelt administration. The new President is his own man. He made no claims to super-capacity during his campaign, and none was made for him; on the contrary, there was a persistent impression that he was vague, too agreeable, playing safe. That impression did not outlast his first bold moves as President. Mr. Roosevelt likes to surprise, and he did surprise the country by the decision and speed with which he went into action. He surprised his chastened Congress. He has already inaugurated three sweeping reforms—in the banking system, in government reorganization, in farm economy—that in ordinary times would require months, perhaps years, to debate and implement.

His readiness to take advantage of the emergency to launch these far-reaching measures indicates that they are part of a prepared program. But it is characteristic that he did not wait to embody them in the long and all-inclusive "Message" expected of Presidents at the opening of a new Congress. Instead he dispatched notes to the legislative bodies, three in a week, refreshingly brief and informal notes, each a specific demand for specific action.

This is a new method of dealing with Congress, safe for the time because the party majority is so large in both houses and because in his emergency measures Mr. Roosevelt has the complete cooperation of the Republicans. During the critical days of the bank holiday, Mr. Hoover stood by in New York, Mr. Mills * and his subordinates hardly left the Treasury, and on the Hill there was perfect team-work between the two parties.

We are still too close to that drama to see it, but to one who attended the first sessions of the Seventy-third Congress

---

* Under Secretary of the Treasury Ogden L. Mills (R), New York City.

there was something both ominous and reassuring in its heavy unanimity. There was stark reality in the Senate that day, and grave and thrilling speech. The Chamber looked out of plumb, with so much empty space on one side of the aisle and so many desks crowded on the other. But for all practical purposes there was no aisle; the Senate voted together as it has voted only once or twice before. An old lady in the gallery wept. She repeated, oddly enough, what the man from Michigan had said on inauguration day: "The government still lives."

A couple of days later the Democratic ranks in the House broke on the economy program. This administration, like the last, will meet its hardest test in keeping solid the unnatural amalgam in its own party. The President, however, holds all the cards in the new deal. He was not above threatening to appeal to the country by radio against the Congressmen who held out against giving him power to cut veterans' compensation and Federal salaries. And Congress knows that the country is almost solidly behind the administration policies.

No one would call this dark prologue a honeymoon. To contrast the beginning of Roosevelt's term with the brilliant Spring of the Hoover era four years ago is like looking at Long Beach before and after the earthquake. Then all the commentators were analyzing the engineer in office and congratulating the nation on substituting economic for political experience in the Executive office. Nobody has yet begun to analyze Mr. Roosevelt. We have been too near collapse for intellectual exercises, and until now he was hardly thought of as a great figure.

Yet he arrives at what every one concedes to be a turning point, and he makes a great turn. During one of his last nights at Hyde Park, with a pencil on a pad of yellow copy paper he wrote his inaugural address, and nothing that oc-

curred subsequently in Washington, all reports to the contrary, caused him to make any important changes in the
original draft. He knew long ago what he meant to do; he
had something definite in mind when he promised a "new
leadership." Until he repeated the words on a black day on
the steps of the Capitol, however, until he promised action
and immediately gave it, nobody paid much attention. The
country had heard a lot of talk about leadership and seen
little.

Two weeks of Roosevelt have changed the atmosphere of
the capital, have raised the morale of the country. It is too
troubled and confused and tense a time to be called a honeymoon, yet no President in so short a time has inspired so
much hope. Miracles were expected of Mr. Hoover four years
ago. His first steps, his first appointments, his first press conferences, were likewise hailed as signs of a new day. But he
had the great advantages of starting at the top. The new
President has the luck to start at the bottom, from the lowest
depths. And already he has performed a miracle in re-estab-
lishing confidence in government, in convincing worried citizens from Michigan to Virginia that the government at
Washington still lives.

[18]   1 9 3 3   *March 26.* "LET'S TRY IT!" SAYS ROOSE-
        velt. That remark reflects the President's way—a
        portrait of the nation's Chief Executive at ease on
        the job.

                                        WASHINGTON
        The new President sits at the big glass-topped desk
in the beautiful oval room which has walled in a succession
of Presidents. He sits remarkably at ease. Energy is the note
he strikes on the ear of the country, but at close range this

ease in office is even more impressive. Already, say the old-timers, he functions as naturally as if he had lived in the White House all his life. His is the free-wheeling type of mind that can turn on the instant from a heavy conference on the state of the world—that cosmic jig-saw—to return an old gold coin sent by an admirer, carefully advising the sender of its value and how to dispose of it.

Months ago, as a candidate, Mr. Roosevelt declared that he had read history and watched Presidents in action and understood perfectly what the office meant and demanded. Now he says that it is just what he expected—emergency and all. He was ready for what he had to do; therefore, his plunge into action surprises everybody except himself. For months, in consultation with advisers whom he refuses to call "experts," because he dislikes the sound and connotation of the word, he has been preparing a program which he proposes to announce point by point and enact measure by measure, instead of whole.

This is for the sake of order, for the sake of strategy, and especially for the reason that the effect of one measure may modify the scope of subsequent legislation, as the economy bill, for instance, or revenue from beer, changes the plan for increased Federal taxes. The program is definite, well-studied, but flexible. In parts, as in the omnibus scheme for farm relief, it is frankly experimental. No tried way, no single way, no way any man can be sure of, leads out of the dismal swamp in which agriculture is mired. It is characteristic of the Roosevelt policy to take a consensus of the farm leaders and go ahead on an exploratory trip in the general direction of their plans rather than to keep on arguing at the cross-roads.

Besides the known facts, the new President allows a large margin for the unknown factors. That is one great difference between the White House of today and yesterday; now it has room, and time, for the unexpected. It is strange to go back after an interval of only two weeks or so and find the setting of the piece almost exactly as it was and everything else changed—new faces behind the desks, new faces in the waiting rooms. The figures of a month ago have faded out of the picture as completely as shadows on a screen.

The same roses, mirrored in the same mahogany, grow in another climate. You look out the long windows on the park-like lawn behind the executive offices. A solitary guard strolls back and forth, casual as all guards are in this free-and-easy capital. He stops to pick a yellow crocus in the grass or feed an antic squirrel under the budding trees. You perceive that the season has changed since yesterday. But not more outside than in here. Visitors crowd in—not casual callers, not even office seekers, but people sent for—the Congressional leaders, the Vice President, the Postmaster General, the Director of the Budget, Ambassadors, the German breathless, a little early. They talk in whispers, as people always do in political vestibules, but from the inner office, at frequent intervals, the Roosevelt laugh rings out, long and hearty.

The Cabinet files into the Cabinet room, next to the President's office. The Secretaries take the places of their predecessors around the long table. They are hurried, eager, discursive—new and ready for new things. Already the one woman among the men is as natural as if she were not the first of her sex to sit at that council board. They are all reorganizing their departments, and as the departments stir with a premonition of change, the whole capital stirs. And as nothing is more set than the pattern of a long-established government, as no organism has harder arteries than a bureaucracy, the feel of uncertainty in this monumental body is oddly disconcerting, like the shaking of the earth.

What distinguishes this administration from the last is not so much tempo, mood, atmosphere. That quickening always accompanies the transfer of power and place from one party to another. It is this sense of movement. Everybody seems receptive, primed to go. "Let's try it," says the President, and there is ground-swell as if the nation waited for the word. In the anteroom you realize that the movement is a movement of the national mind, which has at last reached the capital, penetrated the White House. It is a manifestation that somehow moves you as you wait here at the center, watching a new government taking shape. This is civilization, you say: a people bent on change, yet disciplined and mature enough to move toward new paths together, step by step, patiently and with a tough and valorous humor.

The Executive desk is not quite so clear as it used to be. There is a scattering of papers under the tall bronze lamp. The schedule of appointments is not so rigid. The President smashes through the order of the day by sending for the people he wants whenever he wants them. The secretariat finds it hard to keep up with him, but it is accustomed to his habits and it has survived a period of initiation not unlike the first month at the general headquarters of a revolution.

Congress has revenged itself on a rough-riding Executive by catching up with him; it has been passing laws almost faster than they can be drafted. Statements have to be stitched up while you wait. Cabinet officers rush in out of turn. The international situation has to be taken in as a side line; the world cannot wait until we get our house in order. Hurry calls precipitate extra conferences on some protest on the farm bill, on a snag in a banking situation in a Western State, on an urgent query from Europe on disarmament policy.

To be President in these times is like being at the control board of Station USA, bombarded by all the sound waves of the nation and the world. They focus on the American Executive with the effect of physical pressure. But Mr. Roosevelt does not hurry. He has time to talk, to listen, even to converse, which is rare in high executives, who usually do one thing or the other. His eyes are a little shadowed, due to the loss of his usual ration of sleep. His face seems slightly sharper and firmer than it was a month ago. He is cooler and calmer, however, than any one in the reception room, and confident and cheerful as he was on election day.

Mr. Roosevelt looks thoroughly at home in the White House. He says he feels at home. He likes the space and classic character of the historic old mansion, which has never lost the effect of a stately manor house of a country gentleman of the eighteenth century. The Roosevelts do not belong to that period, but they derive from it more directly than their immediate predecessors. Anyway, they fit in; not since the first Roosevelts have any tenants displayed so much talent for living their private lives in public; it must be a family gift. In contrast to the Hoovers, awkward and ill at ease under an exposure which they hated, the Roosevelts are natural under the spotlight. They break through so many forms and precedents that already they have made official life in Washington as comfortable as life anywhere.

All Presidents sit with their backs to the windows, with their sylvan view, but this one has provided himself with something to look at besides the monotonous expression of his callers, always, one imagines, a little anxious, too ingratiating. Mr. Roosevelt has a strong feeling for place and accustomed things. His last act as a private citizen was to drive off alone in his little car for a final round of his favorite spots at Hyde Park. While he counts on "going home" when he can and plans to spend his Summer weekends on the Hudson instead of the Rapidan, no doubt he foresees that his returns will not be as frequent or unheralded as they used to be.

The upstairs study, another Oval Room, where he works at night, has been made as much like the Hyde Park library as possible, with his timber desk, his favorite chair, his ship prints and war trophies. In the morning, as was his habit at Albany, he runs through his correspondence in his bedroom. He goes over to the executive office about 10 o'clock and works straight through until 5 or later, lunching at his desk—another innovation—and returns to the White House for tea with the family and the friends who drop in to join the circle.

He has not been outside the White House half a dozen times since he moved in. This evening talk has been his only diversion. He likes talk, and he has certain favorite subjects, such as the early American Presidents, the Napoleonic wars, experiments in government, problems of practical farming, tales of fishing and the deep sea, to which he kindles in his weariest moments. People and talk literally enliven and re-create him. He comes out fresh and smiling from conferences that would wear out another man. Nothing wears him out. Even his temper is practically shock-proof; no one in his entourage, through all the strain and drive of the campaign trips, in the frantic pace of the past few weeks, has seen him angry, even irritable. With invincibly good humor, however, he usually gets what he wants.

Mr. Roosevelt thinks and talks a great deal about government. He has very pronounced ideas on the functions of the Presidency. He believes that the President is literally the leader of the people, particularly in the development of ideas. He believes that at every turning point of history some one rises up who can enunciate and in a sense personify the new direction of the public mind and will. In his view America has reached such a crossroads. He does not go so far as to speak of himself as the leader of the economic revolution now in progress, but there is no doubt that he considers the President of the United States at this juncture the instrument by which profound and necessary changes in the American system are to be effected.

When I asked him once, before his nomination, why he wanted to be President in a time like this, he answered, smiling, that some one had to be, some one, with no more than human capacity, to meet a crisis that eventually would have to be resolved by human intelligence. The answer was made lightly. As a reformer, if he is a reformer, Roosevelt has no cant. But even then I saw it was not meant lightly. He might have said: "Here am I, Lord; send me," and the significance would have been the same.

Perhaps that explains the strong line he took immediately upon assuming office. That line, to be sure, was forced upon him by the banking crisis, and if he had not been obliged by circumstances to take the reins there, if the financial structure had not been so near collapse, he would not have started with the momentum that enabled him to achieve in the economy bill the biggest grant of power ever voted to an Executive by a Congress.

He has no desire to be a dictator. He does not think, as many do, that the time has come for a new definition of the Executive and legislative powers, to the end that there may be some central authority to override in the general interest the pull and clamor of a thousand local interests. He feels only that government must function, and that the Constitution already provides ample room for action when the emergency is so serious that there is no time for parliamentary delays.

Further, he is of the opinion that Congress is and should remain the appropriating power, but that in a modern State the legislative body can no longer waste its time and that of the country in arguing on all the details of expenditure, such as the number and kind of pencils used in the consular service or the number of buttons on the trousers of a marine. The present grant of budgetary discretion to the President only conforms to good business practice in leaving spending to the

Executive Department and giving up actual description of
what shall be bought.

As Governor of New York, Mr. Roosevelt had his own
methods of dealing with the Legislature. Already he has discovered, as he predicted long ago, that his legislative experience is his most valuable single equipment for the work of
the Presidency. He discovers also that Washington is the
greatest stage in the world; under this proscenium, every gesture and every word is magnified. The voice of the City of
New York drowns out the voice of Albany, and the Empire
State, including the metropolis, that tall suburb of the
United States, is only one of forty-eight sovereign Commonwealths in the view of the national capital. As President, Mr.
Roosevelt is amused to hear hailed as new and audacious the
methods he employed as a matter of routine as Governor.
But Washington, as I say, has never really heard of New
York State, and the other States recognize nothing beyond
the State lines except Washington.

So when the President, who as Governor was in the habit
of giving weekly radio talks to the people of New York, made
his radio speech to the nation on the banking situation, it was
received as a great innovation. And in fact, timed and keyed
as it was to reassure a deeply troubled nation, in its frank
facing of facts, its tone of friendly intimacy, it did establish
a new, almost personal relation, between the President and
the people. Mr. Roosevelt knows that this connection between government and citizen is broken. He is sure that democracy cannot work without conscious citizens. He means
to make other radio talks, not regularly, as in Albany, where
he found that the weekly broadcast worried him, slowed him
down, but whenever he has anything of real importance to
say.

He uses in Washington, speeded up for the emergency,
practically the same method for dealing with the Legislature

that he developed in Albany. And all the seasoned political observers, the Congressmen themselves, grumbling under their breath, acclaim the technique as proof of consummate political skill. What he has done so far, on each measure, is to send up to the Capitol a message asking for certain legislation and summarizing briefly the reasons why it is necessary. Then, an hour or two later, giving the party leaders barely time enough to laud the message and support the principle, he follows up with the bill and asks for its speedy enactment.

In effect, of course, he is an autocrat giving orders. He tells Congress what to do; until 9 o'clock the night before the special session not even the leaders, Robinson or Rainey,* had any idea of the program they were to be called on to enact. The emergency banking bill was voted by legislators who had not read it.

This is panic legislation, and it goes without saying that even a docile Congress like this will not go on indefinitely doing what it is told. Up to date the President has offered in his measures both a principle and a method of putting it into operation. The majority has had to agree with the principle, which was sound Democratic doctrine, written into the party platform, but they had no alternative method, so their only course was to go along.

Up to date, also, the President has had no need to mobilize public opinion in support of his program. The opinion is all lined up behind him, potential as the dammed reservoir behind a power plant. "Out in my country," said a labor leader from the Middle West the other day in the White House waiting room, "there are no Republicans or Democrats. We are all for Roosevelt. In all my experience I have never seen anything like this united front."

Few Presidents, indeed, have had the power and prestige

* Joseph T. Robinson (D), Arkansas, Democratic Majority Leader, 1933–7; Henry T. Rainey (D), Speaker of the House, 1933–4.

enjoyed by Roosevelt at this moment. He commands a surplus of popular confidence as impressive as the other great American surpluses, wheat, cotton and stock certificates. "Things are going pretty well," is all he says of this astonishing sweep of American sentiment, significant alike of the artificiality of party differences and of the deep hungers that consume us— hunger for leadership, for action, for hope, for national self-respect, for security.

The decision to keep Congress in session until the most pressing measures are passed is based on this public sentiment. In another session the members may get out of control. Even now there is a new group of Democratic insurgents as big as the Republican group, and so much wilder that the old Progressives are disconcerted to find themselves among the conservatives. But for the present the President's authority is absolute. Congress is under a cloud, real and rhetorical. It will take a long time to live down the record of the lame duck session.

It is not only boldness on the impetus of events, however, that exalts the Executive. Mr. Roosevelt was and is ready to act. As an example of his method, take the bill to reform banking practice. The party platform contained a pledge to pass legislation to prevent all kinds of financing frauds and bad banking practice. It promised to regulate the sale of new securities, the relation of banks to the security selling business, the duties of directors toward stockholders in corporations, most of the evils, in short, that shocked the country when they were brought out in the first Senate banking investigation a year ago.

Mr. Roosevelt took the platform pledges seriously, as a program for action. After the convention he asked half a dozen persons, sometimes working together and sometimes separately, without knowledge of one another's findings, to survey the field and recommend laws that would provide ade-

quate remedies for the abuses. For months these surveyors
have been working. They are now ready to report. In a few
days the Department of Commerce will have a complete digest of all recommendations and the administration will draw
up a bill.

This is a sample of the method by which the new President
dominates Congress. It answers the frequent question as to
who are his advisers on the measures he shoots over to the
Capitol in such rapid succession. The question is of special
pertinence when an Executive exercises plenary powers and
initiates his own legislation. The answer is that the advisers
are many, and different for every bill.

If a number of groups working independently to collate
information can be called a brain trust, then here it is. Only
a few of the members are college professors. They are business men, economists, specialists in various fields, even bankers. They do not evolve the ideal plan. The President has not
time to wait for that, even if it could be drafted. He gets
as many reputable, authoritative and honest opinions as possible. Then, on the theory that to do something is better than
to do nothing, that decisive action generates a fulcrum-like
force of its own, that all human progress is a process of trial-
and-error, voluntary or involuntary, he decides: Let's try it!

The new President is very different from the old, different
in personality, in method, in preparation for his task, in quality of mind. But hardly more different, one suspects, than the
Roosevelt of today from the Roosevelt of yesterday. No man
in public life has grown so fast. While the crisis he rides so
boldly is a spur as well as a test, and the very force of events
carries him along and overcomes resistance, he has proved his
capacity to rise to great demands, to be ready for the hour
when it strikes.

A friend of Hoover, an astute judge of men who has known
Roosevelt since the days of the Wilson administration, com-

mented on the change in the new President. "Two years ago," he said, "I saw Roosevelt after a long interval. Today I saw him again. He is no more like the man who was here in Wilson's time than the capital is like the city it was then. He has developed in all directions, far beyond what seemed his natural capacity. I attribute the change to his physical disability. Having overcome that, he is not afraid of anything. The daily course in self-discipline and self-control has strengthened his will, tempered his character; in his years of enforced inactivity he became a student and a thinker. Part of the power of the first Roosevelt was due to the fact that he conquered physical weakness. This man functions smoothly because he has learned to function in chains."

All the problems of the world lie on the White House doorstep, and Mr. Roosevelt knows it. He has already had to take time off from the immediate job of doing "first things first" to hold conferences looking to a new and more forthright policy of the United States in the international field. He has appointed an Ambassador-at-Large in the person of Norman H. Davis to represent him directly in the negotiation in which we have hitherto been represented by one of those amorphous beings like the White House spokesman—an unofficial observer.

Mr. Roosevelt has killed off both those figures of speech. He promises important developments at once in American foreign policy and plainly intends that the United States shall do its part in helping to make the world fit to live in. He believes that an immediate common effort for economic reconstruction is the only alternative to chaos.

The unexpected apparition of Roosevelt as a strong President has caught the imagination of the world, awakened its hope. Mr. Davis concludes, as the result of his observations, that the peoples of the earth are everywhere in advance of their governments. It would be a strange fulfillment of the

Wilson policy if the voice of Roosevelt, dictating a new deal for his own country, should lead the way to an armistice in the economic war. In any case, there is little doubt that the new Roosevelt is going to cut a figure in the world.

[19]   1933 *May* 7. VAST TIDES THAT STIR THE CAPI-TAL. *Behind the revolutionary experiments in Washington there is an impetus that derives directly from a people demanding immediate steps to meet the crisis.*

WASHINGTON

Wherever you go in Washington today you come upon crowds of people. All day they wait in long queues outside the public galleries of Congress. Or they huddle in little groups in the corridors of the Capitol, in the corridors of the State Department, in the White House waiting rooms, around oddly casual dining rooms in the milling lobbies of hotels. Always they are eager, anxious; always they are talking. The place hums and buzzes and quivers with talk. That Dome of Thought on the Hill, where an ever-expanding nation has so long and perfunctorily cerebrated, is not only subdued, a shorn Samson that cannot even shake the roof; it has become but one of many parliaments. The visitors who swarm there now go mostly to hear the echoes of what goes on in the White House or in the executive departments.

The talk is all echo, everywhere the same, yet in these reverberations there is nothing perfunctory. They are vivified by a strong undercurrent of wonder and excitement. You feel the stir of movement, of adventure, even of elation. You never saw before in Washington so much government, or so much animation in government. Everybody in the administration is having the time of his life. So they say, and so you perceive as you watch the new officials, often young, often inexperienced in politics, settling into this great business of national reconstruction. They dash from conference to conference, from hearing to hearing, briefcases bursting with plans and specifications. They are going somewhere, that is plain, and with such momentum and élan that they take the world in the same stride with which they set about reorganizing agriculture, reflating the currency, reforming the structure of business and industry.

The atmosphere is strangely reminiscent of Rome in the first weeks after the march of the Blackshirts, of Moscow at the beginning of the Five-Year Plan. But in those old capitals the high tension and the ferment seemed forced—imported stimulants for which there was no native appetite. Here the rush and excitement are as natural as light and air. It is a little as if at last America had marched on Washington, so that for the first time the capital feels like the center of the country. Or, better, as if the pioneer who became the go-getter, balked in his go-getting, had turned back to discover a forgotten frontier, and was beginning to transfer his energies from revolutionizing industry to revolutionizing government. Consciously or unconsciously, the setting has been made ready; the new capital built by Mr. Hoover presupposes just such a highly centralized, all-inclusive government as is now in the making.

That difference, however, is not the really significant distinction between this and other revolutionary capitals. In all the rest the social and political edifice was changed to fit a theory. Some one arrived with a dogma and imposed it by force until it was modified and overcome by facts. Here the facts themselves are the motive force. There is no theory, nor much volition, in the American movement. It is almost fortuitous, as automatic in producing a new model as is the conveyor system in the Ford factory. If we are going through a process of conversion—and no one doubts that we are—it is not a change of mind or a change of heart but merely a change in our circumstances.

Upheavals elsewhere, moreover, have been signalized by seizures of power. All the dictatorships we observe from afar, and by now they are a common sight, have been forced on people against their will, or at least against the will of large and unhappy sections of the population. Here it can be said that the pressure is on the other side; something far more positive than acquiescence vests the President with the authority of a dictator. This authority is a free gift, a sort of unanimous power of attorney. There is a country-wide dumping of responsibility on the Federal Government. If Mr. Roosevelt goes on collecting mandates, one after another, until their sum is startling, it is because all the other powers —industry, commerce, finance, labor, farmer and householder, State and city—virtually abdicate in his favor. America today literally asks for orders.

Among all the phenomena on the landscape, viewed from any angle, none is more striking than the reversal of the traditional relation between the country and the capital; for once Washington is the center of activity and the States beyond are passive, waiting for direction. Here is the stage, scene of a performance partly rehearsed, partly prompted by events; the nation is like a vast audience, hanging on to their seats to see what happens.

Three visitors met by chance one evening not long ago in the lounge of a Washington hotel. They came from places far apart, each bent on business of his own, each expecting to find the capital remote from the "realities" with which he dealt. The first was from New York. As director of a great relief agency, he had been immersed for months in the bitter problems of the unemployed. "From here," he said, "New

York looks almost segregated. The sense of emergency is so much keener here that I feel as if we had not realized how near the brink the country was; as if on Manhattan Island we but dimly guessed what was going on in the United States, what's going on now."

The second visitor was a manufacturer from the Middle West, come with other manufacturers to find out just what the thirty-hour-week bill means. He was meek, willing to "go along," but bewildered, and what most bewildered him was the docility of his colleagues. "Everywhere," he reported, "they are the same as they are at home, not knowing what it's all about, apologizing for asking questions, but whipped in advance, agreeing to a revolution as casually as if it were just the next step forward. And here that's what it seems."

The third visitor was a Frenchman, a member of M. Herriot's party. "I can hardly believe this is the same Washington I saw three years ago," he remarked. "More than in Europe, I feel here as if I were living in a historic moment. It is a kind of conjunction, I think, of a national mood and a man who expresses it. You who live here have no idea how palpable to a foreigner is your spirit of unity in change. It is as actual as an event. To me it is an event of the highest importance."

It is impossible to interpret what transpires in Washington without reference to this national mood. The action and interaction of the mind of the country with the governing mind explain many things otherwise inexplicable. It is not of their own will that so many Republican members of Congress vote with the majority, nor is it for party loyalty only that the Democrats who grumble in private hew to the line when the roll is called.

That little argument and hardly more than a score of votes could be mustered in the Senate against legislation without precedent in scope and power—the farm bill, for instance, with the inflationary amendment permitting the President to reduce the gold content of the dollar by 50 per cent—represents neither conviction nor yet sheer surrender of function on the part of the legislative body.

The tremendous changes we are enacting are not the result of conviction anywhere, and no one who has watched this Congress voting yes to every administration measure can think of it as an assembly legislating a revolution. Yet that is what it is doing, prodded not so much by the President, who so far has not been obliged to crack the whip in a single instance, as by the same force which pushes him on, too, sometimes, one feels, beyond his intention, faster and further than he meant to go.

This almost involuntary impetus comes from the people. President Roosevelt has a sixth sense for popular reactions. Also he is the kind of man to whom people talk frankly, to whom strangers write freely. Every day he receives hundreds of letters from obscure citizens in all parts of the country. It is amazing how many Americans are moved to offer advice, suggestions and criticism to the President, particularly to this President. Most of these letters require no answer, but they are put in his "bedtime folder" and he runs through them every night or early in the morning. Like Mrs. Roosevelt, the President has a horror of being isolated in the White House. To a guest who sat near him during a motion picture of the campaign trips, showing the throngs of people at every stop, he said: "That's what I miss here—the crowds."

That is what one feels behind Roosevelt—the crowds. To one who has lived in Washington through this "tremendous entrance," to borrow M. Herriot's quotation from Walt Whitman, it is clear that what distinguishes this administration is that it is fresh from the people, in touch with the desires of the multitude. The impression is strengthened if you check up by making an excursion out into the heart of the country, to Detroit or Dayton or Sioux City, any typical industrial town or farming center. Then you perceive that the sense of emergency that moves the government is only the intensification, perhaps the dramatization, of the mood that grips the nation.

The United States has been brought to Washington, the United States in a mood of crisis, a quiet people, peaceable, orderly, very sure it can't stay down, but more dependent on government than it has ever been in its history and demanding omnipotent gestures from government, as many as are necessary to get the machine in motion.

In his present temper the American is not in the least afraid of experiments. He is not thinking of the remote consequences of his emergency demands. In general he does not like dictators; he would not endure the strong-arm methods of Mussolini; he would destroy with laughter the shrill hysteria of Hitler; a Stalin shut up in a Kremlin would be a very unpopular Czar out in Iowa. But he wants action, the immediate action promised by Mr. Roosevelt in his inaugural address and no lobby every exerted so much pressure on Congress as the people now bring to bear to induce the President to use all the executive authority he can command.

I suppose we have never had a President as powerful as Mr. Roosevelt is at this moment. In a century of growth and change we have not found it necessary to enlarge the frame of government as much as it has been extended in the past sixty days. Not only does the present occupant of the White House possess more authority than any of his predecessors, but he presides over a government that has more control over more private activities than any that has ever existed in the United States.

Consider only the fields in which the Chief Executive has been granted an actual overlordship. The banking bill gives

him control of the banking system; under its authority the
government has already stopped runs on sound banks and
tied up about $5,000,000,000 of deposits in banks it declares
not sound enough to reopen. It has placed an embargo on
gold exports and taken us definitely off the gold standard.
The economy bill enables the Executive to proceed to a complete reorganization of the Federal Government. The farm
bill with its amendments practically puts the largest industry
in the country under his management. It permits commodity
price-fixing and inflation of the currency by any one or all
of three drastic methods to be employed at his sole discretion.

The billions allotted to refinance farm and home mortgages, added to the enormous sums loaned to banks and
industry by the Reconstruction Finance Corporation, make
the United States Government the biggest and most powerful lending agency in the world. The railroad bill, taken together with the authorization to start the huge scheme for
the development of the Tennessee Valley, goes measurably
in the direction of nationalization of public services.

In addition, pending or proposed, we have a public-works
program providing a large government investment in self-
liquidating projects. We have reforestation camps under
army control, probably a permanent expedient for keeping
unemployed youth out of mischief. We have a bill for government regulation of the sale of securities. We have beer,
the beginning of the end of prohibition. We have seen the
exit, almost without a whimper, of the veterans' lobby, and
thus have banished at a stroke the two most powerful political influences of the postwar period. We have adopted the
principle, opposed through the whole Hoover administration, of direct Federal relief wherever needed.

Most important of all is the grandiose plan advanced for
the organization and coordination under a government board
of control of all branches of industry. This envisages a fed-

eration of industry, labor and government after the fashion of the corporative State as it exists in Italy.

Even in this brief summary one is dazed by the dimensions of this program, enacted or ready for enactment in the short space of two months. Seen whole, however, it does not appear so inconsistent as did the individual measures as they issued hot, sometimes half-baked, from the hopper. The strictly deflationary measures, such as the cuts in pensions, salaries and government costs and the closing of banks, are surgical measures for chronic tumors in the political and financial systems. The inflationary measures are strong, perhaps dangerous, stimulants to recovery. Whether they work or not, whether the savings effected by the right hand are squandered by the left, it is clear that the unhealthy growths had to be pruned away before progress could be made in any direction.

But that is not all. The administration is not only moving in two directions at once in the domestic field; it charts two opposite roads in world policy and proceeds to follow them both. Mr. Roosevelt drafts tentative plans for a possible state of economic isolation in which the United States will sustain itself and as far as possible contain itself. At the same time he has spent one month out of his two in conference with the representatives of other governments.

In a magnificent effort to turn back the tides into their natural channels, he has dramatically placed himself at the head of the world. He does not ask for a mandate as an international dictator, welcome as such a governor might be to a distracted planet, but if he gets the authority he wants from Congress—to drive trade bargains, to negotiate the best deals he can get and make on war debts—he would be in position to exercise almost as much power abroad as he wields at home. Already it is evident that this government is taking a new line in foreign policy, employing a more aggressive and realistic technique. More, it begins to look as if under the Roosevelt direction the whole world inclines toward the same line.

The observer in Washington today cannot be just an observer. Inevitably he is caught up in the whirl of the drama. He has to read while he runs, but even to the runner certain signs are plain. You see here, for instance, besides all these new laws and powers, any number of other things, new portents. They are mixed with old things, it is true, confused in motive, not too clear or pure in purpose. You see an unconventional, non-political sort of Cabinet, chosen partly for reasons of strictly personal loyalty, but partly, too, because they compose into a new type of governing mind, receptive and flexible. After two months you see most of the local political patronage withheld and Hoover appointees still in some of the most important subsidiary posts. Again, this is partly strategy—a club to drive through a legislative program in the shortest possible time; but mostly it is because there is so much business more urgent than appointing postmasters.

The tightening of authority coincides with a relaxation in the atmosphere, a simplification of administrative procedure, a fade-out of forms and precedents, which convinces you that, whatever this is, it is not what people mean elsewhere when they speak of dictatorship. The academic mind, so called, is pretty much in evidence. Professors are planted at important points in the Departments of State, Agriculture, Commerce and the Treasury; they are among the President's friends and close advisers. "A bunch of amateurs," say the old-timers; but why a professional student of politics or history or economics should not be a better counselor on problems of government than the student of law, the real estate salesman or the banker is difficult to see, particularly after our recent experience with the fond illusions of "practical" men.

The feminine mind is more in evidence, and this not only because the First Lady has a mind of her own and a wide interest in public affairs or because women occupy places in the government they never held before. Rather it is that the women of the administration, like their husbands, are of a new political generation—a little younger, less traditional, less social in the narrow sense, more social-minded. No change is more marked than the transposition into another key of the whole scale of official society. Led by the White House, the Washington that has been growing stiff and in recent years formal, more like a European capital, has gone American again; but very late-American, expressing the mood and mind and manners of a time of transition.

It all works into a new pattern. All the changes come back in the end to that curious community I have spoken of between the mind of the President and the mind of the people. "Let's try something else!" might be the motto of this administration. "Let's try something else!" is the almost unanimous sentiment of America at this moment. Certain sections of the populace are troubled by the idea of inflation. Others have been uneasy as to how a possible six-hour day would affect their business. Millions are still distrustful of all banks and all investments. But nobody, not even Senator Glass, is really terrified by the changes proposed by the President. For two months the country has hardly breathed a protest, though its situation has not basically improved since Inauguration Day, lest a breath should interrupt the progress of the program of "bold experimentation."

Nobody is much disturbed by the idea of dictatorship. Mr. Roosevelt does not fit into the popular conception of a dictator, and there is a general feeling that he collects powers as he collects opinions—to be ready for emergencies rather than with the intention of using them. The people as a whole trust the discretion of the President more than they trust Congress.

It is not too much to say, in fact, that the Executive authority derives from a kind of mass decision of the American will— one of those sudden motions or emotions of the genius of a people which in critical moments serves as a kind of compass to right its course.

Perhaps President Roosevelt is inventing a method to make democracy work. At any rate, here is a new kind of rule— what might be described as the permissive dictatorship, evolved in a few weeks by a concert of powers: The President, the people, the tyranny of events.

[20] 1 9 3 4 *May 20.* ROOSEVELT AS SEEN FROM ABROAD. *The President reanimates in the Old World a fading legend and restores the image of a country rapt again in strange and immeasurable adventure.*

LONDON

Viewed from a distance, the American drama is personified by President Roosevelt. It is easier for Europe, occupied with crowding problems of its own, to see the President than to follow the confused and poorly reported movements of the United States. It is easier at any time to see a person than a people, and never as now has the world turned with such relief from incomprehensible events to human symbols. One reason for the popularity of dictators is that they are so obvious. And when there appears on the scene the ruler of a democracy who can be as spectacular and powerful as a dictator, it is like offering the key of the country to the befuddled foreigner.

President Roosevelt is a godsend to a universal audience composed of very tired business men. Until he began smashing a way out, nobody in Europe really believed in the American crisis. America itself was vague and bewildering before its problems were dramatized in the New Deal. It is still far from clear, but the New Dealer has become so completely both interpretation and interpreter that when Europe now looks toward the United States it focuses its entire attention on the White House.

He is amazingly himself, the Roosevelt Europe sees. And this is a triumph of personal impressiveness, because although for the first time in history statesmen can project their voices, faces, words, gestures and revealing mannerisms to the limits of the earth, only a few seem able to project themselves. Nobody explains why some don't come to life—Stalin, Doumergue, Mustapha Kemal, Dollfuss: while others do— Mussolini, Hitler, the casual Stanley Baldwin with his pipe and tweeds. Or, preeminently, Roosevelt. Of them all I am inclined to think that the President loses least of his own quality in transmission and translation. Seen from anywhere in Europe, through all the varying slants of foreign eyes, he still looks real and natural, even to the American.

Harding and Coolidge never crossed the Atlantic in any sense. Hoover, actually the most international-minded of recent Presidents, long a resident abroad, almoner on the grandest and most efficient scale Europe has ever known, remained shadowy and indefinite to the end of his administration. The first Roosevelt impressed the world by sheer force of personality, Wilson by the magic of his echoing phrases and the Messianic magnificence of his interference in international affairs. But the second Roosevelt registers as even these more reverberant rulers did not; somehow he is better understood, nearer the levels where Europe lives.

Roosevelt is America at last struggling with difficulties common to every nation. All know the pressing necessities driving him into experiments, and to a Continent that has tried everything these experiments do not appear so revolu-

tionary as they do in the more conservative regions of the
United States. In the transatlantic perspective, he seems
wholly unconcerned with Europe, and they understand that,
too; it is a curious but not inexplicable fact that in our least
altruistic moments and this is one, among our foreign relations we are more intelligible, even more popular, than we
arc in our loftier moods. "Right or wrong, at least this President does not pose as a world prophet," says official Europe,
with a glint of satisfaction.

How Mr. Roosevelt registers at all, how the negative of a
little more than a year ago has developed into the enlarged
and sharpening portrait of today, is difficult to explain. When
he entered the White House he was no more to Europe than
a name and a smile. If he surprised his own countrymen
by the vigor with which he went into action, the outside
world was even more startled by the sudden splash of this
unknown, unheard of as Governor of New York, raising no
echoes as candidate for the Presidency.

Even as President, he is most inadequately reported. Probably he occupies more space in European newspapers than
any other American Executive since the war, but the space
occupied by the whole continent of North America amounts
to little more than our papers give to Premier Stauning and
the internal affairs of the Kingdom of Denmark. Try to learn
what's going on at home in the Continental press, try to get
any clear and consecutive account of events anywhere, and
you will wonder, as I do, on what information Europe bases
its judgments. Outside of Great Britain, and to a lesser extent
of France and Scandinavia, the activities of Washington are
but a news flash on an inside page.

Out of these flashes, nevertheless, out of political reviews
(more widely read than with us), out of tales of returning
travelers, but mostly out of the vibrating and electric air,
Europe has built up an image of the new American leader

real enough to trouble its imagination and stir its curiosity.
Talk to the political rulers in any country—Hitler, Mussolini,
de Valera, the head of a Russian Soviet—and their first questions will be of Roosevelt: what manner of man is he, where is
he going, why was he not heard of before? Almost invariably
they compare their policies with his or justify some measure
of their own with a phrase that has become almost a stereo-
type: "Well, look at Roosevelt!"

The ordinary citizen is perplexed by the contrast between
the great authority wielded by this administration and the
democratic freedom and informality of its atmosphere. He,
too, wants to know about Roosevelt—and not less about Mrs.
Roosevelt. The mistress of the White House is a new type
to Europe; so perfectly does she realize the idea of the typical American woman fondly cherished by the average European that he—and especially the wistful she!—is delighted by
a picture of whirlwind activity, bright unconventionality and
social independence that runs gratifyingly true to form. No
use suggesting that Mrs. Roosevelt is exceptional. The European loves his types, as we all do, and prefers his Americans
to be "like Americans."

Part of the President's personal popularity is due to the
same reason; he exemplifies the dash, the energy, the self-
confidence, the good-humor that foreigners expect of Americans. If he had deliberately set out to be conspicuous among
contemporary statesmen he could not have done better than
oppose to their strained, solemn or arrogant attitudes his
easy manner and the friendly, unemphatic voice in which he
converses with the listening world. Abroad as at home, he is
definitely liked, and liked most, oddly enough, for his steady
cheerfulness.

That is not so surprising. Cheerfulness in high places has
become the rarest of sights, grateful as an arc lamp at the end
of a long, dark street. Cheerfulness in Washington is pe-

culiarly grateful, for if anything oppressed the Old World more than its own afflictions it was the gloom of the Western horizon in 1932. "If the United States has no comeback, what hope for the rest of us?" people used to sigh. Now the West brightens, and the illumination heartens even the dubious observers who think it's artificial. Europe is largely inhabited by head-shakers and skeptics who hope the New Deal will surprise them by turning out a success!

"Roosevelt's calm and confidence make me think he knows where he's going," remarked a German after listening to a broadcast from the White House. "Here there is fever, exaltation, but no real cheerfulness, certainly no calm. The contrast between that quiet, good-tempered talk and the shrill passion of our leaders marks the distance between us—between our state of nerves and yours."

Lady Astor expressed the same thought in commenting on the impression the President makes in England. "The English don't worry," she said. "They don't worry because they think they're doing their best. Roosevelt doesn't worry, either, and that reassures them. He does bold things casually, in the approved British manner, and even though they disagree they respect the bland and pleasant stubbornness, so like their own, with which he sticks to his chosen course."

The American member of the House of Commons might have added that this attitude represents a decided revision of British opinion. Nowhere else has Mr. Roosevelt grown in popular and official estimation as in England. The "wrecker" of the economic conference is forgotten in the reformer who is expected, when he gets around to it, to cut the Gordian knot in the tariff tangle. The "too-agreeable" gentleman of last year's international conversations has faded into the resolute currency manager whose decision to take a hand in the game of the Old Lady of Threadneedle Street, at first resented, is now applauded.

In England you can start a hot argument any time by mentioning either the fiscal policies or the more spectacular and costly recovery measures of the New Deal, and the two sides of the argument will be more nearly equal than anywhere else, even in Ireland, which sees us engaged in some sort of obscure competition with Westminster and on principle gives us a record vote of confidence.

On the Continent the rising schools of economic and financial experts are either rigidly radical or ardently conservative—the conservatives have all the ardor now and the radicals the rigidity—and for both the Rooseveltian straddle is a perilous compromise. One gathers that the European equivalent of the Brain Trusters, were they the Washington advisers, would offer counsel quite different from that of their American colleagues. I was told by an eminent young professor in Stockholm that the only time he had ever seen a body of economists in agreement was during a discussion of the Roosevelt policies at an international conference last Fall. Of all those present, he alone believed they would work.

It is, I think, no one measure—because everybody agrees with something Roosevelt is doing—but the grand total the American experiments add up to, the speed with which all are put into effect at once, the feeling that for us they were not the only way out, which accounts for the almost universal attitude of doubt and questioning. This doubt is not confined to people directly affected by specific policies—nations clinging to the gold standard against the force of gravity, for instance, or debtors judged in default and cut off from further credits. Still less is it because the New Deal is really new, except in scale and sum. It includes nothing not already tried or in operation somewhere in Europe.

Under different circumstances, but with similar aims and not dissimilar effects, more than half the world abandoned gold long before we did. Openly or in secret, every Euro-

pean operates under some form of managed currency. Most
have experienced some measure of inflation. The dictatorships, notably, though for the best of reasons they have not
pumped into circulation streams of money or credit comparable to the billions expended by the CWA, the CCC,* the
AAA † or other financing and refinancing schemes of the
American Government, have gone in for public works beyond the limit of their resources.

Italy, while taking a course diametrically opposed to ours,
the course of painful monetary deflation, proceeds simultaneously with a program of building, road-making, land
reclamation, electrification of railways, proportionately more
ambitious than anything Congress conceives in its most abandoned moments. Germany shrinks from inflation with a horror as deep-rooted as French fear of Germany, yet the Nazi
construction camps, the Hitler highways, the new subsidies
to small farmers, are as costly in their degree and as inflationary as similar measures adopted in the United States.

The codes of NRA, the whole conception of governmental
regulation of private industry, are the democratized and so
far voluntary version of the compulsory organization in force
or proposed by the States experimenting with the corporative system. In most industrial countries labor organization
and labor as a political power are decades beyond the point
reached under Roosevelt by the American Federation of
Labor. To pay bonuses for curtailment of agricultural production is probably the most radical thing we have done, but
Denmark is destroying pigs and cattle on a quota plan while

---

* Civilian Conservation Corps, created to relieve unemployment and to
work at reforestation, March 31, 1933.

† Agricultural Adjustment Act, authorization to limit acreage on specific
crops and to pay benefits to farmers, May 12, 1933 (processing tax of this
act declared unconstitutional by Supreme Court, January 16, 1936). National
Industrial Recovery Act, together with AAA, gave the President power to
control industry as well as agriculture, June 16, 1933 (declared unconstitutional by the Supreme Court, May 27, 1935).

France and Germany, where agricultural surpluses are non-existent, by fixing the prices of wheat, butter and other commodities, give them the same high boost above world prices.

As to the social reforms as yet suburban to the New Deal—unemployment insurance, popular housing projects built out of public funds, old-age pensions, resettlement schemes—all the dreams of the American social welfare worker are commonplace institutions under every form of government on a continent infinitely more socialized than ours. We have not reached up to the European level of taxation or settled down to the European plane of living, nor has Washington gone beyond the A B C's of government control as it is known and practiced in three-fourths of Europe.

To see how much further concentration of authority can be carried, we have only to look at the dictatorships, in most cases the effect of economic rather than political desperation. Abroad as at home, people sometimes refer to President Roosevelt as a dictator, but as soon as they begin to compare his powers with those of any real dictator, Mussolini, for preference, at once it becomes clear that there is an enormous gulf between the best of autocrats and the most potent Executive in a democracy.

No two leaders could be more different in method, outlook and temperament, than Roosevelt and Mussolini. The Fascist chief is by nature a solitary: he is his own brain trust. His sense of popular reactions is as intuitive as Roosevelt's, but he does not trust the people. With the same capacity for soaking up ideas and making them his own, he lacks the ability to work on equal terms with others and would probably fail completely as a democratic ruler, subject to the rough give-and-take of party politics.

The two men and their methods are not so different, however, as the two systems under which they operate. Stretched to their utmost, the powers of the American Executive can be, and are now dictatorial, but they represent delegated and not surrendered powers and for the governed that makes all the difference between living in a state of tutelage and a state of citizenship. Democracy is not only a form of government, often unworkable, as at present in France; it is a way of life, and its non-political effects are as important as the political. Looking at Washington from Russia, Germany or Italy, it is evident that the encroaching regulations of the Roosevelt administration stop where government in these dictatorships merely begins.

Nevertheless, the power of Roosevelt, without duplicate in any other republic, puzzles Europeans as much as they are impressed by the airy manner in which, without any signs of struggle visible at this distance, he institutes vast changes and dares to demand more money than he spends, more authority than he uses. If they did not know by other signs, they would know by this reckless candor that he is not a dictator. Neither is he like any President or Prime Minister among the familiar figures traveling uneasily from capital to capital, with their pacts on their backs, so to speak.

He is American, and for Europe that's an explanation; it removes all strange phenomena into another dimension. Beneath all the questions, the doubts, the frank criticisms of the New Deal is one large reservation: it may work because the testing ground is America. Europe is never quite certain of its judgments of the United States; always it feels itself without any true gauge of the forces that give to American life its spring, its tempo, its baffling ups and downs.

A French writer expressed this uncertainty very well one day as we stood on a high terrace overlooking the ordered beauty of Paris. His eyes, like the eyes of all the French, were tired as they swept the gray-green pattern made by the trees, the crystal fountains, the level roofs and converging avenues of the Rond-Point.

"Roosevelt may be all wrong—I think he is—but he is fresh and unafraid, and that in itself is a power that Europe has forgotten," he sighed. "The same scale cannot measure this scene and New York and the same rule does not apply to your civilization and ours. Daring and inexperience—I say it with respect—are the great qualities for meeting the unprecedented. The Soviets fail because they govern by theory, and we fail, though not so dismally or at such frightful human cost, because we govern by experience. If your President succeeds, it will be because his laboratory is the United States, not Europe or Asia, because he is not cursed by too much knowledge of what can't be done, and because he is too shrewd, and himself too early-American, to change the traditional forms while changing the facts."

The conversation took place at one of the "American cocktail parties" that are fast displacing the sedate official teas of Europe. In the group were an English professor, a Swedish banker and an Italian liberal of pre-Fascist days. It was suggestive that though none was young, and all were "Europeans" in the sense that the young of today's Europe are not, the sons of three out of the four were in the United States, one in college, one in a bank, one traveling about the country, all sent by their orthodox fathers to study what's emerging from the upheaval across the Atlantic.

"I can't make out whether Roosevelt's Socialist, Conservative or Lloyd-George," commented the Englishman. "He reminds me of our National government, a kind of coalition in himself. I don't like the Etatism he's developing. I think Americans will live to groan under it. I don't believe your recovery is as real and soundly based as ours, but of course neither we nor any other nation had to deal with your incredible banking system or your fantastic skyscrapers of credit."

"My bet's still on the dollar, even against the pound," said the Swede. "My thesis is not only that America is bound to recover, with Roosevelt or in spite of him, but that the American monetary policy will prove sounder than the British in the long run because it tends to meet conditions in the gold bloc and works as a strong lever to raise world prices. Nobody over here realizes the steam it takes to move the American mountain, and that's what we see now—tons of excess water going up in steam! America can stand it; without an ounce of excess fat, it's still a giant our standard sizes will never fit."

"Don't you both miss the point of the New Deal?" asked the Italian. "Since all Europe is turning Fascist, with the example of France to show why, I feel less humiliated by the subjection of my country. I see that it is not Italy alone that surrenders liberty, we were merely the first to show that the present crisis is a crisis in the order of the world. Under tremendous pressure the individual is being squeezed into a new system, and since that system reached its highest development in the United States, it is to America we look for a lead out of the labyrinth.

"Europe can resist Bolshevism, which is the solution à la barbare. It can resist Germany; Hitler, after all, is the sublimation of the Germany Europe has always resisted. America, as the evolution of our own civilization, I do not think we can resist. What I mean is that what you destroy or create will be more or less decisive for the rest of us. In America the crisis climaxes, and there we shall see what terms we can make with individual liberty. If you ask me," he added, smiling, "I should say it is worth all the waste it costs."

When Europe looks at Roosevelt, the view varies from country to country, changes from month to month and takes on a dozen different shades of local color. To the American the composite is interesting as a new perspective on the subject, but still more interesting as a study in reflections.

In it you see Europe: a good deal of England in the British full-length, with its fleeting resemblances to eminent Britons;

a glimpse of France in the slightly Gallic profile etched in Paris; the Fascist slant in the blurred sketch made in Italy; the hidden hopes of Russia in the large, fresh, left-sided litho- graph issued in Moscow; nothing but Germany in the impres- sion current in a nation which sees her own image wherever she looks.

You see something of the movement of the time. Over here are too many clocks, worked by too many tangled springs. The successive phases of the experiments in Washington, confused though they are, make a sequence in perspective. They serve as a kind of chronometer in chaos, marking the hours as they could not be marked by a figure less striking and independent than the President working in a field less wide than the United States.

Above all, you see America. For, when Europe looks at Roosevelt, I need hardly repeat, it sees the portentous shape of his country. The crazy, syncopated beat of the American movement this Continent gets no better than it gets the true rhythm of jazz. Incomprehensible to Europeans is an advance beginning with forms of socialism they have long since ab- sorbed and rushing on in the same sweep toward a form of socialized capitalism beyond anything they have yet imag- ined. Inevitably, the President has become the symbol of this headlong jump from 1900 to 1950. Inevitably, his cool and smiling performance in a revolutionary role reanimates a fading legend. Roosevelt restores to Europe the lost image of the New World rapt once again in some large, strange, ir- regular and immeasurable adventure all its own.

[21] 1 9 3 4 *July 8.* ROOSEVELT SURVEYS HIS COURSE.
*A picture of the President and his mood at a mile-
stone, when the New Deal moves from the period
of organization toward permanent objectives of his
Administration.*

WASHINGTON

As he left Washington to travel westward, President
Roosevelt definitely set a milestone in his course and the
course of the United States. A third of his administration lay
behind him. He had signed the last of a long series of emergency measures of unprecedented scope and cost. For the
first time since that bleak March day in 1933 when he took
office—how far away and long ago it seems!—he paused for a
look forward and backward along the chartless road he entered then. He paused, and America with him. Out of the
whirl and daze induced by the strongest stimulants administered to any people in this crisis, the nation emerges in that
stage of convalescence when the patient begins to ask questions and take an interest in the shape of the future.

The adjournment of the Seventy-third Congress marked
the end of the first phase of the New Deal. Other, even
greater, recovery measures may still be necessary, many already enacted may not stand the tests of time and experience,
but in a general way the phase of hasty improvisation, of
artificial stimulation, of experiments tried out in the heat of
emergency, is felt to be over. The New Deal is organized, as
any one can see who compares its entrenchments in Washington today with the tentative camps of a year ago. Now
it moves on toward its permanent objectives.

What these objectives are the President indicated in his
last message to Congress and his radio talk on the eve of his
departure for the Pacific. The long-range program he sketched

contains much that is new for the United States if not for other countries, but nothing Mr. Roosevelt himself has not pondered for years, nothing not already foreshadowed in the confused march of the past sixteen months. The chief cause of the confusion, indeed, the ragged tempo, the swings right and left, the advances and retreats, is the incidence of the permanent and the temporary. The rush of the immediate necessity deforms the larger plan just as the beat of the irrevocable slows up the speed and chills the spirit of the emergency helper. In its first stage the New Deal has been a collision on the job between the repair man and the rebuilder.

The second stage looms ahead, but meanwhile there is to be a breathing space. No one knows better than Mr. Roosevelt, whose sixth sense is the keenest of all his senses, that there are limits to popular capacity to digest new ideas. The country is due for a rest from edicts and experiments; it needs time either to learn to walk with crutches or to try out its power to walk unaided. It is too much to expect a vacation from the partisan politics in a campaign year, but at least the blazing stage at Washington will be dark for the Summer season. On 10,000 Main Streets, during the long twilights of the dog days, the America which has reached this point with Roosevelt will be able to look at itself, undistracted by the eye-filling show put on day after day at the White House.

Washington will continue to hum with old and new activities, all speeded up. The alphabetical good works will go on full tilt with increased staffs. Never since wartime has the capital been so crowded in July with perspiring young men saving their country. Only the headliners are absent. The members of the Cabinet will follow their chief into temporary retirement. "We shall have a new form of government this Summer," smiles Mr. Roosevelt. "The Under-Secretaries, even the Assistant Secretaries, will be in command."

It was the fag end of a day before the evacuation. The capi-

tal was flayed by a typical blast of tropical heat. All day long
the President had been besieged by last-minute visitors. He
had signed or vetoed the final batch of Congressional bills.
He had supervised the packing of cases full of reports to be
studied and books to be enjoyed on the long cruise on the
Houston. The books, he confessed, were mostly detective
stories and biographies; "all other forms of modern fiction"
bore him. Now he sat at ease on the circular terrace behind
the White House, sipping iced tea and chatting as if there
were nothing in the world to do but discuss the state of Europe with a returning traveler. Like any American gentleman
relaxing on his back porch in the cool of the evening, I was
about to say, but at the end of his day what other American
executive is as fresh, as serene, as completely focused on the
subject in hand? Or, for that matter, what lesser member of
the Brain Trust?

The most remarkable and crowded year in the history of
the Republic had gone by since I last saw Mr. Roosevelt.
Whether or not he has been engineering a revolution depends
on your definition of revolution. Certainly he has been fighting a war, a war on so many fronts and with forces so obscure
that no war President had half as much to worry him. Yet
here he was, apparently the least worried man in the country.
Or in any country; of all the men in public life today he must
be the least subject to moods, to highs and lows in the spiritual barometer. I recalled other rulers encountered in the
interval, each struggling in his own way with the superhuman
job of governing the ungovernable.

Mussolini, swinging between the deep pessimism of last
year, when his Four-Power Pact hung in the balance, and
the high spirits of six weeks ago, when he slid like a boy
across the glassy marble floor of his office, big as a lake, to
illustrate how he skied. Hitler, running the gamut from
cloudy to fair in a single interview, one moment morose and

wooden, the next smiling and suave or rapt in some remote vision, the medium, so it seemed, of flickering emotions not his own. De Valera, the romantic schoolmaster, blazing with cold passion for an idea, fretting over the exact placing of an indefinite article. Dollfuss, the little Chancellor of a state of siege, depressed or elated according as the winds over Austria blew north or south. Stalin—but who knows what goes on behind that quiet mask, as even in its dark immobility as the sunny surface of Roosevelt?

A procession of statesmen, great or small, gloomy or gay, but all nervous, all dwelling in a climate sharply different from that temperate zone of the mind which President Roosevelt alone inhabits.

Evidently this ruler is not confused by confusion or overwhelmed by the overwhelming. He looks better than he did a year ago, a shade harder, browner, and as confident as ever. If there are chinks in his shining armor of assurance no one reports them. If his cheerfulness ever sags he conceals it from his intimates.

As Mr. Roosevelt looks back, it is easy to see that he appraises the New Deal as an educational method as well as a means to recovery. On the whole he is well satisfied. A year ago facing the heavy pull ahead, he could not have anticipated, he says, that the country would be so far above bottom as it seems to him today. All the economic indices point to steady progress upward. With a long way yet to go in reviving confidence and increasing employment, the mood of crisis is passing. In his view the greatest change that has taken place is the change in the general state of mind and the most encouraging "lift" the rise in the level of public intelligence and social sense.

As a sign of the development of a new public mind, there is the remarkable expansion of the Brain Trust. Originally it consisted of only five members, the President himself, Professor Moley, Professor Tugwell, Louis Howe and Judge Samuel Rosenman. Now, according to Mr. Roosevelt, it is 250,000 strong and includes practically all those enlisted in the new government services.

Washington is full of this strange type of intellectual and enthusiastic bureaucrat. They form the army of "fine young men" that so impressed John Maynard Keynes, in contrast to the scarcity of the young in the public life of England. From the Bronx to Seattle come reports of the effective work they do in interpreting to the country the changed scope and spirit of government. Rather scornful of party politics, these Roosevelt recruits not only exemplify the non-partisanship of the administration but they constitute forces in training which the Chief Executive counts on to supply the national leadership of the future.

The President is proud of the Brain Trust. He likes to think of the past year as a tough term in a great school of adult education. During a period when the Federal Government has functioned almost as a receiver in bankruptcy for a paralyzed economy, constant contact with the business brains of the country has convinced him that too many business executives have gone ahead "with blinders on," unmindful of anything outside their own narrow field. Compared with this one-track mind, the outlook of the average Congressman is broad and patriotic. Teaching business to think in terms of the country, in conscious relation to national policy, seems to him the most valuable effort of the New Deal, and particularly of the NRA.

In spite of criticisms, of recessions, of structural weaknesses, Mr. Roosevelt considers NRA "a magnificent success," the outstanding achievement of the administration to date. It whooped up the revival movement at the low moment. It is an invaluable experimental method, fluid and flexible, for studying and charting the unknown, anarchic states of industry. Certainly it is a storm center of controversy, but that is what it was intended to be, a frame wherein the conflicts between employer and employed can be fought out. It is, above all, an educational agency, forcing those within and without the codes to do some hard thinking on the central problems of modern life, the involved problem of the control of industry, the hardly less irritating issues rising out of its ethics and its social attitude.

Recently a delegation of striking workers in the textile industry brought their case before the President, who has become the court of appeal in an ever-widening variety of disputes. The Cotton Code Authority had met and summarily announced that it was necessary to cut down production 25 per cent during the dull season. Mr. Roosevelt told the workers that he thought the employers were justified. "Well, why didn't they tell us?" demanded the employees, with righteous wrath. "Are we partners in this enterprise or not?" The incident was cited by Mr. Roosevelt as an example of stubborn bad habits, of the Bourbon-like wrong way, more exasperating than real injustice, of doing the right thing.

When he is asked whether the policies of the New Deal tend toward fascism or socialism the President is likely to answer that he hopes they tend toward strengthening American democracy. Though opposed as Fascist by some who a couple of years ago were yearning for a Mussolini, the industrial codes represent the American way of achieving, by what Mr. Roosevelt insists is voluntary organization, the industrial peace and order compulsorily imposed by the corporative system. As to controlling agricultural production, he points out that England exercises far more regulatory power than has ever been contemplated by the AAA. Cotton is the only commodity we produce on a quota system, but the English farmer is integrated into a production plan in which he cannot plant anything without a permit.

The vast relief program put into effect by the administration has one central aim: it works to make more people property owners, to save their property for those who would lose it without government credit, to safeguard small savings and legitimate investment. This is the idea behind the movement for subsistence homesteads, the decentralization of industry, home loans, home building, the banking and securities acts. When Clarence E. Pickett of the Department of the Interior recently returned from a housing survey in Vienna, he reported that the Socialists settled on one-acre garden plots outside the city refused to join their comrades in the urban tenements in the February rising against the government. The homesteaders had a stake in the land. The New Deal seeks to multiply the number of American stakeholders.

"Is this socialistic?" asks the President with the characteristic crinkle of his eyes and backward jerk of his head which accompany his hearty laugh.

For a long time, and on this point in accord with the well-known ideas of Henry Ford, Mr. Roosevelt has been pondering over schemes for decentralizing industry, with the specific object of preventing the development of a proletarian psychology by giving the factory worker a backlog in the land and of a peasant psychology by offering the small farmer a part-time job in a factory. When Governor of New York he requested the head of the General Electric Company to study the problem with a view to determining what units of a big plant might be detached and profitably operated in small communities. For years he has advocated the reforestation of marginal lands and rural slum clearance by the resettlement in more favorable environments of farmers on the lowest levels.

Early in the Spring of 1932 he outlined to the writer the three-point "security program"—decent housing, development of sites offering better living facilities to farmers, a system of social insurance—he now proposes as the next step in the New Deal. Some time in the Fall he plans to call together the 265 executives who control 70 per cent of American industry and ask their cooperation in hammering out a plan to scatter factory units over as wide an area as practicable and at the same time to budget production in order to guarantee the worker the amount of employment he can count on for a year.

On the question of public ownership of utilities the Roosevelt philosophy is purely pragmatic. It is not easy to define a public utility, or, having defined it, to decide whether it would be in the general interest to operate it. It would be next to impossible to take over the milk supply for instance, yet milk should be classified as a public utility. So, obviously, are railroads and telephones, but in this country the latter give better service than any publicly owned system in the world, and the constant effort of the administration has been to devise means to keep the former in private hands.

On the other side the postoffice has been operated by the government for decades and nobody denies that in taking over the parcel post it improved on the service of the old express companies. It simmers down to a question not of ownership but of efficient and economical public service. In the Roosevelt view that is the test.

All the President's tests are simple and non-theoretic. He has changed not at all in a year in which the United States seems to have moved far and to have enormously complicated its running gear. In the labyrinth he has created he retains the faculty of making everything look simple, almost obvious. Surrounded he may be by doctrinaires, yet no occupant of the White House ever seemed so little touched by the winds of doctrine. Hoover and Wilson held theories which they defended stubbornly to tragic ends. Roosevelt has purposes and a program, under his amiable manner he is as firm as they, but his course is less shaped and determined by theory. If anything, he reacts against theories, at least against any one theory; his indifference to party labels is an instinctive response to a like indifference among people in general, but it is also a recognition that in a time of flux you cannot be bound by formulas; you must be free to try anything and to reject anything.

To Mr. Roosevelt the New Deal is a method, a combination of methods. Such planning as he does in his essentially practical and sensitively political mind is flexible and subject to revision: therefore he sees nothing strange or disturbing in the program of social legislation he means to propose to the next Congress as the sequel of the recovery measures enacted in the last session. "Where we go from here is neither right nor left but straight ahead," he says.

There is nothing new in the proposals. In fact, the agencies erected this year and the enormous expenditures they involve are more drastic innovations than the contemplated social insurances. To one who has made the rounds of the European capitals, the news that we are to move "very gradually" toward goals long left behind in nearly every other country sounds neither so upsetting nor, alas, so promising, as it seems to America. Evidently every industrial country, when it grows up, has to make public provision for the chronic industrial diseases of unemployment, disability and impoverished age. We are the last to act because we are the last to leave the happy frontier of unlimited opportunity and undeveloped territory.

Here it is planned to make the insurances compulsory and general, the payments to be shared by employer and employee and the benefits to be administered in some such fashion as in England. Subject to such social costs, however, perhaps larger slices of taxation, the profit system is no more threatened by the New Deal than is the principle of private ownership. In time, size itself may become taxable. That is one way of decentralizing, of meeting the new hazard of monopoly created by coded industries. Mr. Roosevelt has an idea that industries may be too big; he thinks they are too big when they spread beyond the possibility of supervision by the responsible heads. He remembers the executive of a great steel corporation who learned from him, with incredulous surprise, that the miners were reduced to living in his coke ovens.

If there is nothing startling in a plan for social insurance, beyond the reminder that we are passing into the "old-country" stage, neither is there anything in the philosophy of the New Deal to frighten those familiar with the accents of an earlier America. A note of nostalgia sounds through Mr. Roosevelt's utterances; even his prophecies of the future promise a return to "earlier ideals and values." In this he is like the Progressives, those faithful ancients who never forget the Founders. He talks not at all like a Brain Truster but like an old-fashioned Jeffersonian who differs from his predecessors in being willing to accent and actualize the modern implications and connotations of the old phrases about liberty, equality and the pursuit of happiness.

The President believes that the American people are behind him more strongly today than they were a year ago. He takes that as his mandate to go ahead. If his calm spirit is fed by anything outside of the sources of strength in himself, it is by the exalting sense that wherever he goes the masses of the people go with him. That may take him far—into more and more regulation as he sees more and more that should be regulated.

The path of reform has no end. But at least one thing it is safe to predict as he enters the second phase: his genius is for politics, for interpreting the vague but powerful impulses behind popular movements, for measuring the weight of the human equation in the play of economic forces; he will go no further than America is ready to follow. As he sat on the White House porch in the cool of the evening, to the home-coming American he seemed as reassuring as America itself in an otherwise unpredictable world.

[22] 1 9 3 4 *September 9*. THIS AMERICA: A RE-DIS-COVERY. *The returning American finds his country widely different from foreign lands: a separate world, sharing in the universal drama of change, yet weaving a distinctive pattern.*

NEW YORK

Behind the fog shrouding the harbor lay New York, lay America, lay all the changes of an eventful year. From the other side of the ocean the United States had looked turbulent and strange, its large, erratic movements, more startling than anything that was happening in Europe. Only a year, and in some headlong, haphazard American fashion industry had been codified, agriculture regulated, the Stock Exchange subdued almost to a standstill, banks thawed out into liquid reservoirs. The Federal Government had grown to Olympian size, the Constitution had sloughed off an amendment without a struggle,* the financial capital had moved from Wall Street to Washington. The dollar sign itself had become an index of shifting values. Only a year, and nothing was as it had been.

Superficially, the New World seemed closer to the Old. As the process called the Americanization of Europe halted, there were plenty of signs to suggest that the Europeanization of America had begun. We were slowed down by the

* Prohibition (18th Amendment) ended as Utah ratified the 21st Amendment to the Constitution on December 5, 1933, thus repealing the 18th.

shortened hours and relaxed tempo of coded industry. After
nearly five years in low, and the constant drag of unemployment, the levels of life had dropped nearer to the European
plane. We had more time, less money, fewer illusions.

In mood and appearance, New York was more like a Continental city, the speakeasy streets come to life, the sidewalks brightened with outdoor cafés, boxwood hedges, bursts
of convivial laughter; music in the Stadium; fountains playing under the midtown towers. Washington was more like a
European capital, no longer merely a political encampment
but general headquarters of all the interests of the nation.
And beyond New York and Washington, beer gardens,
aperitif hours, government supervision and an economic
vocabulary long current in Europe spread over the land as
easily as a new fashion in berets.

Really, however, the continents were further apart than
ever. The new resemblances served only to bring into
sharper relief the essential differences between the two sides
of the Atlantic. Never as now, contrasting crisis with crisis,
narrow margin with narrower, restricted choice with no
choice, had the returning American been so struck by the
comparative abundance, the comparative exuberance, the
comparative security of his country. The commonest American sights moved him to wonder; the plenty and variety that
filled the shops, the automatic speed and tireless banter of
the soda-slingers in drug stores, the up-to-the-minute style
of the crowds in the streets, the free-and-easy talk of strangers in any sort of casual encounter. This was surface, too,
of course, but at its worst the smoothest, shiniest surface left
in the world.

Nothing of this was visible as the incoming ship inched
up the bay in a Summer fog as smothering as a steam bath.
Nothing at all was visible until the thick curtain suddenly
ripped open at the top and through the high peephole we

had one of those trick views which make the magic of New York.

The fog banks formed a hill and in a patch of light the upper stories of the tallest buildings of lower Broadway seemed to stand on the summit, a cluster of little towers on a hill. A Florentine lawyer straining at the rail for his first glimpse of the famous skyline gazed up in astonishment. "San Gimignano!" he exclaimed, and so for a moment it was an apparition like Dante's City of the Beautiful Towers, or what remains of it six hundred years after, seen across the gray Tuscan valley.

As the mists lowered and the craning turrets lengthened, some one explained to the Florentine that this hill town was the greatest of American villages—the powerful citadel called Wall Street. Rising out of the sea that morning, it looked like a citadel, like something bold and adventurous and splendid, a monumental gesture expressing the audacity and extravagance of the system that developed America.

"The capital of capitalism!" murmured the Italian. But the American, his eyes long filled with other images, recognized something else in the familiar view. He saw that what he came back to was like nothing he had known abroad. This was a separate world, participant in the universal drama of change and crisis, but at its own pace and in its own frame. Wherever it was moving it would make its own pattern at last, distinctive and immeasurable by other standards as were the profile and the stature of its towns.

Take what has happened in Wall Street as the high sign of what has happened everywhere. Perhaps no other place has altered quite so much and no other change illustrates so handily the peculiar character of the American movement. Nothing in Wall Street soars today except the silhouette. All its haughtiness is in its towers. The bold buccaneering of capitalism, the daring and audacity which impel it to great risks and great wastes, which make it a constructive force, give way now to a caution and reserve as thick as fog. Ask why, and you receive a confounding answer, one that could not be valid, if it is, anywhere else in the world. "Capital can no longer take risks," says Wall Street, "because it is too widely distributed."

But that is not the explanation of the almost rural quiet that has settled on downtown New York. In the first months of the regime of regulation by government commission the financial district has a little of the atmosphere of an occupied town, guarded, watchful, frightened and docile. The Stock Exchange, reduced to an investment market, has lost its old excitement. The Curb is a mere echo of what it used to be.

The shadowy streets are crowded still at noon and evening, but the populace is diminished and subdued. The picturesque figures are gone, the big gamblers on margins, the motley assortment of customers' men, running from grand dukes to jockeys. The college boys, jaunty and debonair, are fewer every year; nowadays they begin their careers in conservation camps and building public roads more often than in brokers' offices and bankers' lobbies.

The mind of money has lost assurance and authority. Never a unanimous or an integrated mind, it accepts the new regulations as a defeat in a contest with what it calls the political mind and submits with what grace it can for the same reason that citizens all over the land take orders from Washington; they are afraid to oppose any policy of recovery lest by some miracle it might turn out to be the right one! Wall Street does not know the answers to the universal questions any more than do other villages. Its critics of the New Deal are more numerous, but also more restrained, than those of Middletown. Labels do not mean much in the present confusion, when radicals and conservatives so often act alike, but one hears as much revolutionary talk here as in any typical American community.

It is a fairly typical American community, in fact. It yearns for definitions, for new grooves in place of the old, as who does not? All it asks of the President at the present stage is a clear declaration of where he's going, where he'll stop, and you can listen in on that kind of talk at any corner drug store or any golf course. Its economic experts studying trends and analyzing statistics are as far apart in their conclusions as like advisers in Washington and their laborious reports are as often skipped or disregarded.

What explains the timidity, the humility and the deflation of Wall Street is that it is a kind of deserted village, deprived of its chief attractions. All the audacity in the country has been cornered by Washington. A good part of the national energy, once bent on money-making, animates the head-quarters of the New Deal.

Washington today, even though the peak of nervous tension and activity is passed, is easily the most animated city in the world. It feels as if the adventurousness, the gambling spirit, of America were diverted there, or at least as if the tremendous public wagers and ventures we are making exhaust the national capacity for speculation. No private gamble can compete in interest with the vast enterprises on which we are collectively embarked and no figures Wall Street can again pile up will equal the fabulous and fascinating sums dispensed in Washington.

This transfer of power and interest began in the first months of the Roosevelt administration, perhaps before, with the organization of the RFC * by Mr. Hoover. I doubt if those who have watched the process month by month get

---

* Reconstruction Finance Corporation, January 22, 1932, established with a fund of $500,000,000 and the power to borrow more to release frozen assets in banks and mortgage companies and to help bankrupt railroads.

the full effect of the steady aggrandizement of Washington, but viewed as fait accompli, after a year's absence, it is as startling as if it had been accomplished by force. It wasn't, and the point is that in no other country on earth could so really radical a shift of authority have been made so quickly, so easily, and with so little alteration in the skyline that all the citadels appear as proud as ever.

All other changes one notes in rediscovering America are somehow related to this change. Undoubtedly the story would be different if the New Deal were otherwise headed and personified. Americans have found a hero. That should not be strange to one returning from lands where leaders are a cult, where pictures of kings and dictators paper every wall, yet it is surprising, even disturbing, to see some such cult at home.

When before in this country, except during campaigns, have photographs of a living President been hung in shops and homes, restaurants and gas stations? How often has a President evoked such emotion from a hard-pressed people as greeted Mr. Roosevelt in his recent trip across the continent? This mass emotion is a development; it did not appear when the President was a candidate or during his early days in the White House. Like such hero worship elsewhere, it has little to do with policies or reason. The President is more widely questioned and criticized than he was a year ago—and also more popular!

This is not peculiar to the United States. Neither is the zest for experiment which creates the atmosphere of Washington. Characteristically American, however, are the reactions of many of the men from other walks of life who find themselves for the first time participating in the business of government.

This refers particularly to the 15,000 or so the New Deal

engages in the capital but it is also true of thousands of others employed in public enterprises throughout the country. They constitute the huge new bureaucracy that worries so many overburdened citizens. These new bureaucrats will hang on to their jobs as long as no other occupation is available. For the most part they are not doing the work they were trained to do, and that involves a shaking out of grooves and a readjustment of habits and standards bound to have important social effects.

Still more important, they are seeing government from the inside; two or three million hitherto passive citizens are experiencing how it works. Almost invariably they are critical of government methods, impatient of delays and red tape, appalled at the wastes of public administration. In Washington the difference in tempo between regular service people and the newcomers is a constant irritation to both. So far, at any rate, government employment does not develop in Americans the bureaucratic mind.

What it does develop, what the uncertainties of the crisis and the experiments in recovery have accentuated, is the temporizing mind. We used to live in the future, by the year or the decade; now we live in the immediate present, by the day. And no one can doubt that the zest of the experimenters in Washington is matched by a hearty appetite for change in the country at large. Evidently the New Deal still satisfies something restless in the American spirit, always ready to go, to take a chance, to try anything once.

For years this spirit has been in ferment, stirred by vague but painful dissatisfactions. America is not a happy country, though by contrast with others just now it seems buoyant and gay. It is befuddled to its depths by new ideas, tormented by doubts, worried by the debts piling up and even more by the economic philosophy of extravagance—"spending your way out." Nevertheless, no one can honestly believe that we are more unhappy now than during the feverish, straining years of the last decade. Perhaps we are happier.

In spite of everything—the midsummer slump, the great desert made by drought, multiplying strikes, the ache of a thousand fears—the whole picture is decidedly brighter than it was last year. Washington is incomparably more important and more interesting as a capital. New York is pleasanter, mellower, than it has been for years; it offers more variety, stimulation and ease than any other metropolis. In every city, on a smaller scale, there appears the same impulse to make urban life urban—more music, more public gardens, more open-air shows and open-air dining. Except for the drought area, reports an Englishman who has just crossed the continent, in ten years he has not seen American towns so relaxed or the countryside so well cared for.

My own impression is that people are so weary of the confusion of the world, growing with each year, that they are creating, or striving to create, some semblance of order in their own lives. The general effect of the industrial codes is to lift the level of the low-wage earners and lower the higher levels, with the result that the average living standard is lower than last year.

The adjustment to another plane is still felt to be temporary, as unemployment is still regarded as a temporary condition, but one striking fact emerges: no longer does everybody in America expect to grow rich. The young, especially, are deliberately facing a future in which they count on making no more than a living. Many do not even aspire to be rich. A lot of "front" has disappeared, and with it some stiffening ambition. In the strange America of today one hears the people apologizing for prosperity but not for poverty.

Beyond the material changes is a new mental attitude,

even among those in whom dependence on government aid, of one kind or another, produces the passivity of the English on the dole. Perhaps by contrast with the walled-in mind in most countries of Europe, American talk seems livelier, more critical, better-informed than it was. It does not take so much for granted and at the same time it accepts as a matter of course brand-new conceptions of social responsibility. In casual conversation we bandy terms we have but lately learned; whether or not the professors of the New Deal have altered our thinking, they have transformed our political and economic vocabulary.

As the result of a revolutionary agricultural program and the daily controversies on NRA codes there has been a year of national debate on searching economic issues. In the field of capital-and-labor relations we are far behind most industrial States, where the principle of collective bargaining has long been beyond discussion, but the difference between American club-car talk today and that of 1932 is really astonishing. We have come a long way since "Babbitt." In the public library of an Ohio town the librarian told me that the change in the reading habits of a typical community in the past two years indicated a rise of about eight grades in age and intelligence.

Business, according to President Roosevelt, is slowest to learn, and I suppose nothing he has said or done is more widely resented than his aspersions on the intelligence of business or his putting it in the same bracket with "gangsters and bankers." "We are going through a process which should be called the civilization of business," admits a business man. "I never realized until lately how savage and illiterate it is; you'd be surprised to know the depth of its backwardness and also how it's brushing up lately on the rules of etiquette and the three Rs. We are at the beginning, I think, of the era of the education of the economic man.

"And if government is to become increasingly powerful, as appears too probable," he added, "then the personnel of government will have to be much more thoroughly educated. Probably that is why my friends in the universities tell me that more and more boys and girls request courses to fit them for public service. It's all part of the new conviction, dawning on everybody, that there'll be fewer opportunities for what we used to call making money."

These are but straws in the wind blowing from Wall Street to the Golden Gate. I suspect that they do not indicate any very profound movement of the national spirit. Something is stirring in America, no doubt, and to greater purpose in the past year than in any ten before. But it hasn't "jelled." But if one could sum up one's first impression of change, what they would most significantly amount to is this: In the diverse struggles of today the individual and family readjustments, the industrial conflicts, the economic and political experiments, the search for moral and spiritual certainties, there is a consciousness of America as something other than a nation, as a special environment, a distinct civilization, as that separate world which every American feels it to be when he comes back from other worlds.

Mr. Hopkins expressed it the other day when he returned from studies of relief methods abroad. The answers of other nations, he said, are not the answers for us. "There is an American way which we must find for ourselves." That is what one discovers America engaged in—groping for her own way out, certain of nothing except that she must seek until she finds, or recovers, her own principle of growth and stability.

[23] 1 9 3 4 *November 4.* THE MOOD OF AMERICA ON ELECTION EVE. *Stirred by the New Deal, the nation is still too uncertain to draw conclusions about it and is held back by fear of Government spending.*

WASHINGTON

The American October is always a time of enchantment, and this Fall ironic nature, bent all Summer on beating AAA at the cosmic game of crop reduction, smiles sweetly over all but the worst of the drought-cracked prairie and covers the field between the russet woods with the innocent green of Spring. Soaked by late rains, the desert blooms again with Winter wheat, alfalfa, thickets of fodder corn. Even the marginal lands are carpeted with flowering weeds the city slicker might mistake for a crop if the country folk were not so keen to point out what is margin, which fields are pensioned off to lie fallow, where the top soil is blown off, why the cattle have to be "boned" in one area and "fleshed" in another.

Skimming from State to State in the bright Autumn weather, it seemed to this traveler that the farmers are more conscious of the condition of their land than they ever were before. In the universal debate on government agricultural policies, filling the open spaces with the buzz of controversy, you hear about rain belts, water tables, percentages of fertility, commercial crops, subsistence crops and withered crops, and you sense that as the ground is measured in terms of productive and non-productive value, everybody is more aware of it; it is considered, inspected, spaced out; in spite of everything, it looks neater and better-tended than I ever saw it. And the farmer himself, whether for or against the allotment plan—and either way he is skeptical—does not object to being worried over. In the fertile vocabulary of Kansas and William Allen White, he likes to be "muched."

A new order, transient or not, touches the countryside. The same is true of the towns. Consider merely the extent and effect of the public-works program, unrealized until it is observed over a wide area. It is one thing to watch some government-financed project in your own neighborhood, another to survey a vast series and variety of such projects: new roads or old roads widened and beautified, new parks or neglected parks replanted, bridges, dams, waterworks, sanitation systems, hospitals, schools, municipal buildings.

This government building is only a small proportion of the private construction of a normal year, but in the abnormal quiet of today it bulks large and conspicuous on the horizon. The valley of the Tennessee hums with the activities of TVA, the giant yardstick which already makes so many networks shrink, and even that Aladdin-like performance is nothing beside the grand total of the enterprises of PWA, CCC, FERA, not to speak of far more ambitious plans yet in the blue-print stage but rapidly going forward, for housing and slum clearance.

Here, too, is a suggestion of irony. You learn as you proceed that many communities are attaining in hard times improvements they had to postpone at the height of prosperity. Under ordinary circumstances Cleveland might have waited years for the fine modern postoffice just added to the Terminal group plan. The singing darkies would not yet be laying the last sod in the park on the main street of Charlotte, N. C., which frames one of the most beautiful new Federal buildings in the South. Memphis would not have her grand boulevard along the Mississippi. Kansas City dreamed for years of turning into a spectacular entrance to the town the ragged bluff leading from the railway station to her great war monument. Now, thanks to the emergency, the dream takes shape, a splendid stairway of terraces, gardens and fountains.

So it goes everywhere, and as it goes a surprising thing results: in general the surface of the United States, urban and rural, is actually spruced up and cared for in 1934 as it was not in 1929. By the look of things, the visiting foreigner might judge us better off now than then. His impression would be strengthened by the sight of millions—so it would seem to him—of shiny new cars on the roads, small but indubitably new; by the number of freshly painted houses, especially in the South, where the old clapboards are soaking up more white lead than they have seen in a decade; by the crowded stores in cities, and a certain briskness in the small towns, which he would not recognize as reanimation, a proof that life is more localized, lived in a narrower orbit than it was.

The American notes other aspects of the repair job. He discerns that we have reached the Old-World stage of making over rather than throwing away and building new. Fresh paint and mended fences are as often fruits of depression and the New Deal as are new roads and drained swamps. They represent the home-work of men on new schedules. "I don't see how it helps," grumbled the automobile worker in Detroit, painting his front porch after his six-hour day. "If I worked full time I'd hire a painter and give him a job." "They just don't use letterheads and invoices 'round here any more," testified the town printer in Kansas. "The code makes me charge city prices, $10 for a job worth $5, and people can't pay it."

Consider the effects of industrial codes, not on employers and workers, on competition and prices, but on the unsystematized habits of little business; on the routine of everyday life, meal hours, family budgets, office bookkeeping, domestic relations. The housewife has her own view of the short workday; men eat more, spend more, she says. Once down

on the street level you discover that these are the adjustments people discuss most, discuss without end. Most of our
new leisure, if anybody wants to know, is used up in argument on points never raised in Congress or in print.

Never, I suppose, were these States so murmurous with
echoing, inconclusive talk. And never was there so little
reference to a political campaign. Local battles of national
importance were in progress—the La Follettes against the
field in Wisconsin, with the promise of a new party involved
in the outcome; the energetic fight of young Mr. Landon of
Kansas to succeed himself as the Republican Governor west
of the Mississippi and thus qualify as the party Lochinvar of
1936; the truly epic contest in California between Hollywood and Utopia, as rich in melodrama and naïve Americanism as Los Angeles itself, fade-out of the frontier. Stage
thunder rolled heavily in the deep South. Ohio, Mother of
Presidents, sounded like an old Gramophone record, so faith-
fully did it reproduce the campaign speeches and voices of
the Nineteen Twenties. And everywhere, aggravated by the
desperate desire for jobs, rose to the usual climax the struggles for control of the county courthouse.

Ordinarily, these are the savage, the really decisive, battles of politics. The county courthouse is the vital cell of
the party system. It kept the Democrats alive through years
of national impotence; it keeps the Republicans going today.
But this year no one seemed to care about the local Arma-
geddons except the candidates. It is not wholly because in
nine cases out of ten the result was never in doubt, and
everybody knew it. Nor is it because no voices, except those
of Mr. Fletcher, Mr. Moses and a few others, sounding as
from a great distance, like whistles in a fog, were raised
against the New Deal. Nor because there are no issues.

There are issues, tremendous issues, but none the electorate
is yet prepared to vote on. Five years after the collapse of the

New Era, two years after the Roosevelt landslide, the questions beating in the air all around us are too newly realized, too little understood, in a way too shocking, to be faced or formulated. The issues of the future—two years hence, six years hence, a generation hence—had no place in this dull and lifeless campaign. Nevertheless they are present in the popular mind. The indifference to the results of the election, except where the issues begin to move toward definition, as in Wisconsin and California, is coupled with an obsessing interest in the actions of government.

The net impression produced by a journey through half a dozen sample States, agricultural and industrial, in this fifth year of crisis, is that the average American is withholding decision; he will do a lot of looking before he leaps in any direction. Ask any community how it has changed, and five out of six will speak of themselves as "working out of the depression," but with reservations revealing a newly developed capacity for self-scrutiny.

It may turn out that the chief effect of the experiments of the New Deal will be to force Americans to look at America. Certain it is that the farmer is reappraising more than his own fields as he considers the effects of crop control and processing tax. The townsman contemplates an epoch as he regards the bloated shape of the city for which he is taxed and the bitter human residue of his "promotional" campaigns to attract new industries. Under the pressure of codification and regulation we are more rather than less aware of local differences; the clamor of complaint and exception expresses a real diversity, never before so apparent because never before so well charted, in local conditions, customs, standards, environment and mental attitude.

A country of such spread and variety does not feel events in the same way everywhere. The spiritual distance between New York and North Dakota or between Pittsburgh and

Mobile is greater than the physical distance, and every attempt to enlarge the scope of the central government serves to emphasize how little standardized or synchronized or even nationalized we actually are.

That it is a superhuman job to govern this empire from Washington is clear enough without the feeble rally to the defense of States' rights on the part of the Republicans, whose only issues in the present campaign are those discarded by the Democrats. But that reversal points to the reaction against bigness, evident throughout the country. Nothing much has been done to decentralize industry, but as an idea it is increasingly popular. And as the idea develops, as it is promoted by the administration, inevitably it opposes itself greater centralization of government. Mr. Roosevelt was referring to big business when he remarked: "Perhaps we should tax size," and business is referring to government when it groans: "Look how size taxes us!"

A true picture of the contemporary scene would show a thousand local minds and the minds of a thousand interests—cotton and corn, steel and timber, labor, commerce and all the rest—each oddly shaded by the local environment but of the same general color, so that you can trace the banking mind, for instance, across all the variations of a continent, like a repeated motif in an intricate design. Vast and intricate as it is, however, in its slow, uneven movements, this heterogeneous mass mind has a coalescence to be found neither in so compact and deeply rooted a nation as France nor in a country as strongly united and regimented as Italy. And today it is hardening, this glue that binds us into some sort of pattern. At least there is a deepening consciousness that we have created a pattern.

The picture would show the American looking at this panorama, in a pretty cold north light, and making up his mind what he thinks of it. In the sense that he is intent on one thing, and all alike are in a common state of unsureness and suspended judgment, we have a national mind, but not yet an affirmative mind; the "know-it-all" American, if he ever existed, has gone the way of the volatile Frenchman, the stolid German and the romantic Italian. Something has happened to his self-assurance, the hearty emphasis he gave to happy platitudes—something has happened even to the platitudes themselves. Nobody is positive any more. At present the commonest expressions in the United States are "I don't know" and "What's the answer?"

The land was never so full of echoes. Not only is everyone absorbed in the same topics, but everywhere people are saying the same things, in almost identical words. There is a strong undercurrent of optimism, not always reflected on the surface, and stronger as you leave the big cities. Despite recessions of business and a swamping relief problem hanging over every community like a black cloud, the "feeling" of recovery persists. Perhaps it is more feeling than fact, but it is significant that it is firmer now than it was in the Spring, when the index figures were more favorable.

The buoyancy varies sharply with local conditions and somewhat with the temper of the people. You go into towns, particularly in the West, and meet a hard-hit population, usually small and well-knit, which makes a point of "taking it," as an adventure. Gloom is probably deepest in the canyons of Wall Street, and dissolves in proportion as the plains widen and the economic levels flatten out. The rich are not as gallant as the poor. Of all our population the toughest and bravest in adversity are the middle class in the cities; they suffer most, complain least, and hang on with tragic tenacity to what's left of the "American standard"; if the civilization it represents is to be saved, it is they who will save it.

As far as one can see, such lift as exists is due primarily to

agriculture and is most perceptible in improvement in whole-
sale and retail trade. The industrial centers in general are not
so cheerful as the agricultural capitals, cities like Kansas
City, Atlanta, Des Moines, the market centers for farm produce. There are exceptions both ways, of course, and some
manufacturing towns seem better off than others, Detroit
and Chicago, for example, in contrast to Cleveland and Pittsburgh. The brightest region is the South, where small cotton
planters, as the result of crop reduction, government credit
and a guaranteed minimum price, have cash to spend for the
first time in years and are spending it with an effect of exuberance lacking in sections where money is not such a
novelty.

Such buoyancy, obviously, must be based in large part on
government disbursements. It confirms the view of those
economists who are convinced that there is no recovery beyond that artificially induced by the distribution of $12,000,-
000,000, if that is the sum, of public money. Even that injec-
tion, they say, the most powerful primer ever administered
by a crisis government, has not sufficed to start more than
one or two cylinders of the stalled economic machine and
will have no permanent effects. Some of these agree with Mr.
Ford, who believes in letting nature and science take their
course, on the ground that they will, anyway. Others contend
that the stimulant merely postpones and renders more crushing, when it comes, the inevitable collapse of the doomed system of capitalism or commercialism.

The observer on the ground sees clearly enough that higher
agricultural prices and the distribution of subsidies—"the
farmer's tariff," they call it—account for much of the Fall
business. Everybody knows that, outside of "made work,"
the proportion of re-employment is small and the number of
unemployed on relief mounts with a sickening uniformity in
dark and bright areas alike. But one sees also that in the

South and Middle West the agricultural population needs everything that the factories can produce.

The farmer does not starve like city folk and never will; he has escaped the breadline and the worst horrors and terrors of the urban unemployed. But, lacking money for years, his "goods shortage," from cooking utensils to machinery, sheets to shoes, amounts to a famine. The little he spends now is but a trickle to what he could distribute if he had more, and as a stimulant its effects must and do spread far into other industries. It spreads, but too slowly.

Under the recovery policies of the New Deal the lowest levels, agricultural and industrial, have been lifted, but the most cursory survey reveals how drastically all subsequent levels, up to and excluding the highest, are lowered. Not the unemployed alone, supposing 10,000,000 workless are given a bare subsistence, but millions of the employed, notably among the white-collar class, are too near the verge of want to buy anything but food and shelter. What is missing in the national economy is the purchasing power of the well-paid employee.

It is missing because business is afraid. The characteristic mind of the United States is the business mind, the mind of trade and finance as distinct from the industrial mind. It exhibits local peculiarities, political prejudices, a few differences in taste, not many, but wherever it works or plays, it thinks with a remarkable unanimity. As the middleman of the economic system, this is the conduit through which flow the main currents of American life; in the present set-up it is the most influential mind we have. The intellectual is more expressive, the mass has more political momentum, but the voice of business is the master voice, and no movement can get far without its cooperation.

All its spokesmen agree that business is "rarin' to go." That is one of the echoing phrases; I wish I could count the number of times I heard it. They, too, feel the undercurrent of recovery. Cautiously they report an upward curve that sags, lacks the free swing it should have, but never falls back near bottom. Once in a while they wonder if the upswing is not more advanced than the country realizes. "I suspect we are further along the road out than we let ourselves acknowledge," said a business leader in Chicago. "Sometimes I wonder where we'd be if business were exerting its full weight."

One reason business hangs back is because it is not adventurous. The Chamber of Commerce is the most reckless barker we possess when everything booms, but it is as cautious as a clam in sultry weather. The main reason, however, is the same that makes Fall trade revive: because the government is spending resounding sums of money that somebody at some time will have to pay, either by taxes or inflation. So we have a kind of impasse; government priming up the engine to make it go and business scared to step on the gas because the engine's primed! It is not the experiments that cause defections from the New Deal; it is the cost of experiments. Business conversation everywhere begins and ends on the theme of government expenditure. Among the most spendthrift people on earth the "economics of spending" finds amazingly little support.

The fears of big business become the fears of little business. Both are sincerely and deeply worried by the public debt piling up, more worried than by anything else except the monstrous specter of unemployment. The worst of it is that the two monsters walk together, one and indivisible.

Yet do not imagine that these anxieties cause among the mass of the people the same foreboding that haunts the dissenting economists and the nervous business men. In their separate States and local communities, paradoxically, the people who demand increasing Federal relief insist on balanced budgets and drastic economies. But what most endears

President Roosevelt to the rank and file is that "he goes ahead and tries things"—at any cost.

To the non-analytic mind of the ordinary man the so-called revolutionary experiments mean nothing more than that "Roosevelt is trying to get things started." Sifted down, that is probably all they do mean; that thought bothers the more radical New Dealers as much as business is troubled by the doubt as to whether anybody knows the meaning. Moreover, the term revolution is now too commonplace to be frightening. I heard a mild little woman get up and ask her study club in an Ohio town why it wouldn't be a good idea to start all over again with a second American revolution. Why not? agreed the assembled ladies, applauding.

These are generalizations, and as such subject to large discounts and large exceptions—subject, above all, to volumes of amplification and detail; but for the reporter attempting to sum up his assorted impressions the America he glimpses in the late afternoon of 1934 is:

First, stirred by the application of measures of relief and reform to observe, as if for the first time, the American panorama as a whole system, environment and pattern of life.

Second, too uncertain yet to draw conclusions from these observations; increasingly critical, but not prepared to formulate criticisms into issues, let alone vote on them; waiting not so much for definitions of policy and direction, but—and this is the crux of the uncertainty—to make up its own mind. And

Third, in the mood if not in the state of recovery, actually "rarin' to go," and going in so far as power can be supplied by the mass. The brake, to the extent to which the national economy is independent of the rest of the world, is the fear of government expenditure—and is applied by those who alone can supply a substitute for government spending, and whose terror of inflation and taxation prevents them from taking the initiative to forestall these dangers.

In a Western town I came across a small merchant rebuilding his store in the most modern manner—chromium front, air-conditioning, ingenious parking space for customers' cars. "No," he explained, "I can't say that business justifies this investment, though business isn't bad. But I figured that if I didn't spend money first I'd have to spend it last, and I'd rather pay for the fun of making a little work and realizing a pet dream of my own." Perhaps he had one answer.

[24]   1 9 3 4   *November 25.* "A LITTLE LEFT OF CEN-
TER." *Though his critics contend that the course of the New Deal is uncertain, the President holds that its progress adheres closely to the original line.*

WASHINGTON

In November, 1934, President Roosevelt is a shade grayer, heavier, graver, older but no more than two years older—than the man elected to preside over a national emergency in November, 1932. If even his unconquerable cheerfulness is not altogether proof against the strain of making decisions as complex and momentous as any President ever faced, the traces of strain are faint and elusive.

On the eve of his departure for the South, Mr. Roosevelt looked much less tired than he did on the eve of his election. He appeared fitter in every way, his face thinner and firmer, than when Congress adjourned last June. He is a President who persists in enjoying the Presidency. After twenty arduous and anxious months, to him it is not the crushing burden that weighed down Mr. Hoover; it is still "the greatest job in the world," and easier than the Governorship of New York for the reason that it is less difficult to persuade a Congressman from the most backward district to think in terms

of the nation than it is to induce a New York City politician
to think in terms of the State.

One never sees the President without being freshly impressed by his infinite capacity for remaining himself. Under
all circumstances, that is to say, he remains essentially unchanged, not alone in outward seeming but in the color and
quality of his ideas, and—all reports and appearances to the
contrary notwithstanding—in the general shape and direction of his policies. He complains with a grin that his "in-
terpreters" keep him hopping—to the Right every time he
sees a banker, to the Left whenever he talks with a La Follette or a Sinclair. He is admittedly a pragmatist in politics,
moving as far and as fast as he can along a given line, revising
a method, shifting personnel, balancing one interest against
another with the art that distinguishes political leadership
from business or labor or technical or any other kind of special leadership. But he moves toward pretty definite objectives along a line he describes as "a little left of center." To
those who have talked to him at intervals over a period of
years it is clear that in this phrase he is delineating the habit-
ual direction of his mind.

"There seem to be will and purpose behind the pleasant
smile of your President," sighed a leader of a gold-bloc country when the United States went off the gold standard. This
leader is accustomed to express force by frowning at his
public. "Perhaps his is the better method," he added sadly.

The New Deal is more than anything the triumph of a temperament. If you doubt it, study the election returns. Voters
usually go to the polls to satisfy their likes and dislikes; that
is why dictators are foolhardy when they resort to bullet-
proof shirts instead of ballot boxes. This year less than ever
were the American people measuring the fitness of local candidates, following party arguments or registering final judgment on New Deal policies. They were expressing their

feeling for the optimist who sits in the White House and is generous with cheer and checks.

The election was primarily a plebiscite on the popularity of the President. As such it was one of the most remarkable personal victories in the history of politics; how remarkable may be gauged from its effect in convincing the business leaders of the country that they have no choice but to go along with a political leader who rides the tide so easily and promises to keep on riding it for six years more.

The effect on the President himself of a vote of confidence without precedent in a mid-term election is thoroughly characteristic. He is neither elated nor oppressed by the responsibility of managing a majority so great that it leaves him without an alibi. Predictions of a struggle between the Right and Left wings of his own party in Congress disturb his equanimity no more than does the emergence of Senator Borah or the Liberty League as rallying points of serious opposition. He recalls that the trouble he was always going to have with a Republican Legislature in Albany never developed; the rout threatened in the last Congress did not materialize.

Mr. Roosevelt has had many occasions to learn of what gauzy stuff political prophecies are made and few experiences to shake his assurance in his power to deal with men. He moves forward with increased assurance but no added speed as the result of the election, which he interprets as a sign that most people regard the New Deal as a job of reconstruction and desire the work to go on. That this was the prevailing sentiment of the country he never doubted; therefore the referendum will not cause him to accelerate his program or alter in any degree the course he marked out at the beginning of his administration. The "mandate" is to do only what he fully intended to do anyway, regardless of the election returns.

Its critics may consider the course of the administration variable and uncertain. The commonest complaint against the New Deal is that it is uncharted, balancing each step right by a step left, and vice versa, thus throwing everybody into confusion and in the name of planned economy making it impossible for the individual citizen to plan six months ahead. Throughout the country there is one echoing plaint: "If he'd only say where he's going!" The President's idea is that he has followed one clear and consistent course from the day he took office. In his own mind, at least, he has always been "a little left of center." The tempo varies according to circumstances, immediate necessities cut across and interrupt the long-range plan, but as Mr. Roosevelt sees it the progress of the New Deal has veered very little from the original line.

The project for social insurance furnishes as good an illustration as any not only of the general Roosevelt direction but of the Roosevelt method. Long before his election the President had given thought and study to the plans adopted in various countries for insuring workers against the hazards of unemployment, sickness and old age. Early in 1933, under his orders, experts who had been collecting data prepared a tentative program of social legislation. Mr. Roosevelt postponed action on the ground that the country was not ripe for the scheme and the scheme was not ripe for presentation to the country. This year the matter came up again, and after the adjournment of Congress in June he announced that he would submit to the next Congress a broad plan for a system of social insurance.

"I believe we'll be social-minded enough in another year," he said then, "to make a beginning in a great social reform which must be carefully adapted to our special conditions and needs."

Two weeks ago the National Conference on Economic Security, created to advise the President on this project, was summoned to Washington. Of the 150 members, 148 arrived from all sections of the country to receive the message from the White House. Mr. Roosevelt repeated that he was prepared to make recommendations to the incoming Congress for the enactment of the first measures aiming at social security. But it was evident that when he said "a beginning" he meant a beginning. To the disappointment of the social workers and in contradiction to the bold plans of his own aides, he proposed no more than a State-controlled system of unemployment insurance, to be financed by local contributions and not out of taxes.

Undoubtedly the New Deal envisages broad measures of social security; no project appeals more to the President's imagination and his social conscience; but his approach to the goal is characteristically cautious, realistic, restrained by the knowledge that a nation has to be educated to the point where reforms can be assimilated naturally, without dangerous spasms of indigestion. "The people aren't ready" is a favorite phrase in White House conferences.

Another illustration is the Tennessee Valley development. In Mr. Roosevelt's view the implications of this vast scheme are but dimly understood. It is not wholly, or even chiefly, a yardstick to measure the costs of generating and delivering electrical power and cheapen the price of electric current to the average consumer. It is above all a social yardstick measuring off on real ground a new design for living.

The President is not a theorist; that is why the downright Rights and Lefts cannot classify him or his off-center course. To him those imported terms do not translate literally into American and have no more absolute meaning than North and South. By instinct and tradition he belongs to the school of thought that expresses political distinctions in words like Tory and Liberal. Probably "a little left of center" is the modern equivalent of the slant of Thomas Jefferson in his day, or of Andrew Jackson and Theodore Roosevelt in theirs; Franklin Roosevelt stands in somewhat the same relation to his world and time. In the Tennessee Valley he seizes an opportunity to try out experiments based not on theory but on certain ideas he has long cherished and which are about as radical as anything in the New Deal.

Decentralization of industry is one of these, with its corollary, the subsistence homestead. The scheme differs from the farmed-out industries Henry Ford has established in Michigan only in extent and method. One experiment is privately, the other publicly financed, but both attempt to work out a new blend of agriculture and industry, town and country. The President thinks that if he can produce in the Tennessee Valley a sample of a "balanced civilization" the formula will be worth all it costs. The power issue is large but incidental, and has only an incidental bearing on power contests elsewhere, New York, for instance, where the question is under the jurisdiction of the State and not of the Federal Government.

It is typical of the President that he wants his objectives illustrated and tried out in practice. His gradual approach to social security legislation exemplifies his political technique; what is going on in Tennessee represents a bold employment of executive power to paint on the wall a picture, so big that everybody can see what it means, of his general aims.

In private conversation Mr. Roosevelt never discusses a policy or an idea without finding a specific instance to sharpen his point. His mind always tends to simplify, to reduce the general to the particular. In his presence the problems harassing the United States do not lose their difficulty, but they do lose their complexity.

Thus, in speaking of recovery, this President is not likely to see the movement in terms of carloadings, production charts and market averages. He is apt to recall a small-town doctor he met the other day, symbol of the millions of unrecorded, uncounted private debts that existed two years ago. That doctor had lost a year's income, $3,500, which he had written off and never expected to collect. This year his patients have voluntarily paid $2,500, and payments are still coming in—another symbol of the average American as an honest fellow who pays if he can.

Or Mr. Roosevelt thinks of the farm woman buying her first new hat in three years. The small boy rejoicing in the first suit he ever had that was not cut down from his big brother's. Such reduction of debt and replacements of necessities account for the lift in wholesale and retail trade and represent the first stage of recovery. The second will come when more people are able to buy radios, stoves, carpets, the costlier sort of replacements. The third stage, involving the heavy industries, will be harder to bring about; the worst emergency is past, the general tone of business improves, but neither the President nor any one else can foresee the end of the crisis while prospects are so slim for the revival of basic trades.

A Chicago banker called at the White House not long ago to ask the government to do something to stimulate the durable industries. "What will you do?" asked the President. "Will you lend $10,000,000 to put up a sixty-story building on Michigan Avenue? Will you finance a company wishing to erect a new hotel?"

"For an office building or hotel? Certainly not," replied the banker. "Office space is at a discount now and we have too many hotels. It will be ten years before it will be economically sound to construct big buildings using great quantities of steel."

"Yes," commented Mr. Roosevelt, "and most of that over-capacity, typical of every city, dates from the years 1927–28–

29. During those years, too, most of the railroads were equipped with new rails. How, then, can we speed recovery by getting the heavy industries going?"

It is not believed in Washington that the expanding relief rolls of today mean an actual increase either in need or unemployment. Investigation indicates that in 1932–33 the number unemployed was nearer 16,000,000 than 11,000,000. Of millions of workers there was no record for the reason that they were living on reserves or were supported by relatives. Therefore the reduction in unemployment is probably much greater than the estimates. These estimates represent county averages, usually computed in the cities, where the proportion is higher, and are more likely to overstate than understate the true condition.

Last Winter and Spring the more conservative advisers of the President, men of the type of mind of Lewis Douglas and James P. Warburg, advocated that all public works—PWA, CWA, CCC, the last costing the government $1,000 a year per man—should be discontinued. Proponents of balancing the national budget, they argued that the cost could be cut in half if relief were reduced to direct payments to the needy, without the costly business of making work. Mr. Roosevelt agreed that relief expenditures could be drastically cut if the public works program were abandoned. But if he went on the radio and announced such a change, he added, in two days people from all over the United States would be marching on Washington under banners marked: "We want work, not doles." Uncannily sensitive as he is to the temper of the country, he believes that heading off such a demonstration, dangerous because justified, and keeping up the morale of the people, are more important than balancing the budget.

Signs multiply in Washington that some of the most insistent budget-balancers begin to accept, if not to share, the President's views. The rapprochement between the bankers and the administration, and the Chamber of Commerce and the administration represents a capitulation to the New Deal even more significant than the popular endorsement at the polls. From the White House this tendency to cooperate is regarded as a sign that the social and economic lessons of the depression are being learned in the upper forms.

From the days of the moratorium until now perhaps no administration has had so much conference with bankers, and if there has been an unusual trek from Wall Street to Washington this Fall it is not because Roosevelt has turned Right—any more than Wall Street has turned Left!—but because more bankers have asked to see the President than ever before. What it really signifies is a movement of surrender. Wall Street has been accustomed to think of itself as a government, or the equal of government. It has made treaties and truces with Presidents in the manner of one sovereign power negotiating with another. Now bankers begin to recognize that they represent only one group of interests among many groups, all subject to government.

No change dictated by this administration is more striking than the new relation established between finance and government. Its significance increases when one considers the bold experiments in fiscal policy undertaken by the government itself. In the Roosevelt view the monetary measures have justified themselves. Unless unforeseen circumstances arise, there is no indication of further devaluation of the dollar, for several months now the most stable currency in the world, though the White House attitude is that people make a bogey of devaluation with no idea what it means.

The present policy of the United States is in line with that pursued in the British Dominions, Canada, Australia and South Africa. All are trying to raise values, or prices, to a level corresponding to real or normal values. When that point is reached there will be some basis for the stabilization which

Washington undoubtedly hopes to achieve as soon as the time is ripe. Our fiscal orthodoxy, so it is said, shines in contrast to the unorthodox manoeuvres of the Bank of England.

It is clear, however, that when the President speaks of "objectives," whether they be actual policies or still in the realm of ideals, his mind focuses on the domestic field. What attracts him most is social planning, especially when it can be projected in the form of model communities, which he likes to scatter over the country as samples of what the common life could be with a wider distribution of wealth and a wider public ownership of natural resources. His political-mindedness is essentially social-mindedness; what makes him popular with masses of people is his capacity to translate the abstract into the concrete and to see the general problem in terms of the individual instance.

When it is objected that the recovery program has resulted in a lifting of the lowest wage level and a lowering of the broad plateau just above, he answers that the most healthful thing about this heavy upward movement is that it begins where it should begin, at the bottom. And when the administration is criticized for allotting an undue share of relief money and make-work projects to the poor States of the South, he declares that one of the really constructive effects of the Federal program is that by means of relief it is actually raising the subnormal living standards of the most backward States. Until the level of the South is lifted to some approximation of the national average it is absurd, he believes, to speak of "the American standard" or to hope for consuming power to balance productive capacity.

However zigzag the course may appear, however confused and inconsistent the aims, the President thinks of himself as leading a movement toward what he constantly refers to as "a balanced civilization." The apparent contradictions, one suspects, arise from the fact that his balance assumes a combination of public and private ownership, actually a merging of the roads marked Right and Left.

Mr. Roosevelt unquestionably wishes to make the individual citizen more secure in his individual ownership, and business more secure in reaping the profits of enterprise and efficiency. He is the last to underestimate the truly capital value of private initiative and the profit motive. At the same time he certainly tends, as proved by his enthusiasm for the TVA experiment, to wide extensions of public ownership and a comprehensive system of government control. Not without reason does he point to TVA as a clue to his objective. And not without reason is he accused of moving Left and Right at the same time. He would be the first to claim that the New Deal is a Right-Left march toward a new center, the outlines of which, if vague at first, become larger and clearer in his own mind as he proceeds.

[25] 1 9 3 5 *January 6.* THE MAIN LABORATORY OF THE NEW DEAL. *In the States of the South, the Roosevelt program is now in full operation.*

WASHINGTON

Four years ago, when I saw it last, the depression was just beginning to slow down the belated and headlong industrial invasion of the South. New villages, new skyscrapers, new factories, new voices, loud and insistent, proclaimed the enthusiasm of the most backward States in joining the great American parade. While the Florida boom was not a Southern delirium, it is not without significance that the Southern sun first causes the mind of Wall Street to go dizzy. It was down near Miami that we started seeing ciphers effervescing all over the place until the bubbles began to look like round

sums. The Florida climate dazzled, but the renaissance of
the real South was a logical and solid development, easily the
most important American movement of the post-war period.
At last the withdrawn country beyond the Mason and Dixon
line was in step with the rest of the Union, we said; the oldest America was becoming "Americanized."

To those of us who observed the phenomenon, the awakening South was deeply interesting for another reason. Coming
into industry late, with vast untapped resources, natural and
human, with an almost wholly native population, with the
greatest industrial exhibit in the world at its doors, would it
repeat the mistakes of former developments or improve on a
top-heavy structure fifty years old and already cracked and
quaking? Then the crisis came in earnest, overwhelming
North and South together, but the South less because it was
poorer to begin with, less highly industrialized, living on a
level so much below the "American standard" that it did not
have to fall far or hard to touch bottom. Nevertheless cotton
remained the most depressed crop and the most depressed
industry. And the question one asked of the South in 1930
has become more urgent than ever.

Here is where the South surprises you today. Until you see
it on the ground you cannot realize what is happening. Probably the South itself does not realize it, and other regions are
too absorbed in their own problems to take in the implications of what they vaguely complain of as the "disproportionate amount of Federal money spent in the South." You do not
travel very far or probe much below the surface before discovering that the land of cotton is the special kingdom of the
New Deal. To observe the Roosevelt program in full operation you must go South.

The reasons are fairly obvious. Take a country the prosperity of which depends on one product, subject its production, whether in field or factory, to the control of govern-

ment, and government in a literal sense regulates not only the economy but the business and social habits of that country. When this country occupies three levels, with an enormous waterfall between a wall of mountains and the coastal plain which makes it a natural power area, and when the government owns the strategic power site, the opportunity is well-nigh irresistible, given the mind of the present administration, to use this lever to regulate power production.

When the country is in the early stages of development, so poor compared to the national average of wealth that the States have practically turned over the burden of relief work to the Federal authorities, it stands to reason that it offers the widest, least obstructed ground for government experiments in rehabilitation, subsistence homesteading, resettlement of marginal populations.

Add to all this that industry, outside of tobacco, is newly planted in the South, so that deeply entrenched special interests are few, that political opposition is reduced to the minimum, and you perceive why this section should become the field of the largest and most significant adventures of the New Deal.

Actually the South, the oldest and the newest America, is the main laboratory of the Roosevelt experiments. Not only is it relatively prosperous, the prosperity is in part the result of whole-hearted "cooperation" with administration policies. This Fall the South led the country in increase of sales. The Atlanta district shows the biggest gain in trade of all the Federal Reserve districts, 20 per cent over 1933, and 70 per cent over the index of ten years ago. The upward trend continues and spreads. A hundred signs along the way convince you that there is more ready money in these States, more widely distributed, than there was four years ago. Then the boasts of the New South were belied by the raveled fringes of the towns, the frowzy colored quarters, the tumbling shanties of the share croppers, the misery of the rural slums.

Dilapidation remains, of course, but less poverty under Federal relief I suspect than under "normal" conditions, certainly less contrast with the rest of the country. Prolonged unemployment extends the film of neglect and decay all over the land while the South perks up, paints and repairs. Outside the highest circles, its mood is cheerful. As a section it is the one area of the United States which believes that tomorrow is going to be better than yesterday.

Admittedly, ready money has always been so scarce in the South that a little produces more effect than it would elsewhere. Admittedly, too, much of the money now circulated is provided by the Federal Government in one way or another. Here, as in the wheat country, the little farmer grumbles that the allotments for reducing cotton acreage enrich the big planter, but even the share cropper agrees that the government guarantee of 12 cents a pound for cotton is pulling him out of the hole. In sum these bounties represent a lot of cash in the cotton kingdom.

"The South can come back on 10-cent cotton if we can sell enough," said an old planter. "This reduction program is like a dose of calomel—hard to take but necessary to purge the system of the surplus piled up by the Farm Board. More than that, it is doing more than years of experience and advice to force the South to abandon the one-crop habit. As a cash crop, almost as durable as metal, cotton always tempts us; to grow food, even for ourselves, is a kind of deviation from the line, as they say in Russia. It was our line to be planters, not farmers. We resented the factories, too, when they first appeared. No planter likes the ugly muck of the textile trade. But in the present state of the world market I don't know what would have happened to the South without industry. As I see the modern world, with industry you keep afloat with terrible strain but without industry you are sunk."

As a crop, cotton has profited more than any other by the New Deal. As an industry, textiles were the first to accept the NRA code. Despite bitter dissatisfaction on both sides, despite the first large-scale strike ever known in the South, employers and workers have benefited under the code, and they know it. Nowhere has the short day and the abolition of child labor wrought such social and economic change as in the textile industry. At one stroke, by the enactment of a minimum wage of $13 in the South and $14 in the North, the old differential between the two sections has been canceled, if anything in favor of the South, where the short Winter and cheaper housing reduces living costs 10 to 15 per cent below the Northern norm.

It is true that in neither section is there full-time work, and the stretch-out system and reduced maximum wages tend to defeat the purpose of the new regulations. There will be more labor trouble before the balance is struck, yet no observer can fail to see that what has happened everywhere implies a greater gain when it happens here: the lowest levels of American labor have been jerked up to a point where the "American standard," at least in theory, is within striking distance.

Southerners freely grant that, with the exception of North Carolina and Virginia, where the tobacco industry pours vast sums into the Federal Treasury, the States of the South receive in relief from the government anywhere from five to forty times as much as they pay in taxes. Over and over again they repeat that they "cooperate"—the word echoes like a refrain. They add that it is a new thing for the South to be treated according to its need and not according to its capacity to pay. The business people are as uneasy about the final reckoning as business people in other parts of the country; they are even more aghast than Northerners at the mounting billions of public expenditures. As Southerners, however, they are rather pleased and astonished to be "in on the big money," as one Georgian put it. "It makes us feel for the first time as if we have really been taken into the Union!" he smiled.

The administration is equally ready to acknowledge that the South receives a large, even a disproportionate, share of the relief funds. President Roosevelt goes further; he expresses satisfaction that these grants reach the submerged millions in the cotton country; sub-standard even in good times. The general level of the country can never be raised, he believes, until the South achieves economic equality. The President knows conditions in the Southern States. To a New Yorker who recently complained that the government was cutting into private markets by paying people on relief to make mattresses out of surplus cotton, he retorted: "Stealing markets? Why we are creating a market! I know districts in the South where three families out of four have never bought or even seen a mattress."

Talk to a Federal relief director like Miss Shepperson and you perceive, if the work of her organization is typical, that relief in the South is not so much a matter of carrying the destitute through a crisis as of attacking the problem of poverty and ignorance where both are chronic. In Georgia the FERA is moving 10,000 families this year into a more favorable economic environment; it is starting village industries, financing subsistence homesteads, fighting malaria, typhus, the hookworm and the boll weevil, establishing clinics and nurseries, teaching cooking, gardening and canning, repairing furniture, rebuilding shanties, adding space to one-room schools, distributing books, starting night schools for textile workers and share croppers.

Besides giving a graphic picture of the backwardness of the South, the complex of activities suggests that the New Deal represents a new period of reconstruction for the States of the old Confederacy. Even more than that, it gives the opportunity of the century to the social worker. Until you survey the New Deal in operation over a fairly wide area you have no idea how social workers crowd out both professors and politicians as the typical New Dealers.

Miss Shepperson reports that the Georgia relief rolls have decreased from 15 per cent of the population at the peak to 10 per cent in November. As the Winter advances, the number will mount again, she thinks, and explains the apparently small reduction in unemployment in spite of improved business and vast schemes of made work as a reflection of the growing ranks of the unemployable, augmented each year of the depression by old people, students out of school and by dependents formerly supported by relatives. She adds that the analysis of a State like Georgia discloses that depressed areas are usually places without alternatives—communities dependent on one crop, for instance, or a single industry. Her observation is that villages possessing a small factory come through better than villages that are merely trading posts, and that in general medium-size towns are safer in economic storms than cities or villages.

At a time when there is so much talk of decentralized industry, it is worthy of remark that decentralization is the striking characteristic of the industrial development of the South. The only metropolis is New Orleans, the only industrial city is Birmingham, the only large-scale distributing center is Atlanta. Otherwise there are no big cities and no concentrated industry. The factory towns and the mill villages are widely scattered. Largely because the development of manufacturing followed the development of electric power, itself a distributing agency, the South anticipated in the Twenties the pattern today aimed at in the Roosevelt experiments in regional planning, particularly in the great project going forward in the Tennessee Valley.

The President describes this experiment as the key to the New Deal. As a plan to make over an area as big as many small countries, equip it with electric power and provide a living under entirely new conditions for a population almost as large as Ireland's, this is a government enterprise without parallel except among the unrealized designs of the Soviets. It is neither by chance nor altogether by the accident of geography, political or natural, that such a dream takes shape in the South.

Two years before the election of Mr. Roosevelt I saw a plan prepared by army engineers for the development of the Tennessee Valley which forms the basis of the engineering work today. Years before that Henry Ford coveted this site as the ideal location for the private experiment in a balanced economy which he works out on a smaller scale and under less favorable climatic conditions in Michigan. But nothing less powerful than government could combine the Ford idea with a river and power development on this scale, extending into seven States. Such a scheme could not evolve, moreover, save in a region at the same time undeveloped and over-populated, among a people as helpless and eager to be helped, as quick to "cooperate," as the early Americans stranded for 150 years in the uplands of the South.

Among these early Americans there is no such resistance to the New Deal on the ground of independence as one meets among the hundred-per-centers of Kansas. The South has its reservations, too, one of which was met by the recent decision not to pay workers in relief more than the local wage scale, but it takes to the new order more cheerfully than do other sections. Partly because it is a gift, perhaps, partly because it fits into a pattern already vaguely traced in the least developed regions of the United States, the New Deal flourishes best in the South. And the South, in ways too meager for the North to notice, flourishes with it. No part of America is so interesting or suggestive to the student of the direction and effects of the Roosevelt experiments.

Coming back to the cotton country after four years of depression one wonders whether the questions one asked then of the new industry are being answered now. Will the first sample of a modern industrial pattern come from the region where industry is almost a stranger?

[26]   1 9 3 5 *January 20.* THE NEW DEAL LOOKS OVERSEAS. *Although there have been shifts in Roosevelt's foreign policy, its general direction toward international cooperation is indicated by the World Court issue.*

WASHINGTON

Significant in itself, the emergence so early in the present Congress of the long-buried issue of American adherence to the World Court is even more significant as an index of the general direction of the Roosevelt foreign policy. For as midterm approaches, it becomes increasingly clear that the administration has taken a decided and fairly consistent line on external affairs.

Despite the intense concentration on domestic emergency, the brusque change of front at the London Conference, the higher appropriations for defense, the emphasis on national self-sufficiency, actually we have gone far under President Roosevelt along the road of international cooperation. We are about to go further. There is a new deal in the foreign as in the domestic field.

The President started out with a dramatic if abortive gesture toward the world. Ever since, particularly in recent months, he has been edging back, almost unobserved under the impress of other business, to his original position. In 1929 the United States began to trace a new and inevitable line of international policy. Today, after the earthquake that broke and jumbled all lines of communication, the country and the world with it move cautiously again in the predestined direction.

Who now recalls the speculations and forecasts of a new line of American foreign policy which stirred Washington in the bright dawn of the Hoover administration? The swelling bubble of prosperity had not yet burst. Washington had just become self-conscious as a world capital, head of the great creditor nation upon which all others depended. The monumental plan now nearing completion was exhibited for the first time in plaster model by Andrew Mellon. We had seen the last of two small-town Presidents to whom Europe was a trip—which neither had ever taken.

Entering the White House was a man of the world, a man who personified an opulent Uncle Sam to war-impoverished peoples from Brussels to Odessa, who had lived and worked abroad and had spent eight years in building up a unique official sales force to drum up foreign trade. It was confidently expected that a Chief Executive with such experience would take a new lead in the international field. Beyond curbing the excesses of our abundance he had so little to do at home, we felt, that he might easily devote much of his time to reorganizing and consolidating our position in the world.

Mr. Hoover himself had some such idea. The writer never saw him so animated and assured at any other time as when he discussed his plans for world commerce and world peace in the first weeks of his administration. He kept a voluminous file of clippings from the foreign press. He chose the

ablest man he knew for Secretary of State.* It is hard to
recapture now the mood of the beginning of 1929, when
preparations for the London Disarmament Conference were
carried on in Washington in an atmosphere of cheerful confidence now lost to the world, but the tone was set by the
picture of the American President and the British Prime Minister sitting on a log beside the Rapidan and genially chuck-
ing battleships and naval rivalries, we thought forever, into
the sparkling shallows of that mountain stream.

As things turned out, though Mr. Hoover played a decisive part in the world crisis that followed, soon neither he
nor the head of any government had much thought to spare
for external problems. The international decade ended with
the crash. By the time the Democrats inherited the wreckage
every nation was cowering in its own storm shelter and in all
languages the motto was the same: "Sauve qui peut," "Ourselves alone," "A moi," "Deutschland ueber alles."

Nevertheless, the Roosevelt administration also began with
a burst of international activity. The new President turned
from the bank crisis to plunge at once into action on the
world front. By then economic cooperation seemed the only
way out of the universal deadlock. Another congress of the
nations was about to meet to discuss limitation of economic
armaments—tariffs, quotas, prices, warring currencies. The
project appealed to no one more than to Mr. Roosevelt. He
practically adopted it, and by inviting to Washington for
preliminary conversations not one but a procession of statesmen he magically revived the dying hope and interest in the
London Economic Conference. For a little while the White
House was again the center of the world.

The rest of the story needs no retelling. Nobody but the
President had much faith in the conference; when he suddenly abandoned it to pursue a plan for domestic recovery

* Secretary of State Henry L. Stimson.

which excluded the idea of stabilization it succumbed as weakly as a German political party at the approach of Hitler. With it went the last vague idea of recovery by international arrangement. The nations returned to their compounds and nationalism became not only the de facto but the de jure policy of all governments.

Just as for the individual victim an endemic plague is a terribly domestic affliction, so for every country its own crisis obscured the world. None but this country, to be sure, could actually shut itself up with its own troubles. For two years we have concentrated on national recovery with an energy and single-mindedness that are the admiration and envy of nations in more crowded neighborhoods. The mind of government and people has been, and still is, absorbed by the strain and excitement of the changes and experiments going on within our own system.

It might easily be argued that up to now the administration has taken only an absent-minded interest in external affairs, has traced no line definite and considered enough to be called a foreign policy. In fact, this article was started with the idea of pointing out that the first phase of the Roosevelt effort, after that abortive gesture of cooperation, was directed solely to the solution of internal problems, but that now the strictly domestic stage is ending and there begins a decided shift of emphasis, away from national self-sufficiency and toward more initiative in the international field.

Up to a point this is true. For various reasons the President is giving more attention than he did to the position of the United States in a world moving toward new alignments and changing the economic and political balance as rapidly as we are reorganizing our system of production and our social structure. Nothing outside stands still while one nation concentrates. The map of the world altered very little during the convulsions of 1934, but when you study the potential results of a single twelvemonth of panic pacts and desperate political bargains you see that nearly every boundary slants in a different direction.

For us denunciation by Japan of the treaty on which American naval strength is based means a reconsideration of the whole complex of sea power. The Pacific problem has assumed an entirely different aspect in the brief term of the Roosevelt administration. Our relationships, East and West have altered with the decision of Japan to play the role of overlord in Asia. In a way we are drawn closer to Europe, just as the nations of Europe are pushed slowly but inexorably toward a common front by the resurgence of the German idea of Mittel-Europa.

President Roosevelt has a feeling for the navy no recent President has shared. When a choice of posts was offered him in the Wilson administration, he chose the assistant secretaryship in the Navy Department because of his boyish passion for ships and because as a young man he thought of the United States as primarily a maritime power, with its first line of defense on the sea. He thinks so still; by taste and impulse he is a big-navy man, and favored above his predecessors the construction of the "Treaty Navy." He has no wish to enter into a ship-building competition with Japan, if only for the reason that the New Deal has newer and more exciting ways of spending public funds than pouring them into armies and navies.

No effort will be spared to avoid it, but the administration is inflexible in its decision not to accept the Japanese idea of equality. The President takes the stand that if we had no coast except the Pacific, though even there the line we have to protect, including Alaska and the Philippines, is incomparably longer and more exposed than Japan's, the proposed ratio might be accepted, since the United States claims no "superiority" over Japan. But this country is also a great Atlantic power, with a seaboard in another hemisphere which makes Tokyo's contention unreasonable and inadmissible.

On the economic side, too, the outlook is subtly changing. The question of surplus in relation to the cognate question of tariffs and export and import quotas was never so clearly stated as it is at the end of the first year of the experiment to reduce crops and control machine hours in order to adjust production to home consumption. In talks last Fall with Western farmers and Southern cotton growers, I was impressed by nothing else so much as by the general interest in the subject of foreign markets. The conversations always drifted back to the same anxious inquiry: What chance is there for revival of world trade? Why can't our government do something about it?

Never before had I seen farmers and small townsfolk so interested in the outside world. The idea of political isolation had not heretofore included the disturbing actuality of a United States reduced to a self-sufficient province. But now the limitations of a strictly domestic economy are painfully apparent to these prime producers. They realize how dearly they have paid for a high-tariff policy that dried up their exports in order to shut out imports of manufactured goods. Experience of limitation has convinced them that while it is necessary as a crisis measure, as a permanent policy it definitely narrows and reduces the standard of living.

This view, strongly urged by Secretary Hull and Secretary Wallace, led the President to obtain authority from Congress to raise or lower tariff duties on his own initiative and to put into effect his pet project of reciprocal trade agreements. The first of these treaties, concluded last Summer with Cuba, works better than he could have anticipated, says Mr. Roosevelt. He expects greater trade benefits from agreements in process of negotiation with six European governments.

Half a dozen more are still in the preliminary stage. The

treaty with Belgium, now nearly ready for signature, has been carefully framed to serve as a kind of ice-breaker, pointing a way out of the Arctic night in which all the currents of European trade are congealed. The only obstacle to the long-awaited commerce with Russia is Soviet reluctance to do business through the Export and Import Bank on terms which Washington thinks the lender has a right to impose on the borrower.

Obviously, a system of controlled or regulated production, in which the government itself buys and sells, leads the administration into a new relationship with other countries. The wider the powers of government the greater are its economic as well as its political responsibilities. The AAA, for instance, is obliged to find outlets for the commodities it stores and on which it has advanced money to the producers.

A planned national economy leads inevitably to new international relations, to something approaching what already exists in fact under dictatorships: State monopolies of foreign trade. Carried to the extreme it would lead to a planned economy for the world—in the present state of things a pretty remote prospect. The paradox of this universal tendency toward centralized control is that it must replace rugged individualism down the line by giving tremendous powers of decision, in affairs both external and internal, to a few individuals.

Beyond these reasons for a changing international outlook, plus the fact that this is a world which nobody living can ignore, are the inclination and temperament of Mr. Roosevelt himself. By taste and habit he is an internationalist and a diplomat. His natural impulse was perfectly represented by his first reaction to the idea of an economic conference of all the nations. He can't believe it is not possible to "talk things out" with responsible statesmen from other countries. Fundamentally he belongs to the school of thought which regards the crisis as a world affair. There is increasing evidence that he is confirmed in that idea as time goes on and he recognizes the definite limits of recovery on a strictly domestic plane.

President Roosevelt is no world crusader, as Wilson was. As a political realist he perceives the psychological obstacles to any simple, common-sense solution of difficulties between nations. Those who have had an opportunity to talk to him on world affairs know how real is his interest, how keen and open-minded his observation. He is curious about other governments, the people who run them, the mentality of nations, especially in Europe, the forces behind movements and events. "I wish I could go, too!" he said to a visitor recently departing for Europe. "I'd like to get the feel of what's happening, take the temperature of two or three other countries and get the perspective of distance and contrast on our own struggle."

Looking back on the Roosevelt administration from the point of view of foreign policy one discovers that while the present tendency is to scan the far horizons a little more diligently than heretofore, in reality the course from the first has tended quietly but surely toward international cooperation. Reviewing the record to confirm an impression—a general impression—that "the domestic phase" is shading into a broader policy, you perceive that events at home have merely overshadowed an activity in foreign affairs that in ordinary times would have been debated as a distinct change in American policy.

During this so-called domestic phase, for instance, the United States has cooperated with the League of Nations in a manner unknown in any previous administration. We have abolished the "unofficial observer" and have used the American Minister to Switzerland, Mr. Wilson, to represent this government on occasions when the interests of the United

States were involved. We have definitely joined an organization closely affiliated with the League, the International Labor Office.

The position of Norman Davis, under Hoover a kind of roving correspondent of the government, interviewing foreign officials and reporting their views, is greatly enhanced under President Roosevelt. Mr. Davis is now a traveling ambassador with full official rank. His incessant labors month after month in negotiations for disarmament are in themselves a proof of the persistence of the administration's efforts to prevent a relapse into the old system of competing war machines.

Two other moves in the same direction, steps toward peace more concrete and practical than the magnificent but vague renunciation of the Kellogg pact, are of even greater significance. One is the completely worked out draft of a treaty for the international control of armaments presented to the disarmament conference by Mr. Wilson in the name of the United States Government. Not only is it the first plan of this kind sponsored by any government; it is a plan dependent on and tied up with the League of Nations. It binds the United States into a world system of arms control and expresses for the first time in official form the willingness of the American Government to accept an active responsibility in the international order.

The second step is the proposal to abandon or modify the traditional doctrine of freedom of the seas for neutrals in time of war. This policy, if adopted, would save America from being drawn into a conflict between other powers, and by removing a serious obstacle to collective action against an aggressor nation would operate as a form of passive cooperation should the League ever invoke the sanction provisions of the covenant. It constitutes a change of front hailed in Europe as one of the most important developments of the post-war period.

These are bold advances in foreign policy. Nor can it be overlooked that Mr. Roosevelt appointed and has retained at the head of the State Department, despite Professor Moley and a considerable barrage of opposition, the one man in the Senate who stood out against the overwhelming pressure of the high-tariff lobbies and who has never wavered from the conviction he upheld at the London conference that the removal of political barriers to the flow of international trade is the basic condition of economic recovery.

To Secretary Hull the tariff is a moral question. Day after day, with a steady and indomitable patience, he works to break down the suffocating barriers which, he warned Congress in 1929, would result in a tariff war, a war of reprisals, sure to wreck the economic structure of the world. Mr. Hull was respected in London; he is increasingly respected at home, and most by his political opponents. The President placed him in the Cabinet because of his tariff views; fundamentally they are the President's own views. The Roosevelt monetary measures have stiffened commercial and social relations with the gold-bloc countries—proof that where you do not buy you cannot sell at any price—but at heart the President remains an old-fashioned Democrat, an economic liberal with a leaning toward free trade.

The foreign policy of Mr. Rooosevelt has not been dramatized like the domestic experiments. Neither at home nor abroad is it fully recognized that under his direction the United States has moved into a new zone and taken a new line in relation to the world. With hardly a murmur of argument, so riveted is the mind of America on the home scene, he has employed his unopposed power to make changes that sum up into a rather astonishing total.

He has recognized Russia. Despite the impasse on naval policy, normal relations with Japan are much more amiable than in the Hoover administration. Replaced by a policy of non-intervention—the "good neighborhood" program which is Mr. Roosevelt's idea of world amity—the old Monroe Doctrine has been unobtrusively shelved. The regimes in Puerto Rico, Haiti and the Virgin Islands have been modified, whether for better or worse remains to be seen. The decisive step has been taken for the independence of the Philippines. Without prejudice to the American claims, the question of war-debt defaults has been handled with so little emphasis that it no longer embitters the international atmosphere.

We have moved; we are still moving. Adherence to the World Court is on the agenda. We have reached a point of cooperation with the League of Nations where formal membership does not much matter and is no longer impossible. At the same time, we are further than ever from foreign alliances. We are taking precautions to avoid drifting into a situation, such as that of 1917, which would lead us into a future war. We are strengthening our defenses by building up fleets of the sea and the air, by plans to construct a new canal in Nicaragua and by a definite project for mobilization of all the material and human resources of the country in case of attack.

The movement, in other words, is in two directions at once, like the Right and Left march toward internal recovery. The broad lines of the Roosevelt foreign policy are now clear and, as in all his policies, they are difficult to characterize because at the same time they are nationalist and internationalist.

The President has taken a wholly independent course in domestic policy, with painful repercussions abroad, while cooperating in all collective efforts for the maintenance of peace. He has gone back further than any of his immediate predecessors to the traditional American moorings in the home waters and also carried many steps forward "the return to the world" inaugurated by Mr. Hoover.

The result is that, while nobody thinks of Mr. Roosevelt as an "internationalist," least of all himself, his policy toward the world is better understood abroad than that of Wilson or Hoover. "In Roosevelt America is neither Messianic nor aloof," remarks a French observer. "Like the rest of us, he is just human, working frankly and selfishly for his own country first, letting the chips fall where they may, but obviously full of good-will toward the world, willing to help where he can."

Mr. Roosevelt's own attitude is that something like that is good world policy. He believes strongly in regional agreements—the "good neighborhood"—as the first step toward economic and political pacification. He thinks the problem of Europe is a regional problem, the creation of economic as distinct from political empires, a gradual enlargement of free-trade areas.

For the United States, his outlook represents something as typically American as are, at base, the push and drive of his experiments; he moves inevitably, but with constant reactions and withdrawals, toward that new position of responsibility the world recognized before the war and which has ever since been worrying, oppressing and fascinating the American people. The world fascinates Mr. Roosevelt. Only a terrific job at home prevents him from doing something spectacular about it. Even as it is, as this brief review suggests, he has gone far to put the United States in a different relation with the world.

[27]   1 9 3 6 *June 21*. STILL "A LITTLE LEFT OF CEN-
TER." *A visitor finds the President holding his
course firmly*.

WASHINGTON

On the eve of his renomination at Philadelphia nobody knows better than the President that there is but one
issue in the coming campaign. That issue, he openly admits,
is Franklin D. Roosevelt. In contrast to the tendency of other
nations either to coagulate into one-party States or curdle up
into innumerable shifting blocs, the two-party system miracu-
lously survives in the United States. But the two parties performing this Summer in the traditional manner are only
shadows of their former selves. The echoing names they bear
are for the most part commemorative.

To recall the normal Republican or the normal Democratic
vote is pure reminiscence, because the norm on which either
is based is gone forever. Even less than four years ago is the
country today divided on the old lines. For the moment—and
the moment is clearly transitional—it is split into New Dealers and anti-New Dealers. Put still more simply, it is divided
for and against Mr. Roosevelt. The New Deal is Roosevelt,
his policies, his agencies, his social philosophy, his personality
and the color of his mind.

Mr. Roosevelt is better known than when he flew to Chicago after his first nomination. He runs as President, and in
all its history the nation has never before been so intimately
acquainted with the voice, the smile, the ideas and the domestic life of a President.

He runs on a record written large across the face of this
continent. Every one reads it because every one is affected
by it. From Maine to California a good part of the population
of every State is dependent as never before on the Federal

Government, and no community, urban or rural, is not in visible and tangible contact with the administration at Washington. He runs in a way, with history, for however we dislike the pace and whether we think the pace-maker goes whirling around in circles, arriving nowhere, or veers right and left in a struggle to hold the course, it is plain that he rides a world-wide storm.

And still the marvel grows that he is so little shaken by the seismic disturbance over which he presides. All the rulers of Europe have shriveled or aged during the past few years. On the faces of Mussolini, Hitler, Stanley Baldwin, even the rotating governors of France, strain and worry have etched indelible lines. Caught off-guard, when they are alone, they are tired and baffled men who have paid a heavy price for power.

The face of the world has changed. You walk familiar streets and they are strange. People everywhere are like houses with the shutters down, withdrawn and waiting, as if life were held in suspense; or they are quarreling within their houses, hating one another because long-drawn-out uncertainty has rasped their nerves to the breaking point.

The United States has changed. To a traveler fresh from the murky atmosphere of Europe, the American air seems light and clear, but things and thoughts that were vague a year ago begin to crystallize. What was in dispute is taken for granted and what was taken for granted is in dispute. The political vocabulary is oddly different. We are not yet ready for great questions, but everybody seems uneasily conscious that the answers are catching up with us, and that in another four years we may face a division on principles as fundamental as the issues of the Civil War.

Washington is changed. It is not merely that the weight of government represented by the monumental offices begun in the Hoover administration keeps spreading far beyond the Triangle, or that a Congress lacking a vigorous opposition seems staler than usual. Washington is increasingly a political city, where life merely echoes, as in Geneva, but the echoes and the accent are new. Social service is mixed with civil service, to the dilution of both. More than the weather wears down the early excitement of the experts and young idealists who flocked in the wake of the New Deal: the infusion of fresh blood stimulates the old bureaus, but all bureaus in time tend to calm the pulse and temper the enthusiasm of the most ardent.

In this universal flux only the President remains unchanged. On none of his predecessors has the office left so few marks as on Mr. Roosevelt. He is a little heavier, a shade grayer; otherwise he looks harder and in better health than on the day of his inauguration. His face is so tanned that his eyes appear lighter, a cool Wedgwood blue; after the four grilling years since the last campaign they are as keen, curious, friendly and impenetrable as ever.

As he sits in the cool of the evening on the back porch of the White House, sipping iced tea and munching jam sandwiches, a pair of Irish setters at his feet, Mr. Roosevelt is a unique figure in the modern world: the one statesman this writer has seen who seems able to relax.

Even the visitor relaxes, listening to the easy voice and gazing across the quiet green lawns to the white shaft of the Washington Monument springing out of the trees like a child's dream of the North Pole, telling direction as a clock tells time. The President likes to talk and he likes to listen. He talks well, not so much in terms of ideas as of concrete cases. Collectivist he may be, but he reduces all general problems to individual instances, the experience of this banker, that manufacturer, one homesteader, a particular relief worker. He sounds rather like the head case-worker in a tremendous social service organization.

Little as he has changed physically, unless for the better,

one suspects that President Roosevelt has changed even less in his mind and temper, and least of all in the direction which he follows and means to follow. Some of his supporters say that he is naturally a conservative, heir of the most conservative American tradition, and that in his second term he will feel free to be himself, a moderate liberal with humanitarian impulses. Others believe he will interpret re-election as a mandate to revise the Constitution and push through a program more frankly radical than he has so far dared to propose.

Mr. Roosevelt himself holds that he has not deviated by a hair's breadth from the course he set in his inauguration speech. In his own view he is still "a little left of center," and he declares categorically that he intends to follow exactly the same direction in the next four years. To go straight center is to stand still, he explains, and stand-still agreements are only for financial and political bankrupts. To go right of center is to go back; to go left of center is to make progress. "Right" and "Left" he considers convenient omnibus words for hurried journalists, and the fact that Socialists and stand-patters alike repudiate the New Deal seems to him convincing proof that he has hewed pretty close to the line which just leans away from the middle.

Unless all the political prophets are wrong, the President is as sure of re-election as he thinks he is. There is a strong probability that he will have four years more to develop, revise or discard the experiments, reforms and projects embodied in the New Deal legislative program. He has every chance of retaining a position regarded enviously by all European politicians—including the dictators—as the most important and powerful in the world.

Mr. Roosevelt has made it more powerful; he has extended the powers of the Presidency—and thereby bumped into the Supreme Court. The distinguishing feature of his administration is that instead of the usual struggle between the Executive and the Congress, the only real contest has been between the Executive and the judiciary.

Even with the restraints of the court, however, the Presidential prerogatives are enormous, and this President exercises them to the limit. Re-elected, he will certainly continue to dominate. Behind the good humor and ingratiating manner of the "gay reformer" works a persistent will. It is easy enough to argue with Mr. Roosevelt, very difficult to deflect him from his purpose.

Of supreme interest to Americans, therefore, is the knowledge of what this purpose is. Nothing is more important, in a campaign that turns on him, his record and his intentions, than to find out what he thinks of the progress of the New Deal up to this point, how he interprets the effects of the Supreme Court decisions nullifying his key policies, which parts of the crisis program he formulated seem to him essential reforms, to be pursued further, and which are temporary measures, to be dropped. This article, based on recent conversations with the President, attempts to reflect his own views and the bent of his mind.

Now it should be said at once that Mr. Roosevelt has neither the mind nor the temperament of a revolutionary. He is not even a crusader; he doesn't burn up or tilt at windmills. He is a practical politician, the best in either party, who will go as far as he can with popular support on the path most congenial to him, which is the path of experiment and reform. He believes that democratic governments as well as dictators have to propose and carry through policies of action, that "new things" are necessary to keep people behind governments instead of against them. Mr. Roosevelt is not a leader to go farther than he is followed—farther, he would say, than he is pushed by the forces and events of the time. His significance is that his ideas and innovations have so far found mass support.

The President's attitude toward the Constitution is indicated by the extreme reluctance of the Democrats to make constitutional amendment or revision an issue of the campaign. Most of the changes in the historic charter, they point out, have been made by Republicans. Mr. Roosevelt is "for the Constitution" as strongly as the preacher in the famous Coolidge story was "agin sin." He would never admit, as Walter Lippmann charges, that he cannot act because his personal philosophy of government is irreconcilable with the charter under which he must act.

His philosophy as he expresses it sounds very simple: he wants to correct abuses which have developed against the spirit of the Constitution and so to revamp the machinery of government that the Federal authority can do what the several States cannot or will not do. He does not believe that the Constitution contemplated what he describes as a "twilight zone," an ungovernable "no man's land" where no authority has power to deal with things like working hours, wage standards, labor conditions, flood control, soil erosion.

A solution based on regional agreements among contiguous States Mr. Roosevelt dismisses a "fine editorial-office idea," unworkable elsewhere. He recalls that when he was Governor of New York he tried to put through an old-age pension scheme which called for contributions from employers, employees and the State. The New York Manufacturers Association objected on the ground that the passage of the law would mean the flight of many factories to New Jersey. Governor Roosevelt then tried to induce the Governor of New Jersey to cooperate by passing an identical law. "I couldn't," was the reply, "because New Jersey wants to profit by the exodus of manufacturers from New York."

Obviously, the fight on the New Deal will center on the questions it raises touching the powers of the Federal Government. In fact, the battle is already on for the conquest of Mr. Roosevelt's "twilight zone." Senator Borah says that one line runs straight as a pointing arrow in the confusion of New Deal policies. The President's cardinal aim, as Mr. Borah sees it, is to break down State lines and unify the country under a powerful central government, thus transforming a republic organized as a federation of forty-eight sovereign Commonwealths into something entirely different.

Mr. Roosevelt's answer is that not he but the development of industry, transportation and communication has changed the relations of the States. In his view the questions pressing for definition today rise not from the Constitution but from the 1936 construction of the Constitution.

Whatever he feels privately, publicly he is philosophic in discussing the series of Supreme Court decisions which in a few months reduced to ruin all but a wing or two of the spreading structure of the New Deal. He notes that the court divides, reverses and overrules itself, and in its latest rulings, particularly the last, serves to focus public attention on the necessity of placing a modern construction on certain points of fundamental law. The American system is designed to slow up the process of change, he discovers; under this system it takes at least ten years for a necessary reform to be proposed, accepted and enacted.

So the architect, with a characteristic shrug, surveys the wreckage of his plans. It would be a fatal mistake, however, to imagine that he means to stop there. By next January, when Congress reassembles, he will certainly have evolved another set of specifications whereby the edifice can be rebuilt. Supreme Court justices are long-lived but they do not live forever. Mr. Roosevelt refrains from mentioning that. What he does imply is that if the country decides that certain regulatory powers over all the States must be conferred on the Federal Government, a way will be found to implement this desire within the framework of the Constitution.

To the Roosevelt mind Federal regulation in some form is inescapable. Two manufacturers from the Middle West visited the President a few days ago. The conversation, as reported afterward by one of them, was interesting because it touched upon most of the subjects now engaging the attention of business men. The manufacturers suggested a more rapid curtailment of Federal relief. They broke down the unemployment figures, estimating that if from the total were subtracted part-time and seasonal workers, like substitute teachers, clerks working in rush seasons for extra spending money, carpenters, farm hands, people who never work all the time plus unemployables, the actual number of unemployed would be nearer 4,000,000 than 12,000,000.

"Can industry absorb these 4,000,000?" asked the President.

The manufacturers thought that given a fair break industry could add one worker to every ten now employed by shortening the work week to forty hours at forty-eight or forty-four hours' pay. Asked if all employers would do this, they replied that 75 to 85 per cent could be counted on to cooperate. Asked further if each industry could force the recalcitrant minority into line, the answer was that so far industry had been unable to police itself. The rules could be enforced only by government.

But what government? the President was quick to inquire. If industry cannot regulate itself, if the States cannot do it outside their own borders and the Supreme Court rules that Washington has no power to do it, then nobody can do it. It can't be done!

All this leads back to the Blue Eagle and the vanished codes of NRA. NRA is the core of the New Deal. From the

President's public and private utterances, it is fair to assume that the one project on which the ruling of the Supreme Court was unanimous is the experiment he values most.

He is proudest of the CCC camps and vast regional development in the Tennessee Valley. "Go South!" he said to a recent visitor. "There you will see best what we have done and what we are trying to do." Undoubtedly he believes that if his administration has done nothing else, the Federal activities in the South—TVA, the resettlement schemes, the large-scale relief work—have operated to jack up the backward States below the Potomac to a point nearer the level of the rest of the country.

The agricultural problem can be solved, he is convinced, by the substitute measures that followed the abrogation of the AAA. As far as surpluses are concerned, indeed, the administration regards the problem as already very close to solution. Helped by drought, by reciprocal trade agreements which have increased agricultural exports to certain countries by 15 per cent, the program of curtailment, it is claimed, have brought within reasonable bounds those drastic fluctuations in the prices of basic commodities—cotton, copper, wheat, &c.—which upset the whole rural economy and made farming as speculative a business as stock gambling.

But nothing takes the place of NRA. There is little doubt that regulation of industry in some form remains one of the President's chief objectives. The outlawed codes may not be revived, the means to the end may be changed, but one safe prediction is that some method will be devised to accomplish the same result. Since it is clear that as many Republicans as Democrats favor an amendment to the Constitution, it requires no political courage to advocate an extension of government to the undefined borderland between the States and the nation. But the President wants more than that. He wants nation-wide standards that only a central government can enforce.

Thus he is bound to come back to some variation of the original plan. Does this mean moving in the direction of the corporate State? Is not State control of private industry essentially a Fascist idea? The President's reply to these questions is that regulation of standards does not imply either interference with the management of business or doing anything by Federal law that either a State or an industry is able to do for itself.

He has repeatedly declared, moreover, that control of relief should be permanently vested in the Federal Government. Now the administration of relief, its cost and abuses, will certainly be the grass-roots issue of this campaign. Mr. Roosevelt is fully aware of this; nevertheless he argues that there is "less politics" in relief funds administered from Washington and that many localities would get no relief at all if the Federal authorities did not assume responsibility. He is strongly against returning to the old system. There is little hope in his attitude for those who demand decentralization of relief control.

The relief projects most criticized were those chosen by local bodies, he points out, and while he admits that a certain amount of waste, inefficiency and red tape are almost inseparable from democratic procedure, "which can never be as efficient as the police rule of a dictator," he boasts that billions have been spent with the minimum amount of graft.

These are very debatable questions. We shall hear them argued ad nauseam from now until November. How many local administrations themselves graft on the Federal Government? How many use relief funds for political purposes? Where is the boundary line beyond which government regulation becomes something else?

Looking back and forward from this milestone where the race begins again, Mr. Roosevelt says he has learned by experience. "We all have," he adds. If he were doing it again, he would not include so much in great experiments in managed economy, like the NRA and the AAA. Such mistakes as he recognizes in retrospect, he attributes to the effort to make fundamental readjustments too hastily to meet an emergency, and also to the slow pace at which emergency projects could be put in operation. In other words, the New Deal was an authoritarian program executed by democratic methods, and thus demonstrates the worst aspects of both systems.

On the whole one gathers that the President recognizes few mistakes. He looks back with more satisfaction than regret. Perhaps he sees that Washington was not prepared for the expansion of government he decreed and that the administration of his program failed to do justice to an ideal which calls for a highly trained body of civil servants. Perhaps he rests on those large margins for mistakes and experiments which this country still possesses, almost alone in the world. Certainly he regards himself as the captain of a craft which is shooting the rapids. If he manoeuvres the boat safely to the next level, the rocking in the shoals will be forgotten. The one thing he is sure of, that everybody is sure of, even the carpenters of the Republican platform, is that there is no going back.

The historic role of President Roosevelt is to shape and dramatize a transition which nothing now can stop. Before the campaign is fairly started, it is evident that the contest is not over the New Deal. The opposition has practically adopted the whole Roosevelt program. The only question is by whom and how the New Deal is to be administered. It all comes back to the fact that the single issue is Franklin D. Roosevelt and his infuriating or fascinating smile.

[28]   1 9 3 7   *January 17*. As Mr. Roosevelt Sees His
Role. *He conceives of a leadership that may stand
as a rallying point for world democracy.*

Washington

President Roosevelt enters upon another term of office
as the most influential, if not the most powerful, figure in the
world. The distinction is his own. He is not the man to underestimate the eminence he occupies, nationally or internation-
ally. He knows that the prestige of the head of the American
Government and his personal ascendancy were never higher
than at the moment of his second inaugural. But he is quick
to point the contrast between the possible reaches of the sov-
ereignty of the Chief Magistrate of the United States, when
extended to the utmost by extraordinary grants of authority
in domestic emergency or foreign policy, and the absolute
and instant decisions that can be taken where one man expresses the will of the State.

The difference between dictatorial power and moral predominance is vital to Mr. Roosevelt's conception of his role in
the world. This conception was strengthened by his campaign trips through the States of the Union. It was amplified
by his reception in South America. Simply stated, it is that
leadership is possible in a democracy; more, that a leader
chosen by overwhelming popular vote in a free election may
stand as a symbol and rallying point of democracy. It implies
that the democratic idea can be personified in the same way
as opposing ideas are incarnate in the person of Stalin, Hitler
or Mussolini.

When the President rode through the crowded streets of
Rio and Buenos Aires there were only scattered shouts of
"Viva Roosevelt!" The cry that greeted him over and over
again was "Viva Democracia!" This greeting made a deep im-

pression. It stirred his imagination, struck a bell already ringing faintly in his own mind. In a way it may be said to underline a change of emphasis, subtle but significant, that marks the passage from one administration to the next.

Four years ago, and most of the time since, the Roosevelt program has stressed two things: recovery and reform. Now his chief concern is with other questions. In a conversation on the eve of the inauguration the President's talk was all of peace and the vindication and strengthening of democratic government. His general aims remain the same. His mind is the same.

At every meeting, whatever the circumstances, what strikes you most is that he is always the same Roosevelt; it would be difficult to find a man who changes less, in manner or substance. But the accent has definitely shifted. There is a difference in the interpretation he puts on his policies. It is as if, looking back, he perceives something not clear at the time; he sees that the crisis he has administered was more than economic; it was really a breakdown of the democratic system.

The memory reverts to the gray morning in 1933 when Mr. Roosevelt first moved slowly up the incline to the stand on the steps of the Capitol. Under the gloomy sky and the gloomy gaze of the Washington crowds he appeared as a sign of hope and change. But he was also an unknown quantity. The promise of a New Deal was not very reassuring to a people stunned by the collapse of a New Era. The worried spectators watched the parade with thoughts elsewhere, wondering what lay beyond an inaugural accompanied by the thunderclap of closing banks and shaken citadels: the falling walls of Babylon.

Today an older and more experienced man mounts the white-pillared, glass-enclosed platform, grandest grandstand ever provided for the historic ceremony. There is no outgoing President, so this time he takes the spotlight alone. The only comparison he faces is with himself, and never since has he looked so much as he did four years ago. His bronzed face is firm again, his figure trimmed down by nine pounds since November. Far from wearing on his physique or his spirit, the burden of the Presidency seems to have acted as a stimulant to buoy him up.

He has altered little, but the atmosphere of the capital is completely reconditioned. The first inauguration to take place in January might have been planned as a climax to the holiday season. Lighted Christmas trees made way for banners and bunting with the festive effect of a continuing holiday. The White House itself is never gayer than at this season, when candles and banks of red poinsettia glow in the crimson-carpeted corridors and children run up and down between the sparkling little trees set on the stairs. It is easy to imagine that this house, in love with ease and familiar order like all old mansions, is rejoicing not to be stripped and turned over to strange tenants. So certainly are more transient institutions, especially new boards and bureaus and officeholders, saved by an incomparable vote getter from having to pack up and move away.

This is part of the general cheerfulness. But its sources go deeper. Washington naturally reflects the heightened optimism of the nation; even more, I think, it reflects the optimism of the President, and his feeling that the capital is more representative of the country than it used to be, is, at last, indeed, the center of the most important goings-on. Mr. Roosevelt is no longer an unknown quantity. He has been a very public President and the unflagging zest of his performance has invested the office with a drama that attracts and constantly whets the interest of the audience.

There is no doubt that not only the influence but the actual power of the Presidency has been increased and extended during his administration. One guesses that it would be even further if he had his way. He relishes leadership. He enjoys the used and usufruct of the authority residing in the position of head of the American Government, and he is not in the least oppressed by the unwieldy size of the majority he now commands. He believes that government must be more regulatory rather than less, therefore more authoritative; he is convinced that power over labor, industry and social welfare must be increasingly centralized under Federal rule.

It is hardly too much to say that he is working out in practice his idea of what the Presidency should be and do. The idea is still in process of development, like the structure of democracy itself under the social pressures of the Power Age. If Mr. Roosevelt followed his own bent, it is quite likely that in law as well as fact the Executive chosen by a clear majority would be given a pretty free hand in carrying out his program. He would have something of the status of a national manager, checked, of course by the legislative and judicial branches of the government.

The Constitution does not define either the extent or limits of the duties of the Executive. It says simply that "the executive power shall be vested in a President of the United States." The President has full authority to organize the executive departments as he pleases; he can have a Cabinet of two or a dozen members, or no Cabinet at all. The Federal departments he is free to multiply, merge or abolish at will. He has the broadest scope in the administrative field and almost equal power to initiate legislation.

Mr. Roosevelt is not inclined to minimize this warrant of authority. Having asked a blanket permission from Congress, he allows himself the widest latitude in his plans for the reorganization of the government. As to policies, especially the great policy of experimentation on which all the rest hinges, in Mr. Roosevelt's view, an election represents a popular mandate to follow a certain course; the next election supplies the popular referendum on whether the course is satisfactory and shall be continued.

Now, it is a curious fact that there is little talk nowadays of the Roosevelt dictatorship. The President boasts of the power he has recovered for the government, and nobody denies it; even the directors of the Federal Reserve Bank of New York, whose financial dominance was once supreme, now admit that the financial capital is moved to Washington. There is every reason to suppose that the present Congress will be more of a rubber stamp than its predecessor. Mr. Roosevelt has a backing that would permit him to go as far as he wishes, anywhere. Yet the dictator bogey has all but disappeared from the public mind. He owes that partly to the Supreme Court. A good many citizens scoff at the "nine old men" and disapprove heartily of their divided judgment, but at least they have proved that no President can be the whole government. Mostly, however, the charge fades out because nobody seriously believes in it.

In the past three years the world has observed dictators at work. We all know pretty well how they operate as governments and how they behave as human beings. Mussolini runs the whole show in Italy and does it extraordinarly well. Hitler is the whole show in Germany; he makes the big decisions but the business of government he leaves to others. Stalin is not a show piece at all; he acts behind the scenes to control the party which controls Russia, as completely under the new Constitution as under the old.

They all act alone, and of the millions who have to obey their orders none knows why they act, who advises them, where they are going. They make their own rules, change them when inconvenient, interpret all laws to suit their own improvised notions. You cannot say they act like God or the force of nature, because God leaves men free choice and natural forces follow a certain logic. There is no limit to their police power and no term to their tenure of office. They clamp the lid on a whole population and then issue warnings that it will explode unless somebody else provides an outlet.

This could not describe any possible President of the United States. The President cannot overstep the constitutional bounds very far without being caught up, by Congress, by the courts, by the press, by the people. The Constitution cannot be revised without a vote of the States, and Mr. Roosevelt is so little desirous of raising that issue that he proposes instead to revise the methods whereby he hopes to accomplish the reforms that were thrown out as unconstitutional. On sober second thought, it is doubted whether he would abridge, if he could, the powers of the Supreme Court. All he asks of that body, he says, is that it should be reasonably contemporary. He holds that the court should live and think in the same decade as the other branches of the government—and that is a condition any President can help realize by the exercise of appointive power.

Mr. Roosevelt has not in any case the temperament of a dictator. He has no taste for playing lone hands. The characteristic common to the supermen presiding over the destinies of nations is that they are never "mixers," and the President is probably the best living practitioner of the art of being friends with all the world. He would hate to sit in lonely grandeur in a room the size of a railway station, like Mussolini in his marble hall in the Palazzo Venezia, or retire for weeks at a time to solitary cogitations on a mountain top, like Hitler at Berchtesgaden, or live secluded within the guarded fortress of the Kremlin, like Stalin. All day long the President confers with people. He loves to talk. He could not hold the pose of the man in whose presence all other men are subordinate; he has a pretty shrewd idea of what the American crowd would do to that pose!

A Congress 80 per cent Democratic may be only a chorus for the President, but if it were not he would still invite the leaders, the committee chairmen or odd groups of the rank and file into his study in the evenings and there they would sit smoking and swapping jokes and discussing this bill or that. A one-party Congress is rather more difficult to deal with than a session with a respectable opposition, because it is outside attack that unites and stiffens the defense. "But we talk things over," says Mr. Roosevelt. "We get together."

Beyond all that—and this is the important point—the President has not the will to be a dictator. Certainly not now, when he sees himself as the symbol of democratic leadership. That notion of the part he is cast to play in the world grows on him as he perceives that the democratic idea is once more in the ascendant after a period of doubt and disillusion. In Buenos Aires he inquired why the crowds shouted "Long live democracy!" as he passed. He was told that the Argentine and various other republics to the south had experienced a crisis of the same order as that of the United States. They had gone through their period of "Hooverism" in the attempt to solve their problems by conventional methods. They had tried temporary dictatorships. They saw in the Roosevelt landslide a proof that he had broadened the basis of popular rule, restored government of, by and especially for the people.

So they hailed Mr. Roosevelt as a sign. In their various stages of political development, and no one imagines that the omnibus term does not cover widely different degrees and many counterfeits of democracy, the peoples of South America interpreted the triumph of the New Deal as a triumph of popular government. Instinctively they felt that the New Dealer was a figure to set against the eye-filling images of triumphant autocrats. Here at last—and in person—was a leader representing the Supreme People in contrast to that subjugating and sublimating monster, the Supreme State. It was almost as if the crowds in nations newer than ours, half-literate, not fully enfranchised, accustomed to changes of administration by coup d'état, as well as by ballot, beheld what they wanted personified: a ruler chosen by the people with power enough to make democracy work.

As a matter of fact, supposing that ideas must be personified, there is no comparable figure to stand as symbol or rallying point for the idea of democracy. Democratic States are still numerous in the world. In Europe a majority of the small nations cling to representative government. The Western Hemisphere is pretty solidly democratic, in name and form, if not invariably in practice. But of the three leading democratic powers, the oldest and strongest parliamentary governments, Great Britain, is presided over by a monarch, actually a figurehead but a symbol dwarfing the political figures, particularly those now charged with the direction of British policies; France creaks along under a chief of state ruling in the name of a Popular Front whose unity is so precarious that the Blum leadership expresses more skill than power. Certainly neither Blum nor Baldwin kindles the imagination as Roosevelt does or has anything like the same national backing.

When the American majority re-elected the President they elected the only available candidate to lead the Democratic Party of the World. Perhaps this is Mr. Roosevelt's chief significance in this hour when the wars of principalities and powers are translated into wars of ideas. More and more, one surmises, it expresses his significance to himself.

Wilson's idea of making the world safe for democracy is not Roosevelt's; his sensitiveness to the currents of opinion in this country renders him as chary as any Midwesterner of the most tenuous commitments abroad. But the persuasion grows in his mind that as the greatest and most independent democracy the United States stands as an example of a truth that must be spectacularly demonstrated. The first responsibility of such a democracy is to prove that the representative system works, that it is applicable and adjustable as conditions change, that as government it is not only more satisfactory to the governed—even dictators do not question that—but can be made as efficient and decisive as one-man rule.

He believes this truth is in process of demonstration. If he tends to strengthen the executive by holding on to emergency powers, if he seizes on an incident like the sale of airplanes and war equipment to Spain to advertise the need of giving the President broad discretion to act quickly, it is because he thinks that without power of initiative the representative system deteriorates, as it did in Italy before Fascism, or weakens, as it did in France before Blum.

Mr. Roosevelt interprets what he has done so far as a restoration of government to the people. The job is far from completed; in his second term he will undoubtedly try different methods to attain the same objectives he worked for in his first. He will not be satisfied until by some means he enforces certain minimum standards of life and labor on the whole country, though he admits that the same scale of working hours cannot be applied to all localities and industries, to unskilled labor, for instance, of which there is an almost irreducible surplus, and to trades that suffer from a shortage of labor. He will not rest until a way is found to regulate production.

He begins to see, in short, that the task this country is engaged in is creative. Slowly, vaguely, in the vast melting pot of races, theories and dreams, we are working out a synthesis

—some endurable and viable blend of freedom, authority and justice that will make man whole again, not a mutilated creature torn Right and Left and marching nowhere but to war.

Having "re-established democracy" at home, what is the responsibility to the world of a leader who symbolizes the democratic idea? Certainly the call of the world echoes in Mr. Roosevelt's consciousness. In his position, no man with imagination can help being haunted by thoughts of what could and should be done to ease the tension and terror that rests on all the nations like an evil spell. He is attracted by the idea that the democratic peoples in cooperation might make a demonstration of moral force as overwhelming as military force. He is under no illusions as to the power of moral suasion versus force, or as to the possibility of peace without changing conditions that make peace impossible. He thinks that to avoid war the bases of the international order have to be broadened in much the same fashion as the bases of the national order have to be democratized to avoid revolution. It is clear to him that nations pinched by the status quo have not the same incentive to maintain it as the nations that benefit by leaving things as they are.

The satisfied have to pay a price for peace. To a mind like Mr. Roosevelt's nothing is impossible. He will not believe that the human brain has not the capacity to solve the problems it has created or that nations are so sunk in selfishness that they will commit suicide. His imagination still plays with the idea of a meeting of the rulers of the world. He will not use the word conference; he knows an international conference would get nowhere. What he reverts to—not as a plan but as a fascinating fancy—is a private exchange of views by the heads of five governments, five men with such power that if they could be brought to agree on anything their agreement could prevent war.

· · ·

In playing with this idea, more in whimsy than in seriousness—but the whimsy sticks!—the President has been caught,
in relaxed moments, developing details. Before they began to
talk, the Big Five would have to renounce all territorial ambitions. This done, the ground would be cleared for a discussion of how the needs of the Have-Nots could be satisfied by
other means than force. At some point they would have to devise an international currency to solve the transfer problem,
a problem nobody has really tackled. The possibility of pool-
ing surpluses of raw materials would have to be explored,
also a practical system for the export of surplus man power.
A dozen other vital problems take precedence over disarmament, on the theory that nations will not disarm except for
two reasons: either they know they cannot win by fighting or
they see an alternative way to obtain the things for which
they prepare to fight.

The idea sounds like the first rough sketch for a planned
world economy at a time when a planned national economy
has not gone beyond the primer stage. The trouble with it is
not that it is mad, but that it is not mad enough. The ruling
minds, saner, prefer the more conventional councils of war.
And since the mind that toys with the notion of a meeting of
at least two dictators, Hitler and Mussolini, with the representatives of the three great democracies, is primarily the
mind of a cool, practical and intuitive politician, there is only
a remote danger that the fantasy of the imagination will become a reality or that men who share the responsibility for
the fate of civilization will come together to negotiate a pre-
ventive peace.

The remote possibility lies only in the fact that we live in
an age of symbols and strange gods: a world of the impossible. Throughout this world, as he renews his oath as President of the United States, Mr. Roosevelt is acclaimed as the
symbol of the freedom to which men turn back with a home-

sickness as strong as love or hate. The difference between the
President of 1933 and the President of 1937 is that his paramount purpose today is to "make democracy succeed."

[29] 1 9 3 7 *August 15*. AN UNCHANGING ROOSEVELT
DRIVES ON. *In spite of criticism and party dissen-
sion, the President holds firmly to his course.*

WASHINGTON
Among the china pigs and wooden donkeys his friends
contribute to the collection parading on the President's desk
to add to the gayety of the executive office, stands one lonely
elephant. It is a very small elephant made of white flannel,
the ears flopping and the wobbly underpinning inclining him
to list.

"He used to be bigger," Mr. Roosevelt explains. " I remember him when he was quite a fellow. That was before we
washed him. Every time the elephant is washed," he adds
with a grin, "he shrinks."

The quip had a certain bearing on the topic under discussion, though the splits and shrinkages we were referring to
were under the sign of the donkey instead of the elephant.
The President admits a cleavage in the Democratic party.
He remarked it in the Chicago convention of 1932, he says,
when he was nominated. It reappeared in 1935 in the Liberty
League. From the beginning of the New Deal the party has
been sloughing off members with conspicuous names. In Mr.
Roosevelt's view the cleavage is always on the same lines,
reflecting the same classic conflict of interests and ideas.

It is thus that he interprets the angry split in the Democratic ranks on the Supreme Court issue. After the signal

Congressional defeat of his enlargement plan,* he is as stubbornly convinced as he was throughout the long debate that a popular poll would prove that the people back him on this issue by as big a majority as he received last November. This is the report of his political scouts in the Middle West, the South and the Southwest. If the President revives the argument in a fireside talk after Congress adjourns, it will be because, regardless of the Senate vote, the press, the legal profession and other vocal opposition, he continues to believe that public sentiment supports his objectives and is not much concerned about the methods adopted to realize them.

As Mr. Roosevelt cheerfully discusses the first major legislative battle he has lost, the listener cannot doubt that in his mind it figures as just another round in the familiar struggle of conservative against liberal, economic royalists against the masses of the people. Not all the opposition is attributed to interested motives: some of it is ascribed to unwillingness or incapacity to keep up with the pace of change. But the people understand clearly what is involved, the President is sure. He now concludes that the controversy was useful in focusing public attention on a branch of government hitherto remote and unreal to the ordinary citizen. "At least I have introduced the Supreme Court to the country," he smiles. "After this judicial decisions will be everybody's business."

Nor can it be doubted that the President means to press on toward "liberalization" of the court. He refers to the end of one round as a setback, not a defeat, and although the road ahead may seem longer and rougher than he once foresaw, apparently he has no thought of stopping or turning back. Questions concerning a third term he either laughs off or answers by reiterating such phrases as "when I return to

* This was President Franklin D. Roosevelt's famous "court packing plan," which was defeated by Democrats and Republicans, led by Hatton Sumners of Texas, who was Chairman of the House Judiciary Committee.

Hyde Park in 1941" or "when my successor is named three years hence." At the same time he intimates that he has no intention of retiring from politics or public service when he leaves the White House. "I'll still be around, fighting," he declares. "And as a Democrat."

This is Mr. Roosevelt's comment on the talk of a permanent schism in the Democratic party, a realignment of parties or a new party under his leadership. He scoffs at all three predictions. As he sees it, the reforms initiated by the New Deal do tend to sharpen the division between liberals and conservatives. They emphasize an evolution going on within the party itself. But in his forecast of the future the Republican party continues to represent the conservative and the Democratic the liberal point of view, as in the past.

The important difference is that as the definition of liberalism broadens to fit social and economic change, the Democratic party, because it marches with history, is inevitably transformed into the majority party. This is the President's interpretation of what is happening now. The party defections the process entails he finds small by comparison with the new adherents it attracts. As for the division growing out of the court fight, he believes that it will not only be healed but as quickly forgotten as the Liberty League or the movement headed by Father Coughlin.

If anyone imagines that the reverse he has suffered dashes the spirits or shakes the poise of Mr. Roosevelt, a half hour's conversation with him is sufficient to dispel the notion. If he reels from the blow to his prestige or is eaten by disappointment over the failure of his plan, he conceals his feelings remarkably well.

He is able to poke fun at his opponents and philosophize over the quirks and mixed motives of politics. He is able to shift ground so easily that the rejuvenation of the highest tribunal is made to appear incidental to the reform of the entire judicial system, merely the apex of a pyramid in need of repair from the ground up. Before you know it you are contemplating the speed and efficiency of English legal procedure and administration of justice, persuaded that the Administration intervenes to renovate the judiciary only because American bench and bar have been singularly remiss in correcting abuses or backing elementary reforms in their own field.

The writer has talked twice with the President in recent weeks, at the climax of the court battle and after it was lost. Both times his temper and attitude were exactly the same. Despite the physical and the political heat of Washington, he looked cool, comfortable and fit, the smile as wide and instant as ever, the bright surface as undented. The first visit was on the day the House passed the Farm Loan Bill over his veto. As he announced the news my mind went back to an interview with his predecessor under similar circumstances, after the Senate had overridden an Executive veto. Mr. Hoover was curiously disappointed, and showed it. Mr. Roosevelt took it casually, even gayly.

Whether this good humor includes magnanimity toward the deserters in the ranks is another question, just now disturbing a good many Democrats in Congress. For it is evident that the President feels himself unweakened as head of his party. He knows and they know that as a national leader he has no visible runner-up. When he predicts that certain opposition Senators will not return to the Senate, it is from conviction that the voters do not approve their course.

It all comes back to his complete confidence that the man in the street is on his side, unmoved by the arguments of the opposition. After four and a half years of his Administration, business is better in town and country, the specter of starvation has been banished for the poorest, and the American system remains intact. In the Roosevelt logic, that's the answer. He has not the slightest doubt that the people trust his voice above all contrary voices.

It all comes back, that is to say, to the character and personality of the President himself. Of all the leaders of his time, he is perhaps the least variable. Physically he ages remarkably little. His hair is thinner, his face and figure thicker, the shadows more deeply etched around his eyes. The characteristic expression, the backward jerk of his head when he laughs, the laugh itself, are the same.

Mentally and temperamentally, the changes are even less apparent. After observing the moods of the heads of other governments shifting up and down according to the play of circumstance and political fortune, one concludes that Mr. Roosevelt is either a man of a single mood or that he holds the pose better than the others. It isn't simply a matter of manner and gesture, the public man strutting his stuff. In that fluent mind is a fixed bent, a changeless color.

This reporter first talked to the President in the early Spring of 1932, when as a candidate he was just beginning to think presidentially. Then he discussed the reforms he thought the country needed and the measures he intended to take to realize them. Last week he talked of precisely the same reforms, in nearly identical terms. Some he believes accomplished. Others the court decisions have nullified, so that it is necessary to begin over again. Others remain in the realm of plan, project and hope.

But the basic ideas remain unchanged. The extraordinary thing about Mr. Roosevelt is the consistency with which under all conditions he remains himself. He is attracted by novelties, receptive to any interesting suggestion, careless in the use of instruments and methods to further his purposes. His objectives do not alter. With a deceptive effect of darting in all directions, his mind revolves around fixed points. He likes short cuts, and this explains his bids for special powers, as in the bill to enlarge the Supreme Court. He likes visual demonstrations, samples here and now of the better world he aims at building. Such are the resettlement experiments, the TVA. He is a man in a hurry, who holds that progress in this country is made in spurts, followed by periods of reaction and inertia. This is his spurt, the historic chance to master a transition and bridge in a decade the dangerous gap between two epochs.

Add to this a monumental self-confidence and a tendency to oversimplify the complex which makes problems appear easier to work out than they ever are in real life. Add the habit of mind in which "Let's try it!" is not just a slogan for the depression. What it adds up to is obvious: for better or worse Mr. Roosevelt is what he was, neither more radical nor more conservative than when he entered the White House.

Here lies the answer to many questions. In essentials the President has not altered his course since the beginning of his Administration. There is little possibility that he will change his mind, his temperament or his general objectives during the remainder of his term. If anything makes that clear it is the legislation he has been trying to push through in the last weeks of Congress.

The Wages-and-Hours Bill is a revival in limited but in some respects more absolute form of the basic codes of the NRA. The Government Reorganization Bill was planned in the early days of the Administration. Government-aided housing is an important item in the original program. He is determined to regulate farm surpluses and thus restore AAA, and convinced that this year's experience of unregulated production will cause the farmers to come begging for a resumption of crop control.

The last thing he desires, nevertheless, is to revive the emergency measures in their original form. Experience showed up the weak spots in the early New Deal legislation.

The President freely admits that in the trial-and-error method the margin of error was so great that he is now much better equipped to tackle the same problems. In reviewing the record, his faith in the necessity of Federal regulation is confirmed, but he sees that the tendency of the NRA to create monopoly must be checked in the new laws and that some device for dealing with price-breaking surpluses is better than the AAA contracts for limiting acreage. While he insists that the gains made under the outlawed legislation are being lost every day that passes until new legislation takes its place, one guesses that the interval for stock-taking has not been unwelcome.

Asked how far government regulation should go, or where State control should stop, Mr. Roosevelt implies, though he does not say so, that it should be kept in the experimental stage until it has proved itself. By that he means that one Congress should not commit the country to an untried policy which another Congress could not revoke if the policy does not work. Thus he was frankly dubious about a housing scheme which requires appropriations over an indefinite period or over a very long period.

This streak of caution is as characteristic of the President as his more spectacular tendencies. Before M. Bonnet, the French Ambassador, left Washington to administer oxygen to French finance, the President advised him to make a drive on French tax slackers, explaining that he published the names of prominent evaders in this country as a sure-fire method of arousing popular interest in the subject. This is the well-known Roosevelt, the political showman who sees the value of dash, drama and attack to put things over. He believes that the public must have "something new"—a fresh idea, a novel approach—to keep them interested. Less known but just as real is the Dutch householder who carefully totes up his accounts every month and who is really annoyed, now that he is bent on balancing the budget, when Congress can't stop spending.

Another thing that has power to exasperate the President is the word "dictator" as applied to himself or his ambitions. Last January he talked to the writer about leadership. His huge majority in the election and the ovation he received on the trip to South America made him think of himself as a leader of democracy, a symbol to set against symbols of the systems entrenched in Moscow and Rome. Then he was beguiled by the role the head of the Government of the United States might play in the world—always as a symbol of the democratic idea. Now he shies away from the word leader, inclines instead to draw attention to the limits of his power.

There is no doubt that Mr. Roosevelt regards himself as the champion and safeguard of the American form of government. He is sure of his own devotion to that ideal, sure that the people ridicule the attempt to represent him as a potential dictator. If you inquire whether democracy is not threatened by his policies, by extension of government control over the economic life of the nation or by the progressive centralization of power in Washington, the answer is that government must act to correct abuses that have accumulated like barnacles under laissez-faire administrations and that it is science and invention that have robbed the separate States of their power to regulate except in concert.

Under these explanations is the fixed belief that the reforms he is seeking and applying tend to strengthen and save popular government against the forces that undermine democracy. He describes the fight on his program as "a fascist fight for fascist objectives," meaning fascism in the conventional sense of rule by Big Business, although that definition no longer applies where the system actually prevails. In Mr. Roosevelt's view, such opposition breeds communism just as truly as communist activity produces a fascist reaction. In these two despotisms he sees the only alternatives to democracy, and the importance of his function as he conceives it in the present crisis in the democratic system lies in the fact that the imperative changes required to make the system work must be made by "a passionate believer in democracy." Where democracy has failed, he thinks, power first fell into the hands of leaders without real faith in the idea of representative government.

In this connection it is interesting to realize that the President considers that his "hands-off policy" in the strike situation, as he calls, it, constitutes a contribution to the democratic solution of the labor struggle. Observing that people who strongly object to government interference in other affairs protest as strongly when government does not interfere in labor disorders, he contends that the Federal authorities can intervene in a local disturbance only in case of rebellion or in response to a call from the Governor or State Legislature, and not to protect property or deal with trespass or misdemeanor.

In none of the strike areas has there been a call for Federal help; but in any case Mr. Roosevelt believes that the three parties in the struggle—employers, employees and the public —must work out the problem for themselves. This is the difference, he thinks, between the way of dictatorship and the way of democracy. Pointing out that up to the end of July the NLRB settled 107 out of 115 strikes, he expresses the opinion that if collective bargaining and arbitration are to be established as orderly methods of regulating labor relations the people must learn by experience. He is convinced that they have learned a great deal from the extremists on both sides. As to the charge that he is in alliance with John L. Lewis, the retort—without the smile—is that the President of the United States is not in alliance with anybody.

If Mr. Roosevelt dislikes the word dictator applied to himself no more does he like the word socialism applied to the New Deal. Either it means Marxism, to his mind an obsolete theory, inapplicable to the present stage of industrial development, or it expresses so many different things that it has no meaning. "Social-mindedness" is the term he uses to describe the philosophy which extends the nineteenth-century concept of political democracy to fit the mechanized, tightly interwoven pattern of twentieth-century civilization. He defines it as freedom conditioned on mass production and the new tempo of change and limited by social responsibility, a freedom much more difficult to maintain now than in the simpler, roomier world of the past.

The President is no theorist, to think his premises through to conclusions. He is the figure of a confused and groping time; but his political philosophy, translated into action, is clearly manifest in the general lines of regulation he persistently pursues: regulation of agriculture, to prevent fluctuations of farm income by crop control; regulation of industry, to establish a living standard and old-age security for industrial workers; regulation of banking, the stock market and business practices, to curb financial power and secure investments and savings.

Redistribution of wealth? Mr. Roosevelt objects to that phrase, especially. In nothing is he more insistent than in emphasizing his belief in capitalism. He doesn't want to take anything away from anybody, he declares—except, presumably, by the tax method—or prevent any business from making all the profit it honestly can. He draws a distinction between old or accumulated wealth and new wealth, in process of accumulation through the increase in farm income and increases in production and earnings.

Suppose, he argues, that the national income rises, say from $60,000,000,000 to $80,000,000,000, as seems possible, should not the Government seek to spread the increment so that instead of raising the roof of the economic structure it shall level up and carpet the floor? In other words, he believes that the lion's share of the new prosperity should be diverted downward, to lift the living standard of that third of the population he refers to as "ill-nourished, ill-clad and ill-housed."

The President will not admit that his "spurt" is finished. He recalls that in 1934 it was announced in many responsible quarters that the emergency was over and the nation had had enough of experiment and reform. But he is probably fully aware that he has reached a turn of the road where the traffic lane narrows and the red lights outnumber the green. This awareness does not and will not prevent him from running true to type and continuing to perform in his own character. For five years observers have been expecting Mr. Roosevelt to go Left when he veers in that direction or to go Right when he makes a swing the other way. And for five years he has been weaving a course back and forth.

If all that is reported above could be capsuled into a one-question, one-answer interview, the question would be: "What next?" and the answer, "More of the same!" The President will continue to lead as far as he is followed. No farther. Maybe not so far, for he attracts by his person more than by his policies, and in his person, besides being adventurous, empirical and enthusiastic, he is also cool, canny, sensitive and as responsive as any man alive to the pull of the American past. It is not to be forgotten that a man named Franklin Delano Roosevelt is enmeshed as few Presidents have been in the curiously vague, fluid yet curiously strong tradition of America. Perhaps that best explains why he is what he is.

[30]   1 9 3 8   *October 16*. As He Sees Himself. *F.D.R.*
defines his role as that of "fighting liberal" trying to
consolidate democracy here.

WASHINGTON

President Roosevelt has dropped the phrase "a little
left of center" to describe the direction of his policy and the
slant of his mind. He has revived the old-fashioned word
"liberal," long rather obsolete in the political vocabulary. He
refers to himself as "a fighting liberal," and declares that he
will be found battling for liberal principles as long as he lives,
up to 1940 and after 1940, in the White House and after he
leaves it.

The President also designates the Democratic party as the
liberal party in American politics. With some lapses, with
frequent exceptions within the ranks, on the whole and as a
usual thing it has been the party of progress and the instrument of social reform. Since that is proved by the record, he
intimates that there is every reason to continue the liberal
fight within its ranks and no good reason to establish a new
party for the same purpose.

As for the New Deal, the framework of its reforms is laid
down. The objectives and the program are embodied in legislation either enacted or in preparation. Nothing new is contemplated. No "surprises" are in store. From now on the efforts of the Administration will concentrate on the natural
extension and development of principles already accepted.
"More of the same" may be expected, also some corrections
and amendments to measures now in force, but not what Mr.
Roosevelt calls "new departures," real innovations.

The President confesses that, like most good bargainers, he
often asks for more than he expects to get, in order to achieve
what he deems essential. Perhaps the fight for the liberaliza-

tion of the Supreme Court is an instance of this tactic. Looking back, at any rate, Mr. Roosevelt expresses satisfaction with the consequences of that defeat. The reason he did not claim it as a victory at the time, those in his confidence assert, was because of the possible effect of such an assumption on the court itself.

Whether or not the most militant phase of the New Deal ended with the unsuccessful interventions in the Democratic primaries last Summer, it can be said that a period of pacification is beginning. The new efforts to conciliate business and reconcile the differences of the C. I. O. and the A. F. of L. are not merely a pre-election gesture. They are the outgrowth of the European crisis and the settlement made at Munich, but not in the sense in which the President's statement to that effect has been interpreted. Europe's plight brought home to Washington the urgent necessity of internal unity and the consolidation of forces in the United States. The tense weeks of crisis convinced Mr. Roosevelt not only that the first defense of democracy is strength on the home front but also that if a new synthesis of interests and energies is required to save representative government it must be worked out in this country.

The foregoing views and opinions were amplified by the President in recent conversations with the writer, in which he discussed the world at large, changes in the United States, philosophies of government, his own program in retrospect and prospect. It is needless to report that he discoursed on all these large subjects with equal zest and fluency. The more an interviewer sees of the leaders of other nations the more he is impressed by the unique quality of interest and energy, and particularly of ease in energy, which Mr. Roosevelt possesses. Because of his interest in everything under the sun he can talk all day and refresh himself in the evening with more talk.

He is as fascinated by the status of the Ruthenians in Czechoslovakia as by the latest idea to cut costs in housing projects. His quicksilver mind invariably moves from the general to the particular, is never at a loss for a "simple illustration" to explain a complex problem.

The fundamental ideas change very little, however; so little that each time one sees the President after a long interval it is like going back to a well-known country which for months has been seen only in the headlines or through the eyes of others. "It must have changed since I left," you decide, puzzled, and then you return to find everything the same.

At close range, in the setting of marine prints, ship models, stamp albums, chairs piled with books, the President never fits the picture drawn either by his ardent critics or his ardent disciples. After nearly six years in the White House, the center of deeper domestic controversies than have shaken this country for generations, the focal point of whirling social change, his personality is still oddly intact and unclassifiable. Listening to his discursive talk, it is difficult to think of him as any kind of extremist. It is difficult to imagine stone or steel under that smooth, bright flow. Only once, when speaking of some one else, did the fighter flash through. "He is a man who wouldn't risk a blow, much less a battle, for anything," he shot out, with biting scorn.

The President sounds, in fact, like the liberal he proclaims himself, and there is a peculiar significance in his new emphasis on the old word. Mr. Roosevelt's shrewdest instinct is for the variations of the popular mind. In his public utterances he seldom fails to strike the note to which the American chorus is attuned.

The failure of his appeals for New Deal candidates in the primaries does not worry him, nor will he be greatly cast down if the coming elections result in further setbacks. He is pretty confident that if he were speaking for himself, on a test of his leadership in national issues, the story would be different. His sensitiveness to the feeling of the majority is so acute that he is probably right.

So when he talks of domestic affairs, without once using "left," "right," "communist," "fascist" or any of the words we have lately imported in wholesale lots, it must be from an intuitive sense that the American people are coming home, so to speak, returning to political designations more suited to their own special pattern of life.

The change is significant, because to the President "liberal" and "left of center" mean the same thing. A line divides liberals from conservatives. To the left of this line are those who desire change and are willing to support the methods and adopt the machinery to bring it about. All liberals therefore move left, "move with history," as Mr. Roosevelt puts it. But they are not radicals. "A radical," he says, "is one whose inclinations and beliefs are liberal but whose methods are badly thought out and if put into practice would not work."

Conservatives, on the other hand, do not attack reforms; they oppose the measures and methods proposed by the Administration to realize reforms. And since they do not propose alternative methods, but work to slow up progress by demands for pauses and breathing spells, the President concludes that they do not want to move at all. He defines conservatives as people who by various devices resist change because "they like it where they are."

Nevertheless, they do not stay where they are. The dividing line shifts constantly to make the liberals of today further left than they were yesterday, and by their movement they drag the conservatives after them. In Mr. Roosevelt's view, there is no static in human progress. There are periods of speed-up and periods of slow motion, and the latter, because the process of invention outstrips the political process, are really periods of retrogression.

In the time-table he is fond of using to illustrate what he means by spurts and lags the years between 1917, when the World War put a stop to the Wilson reforms, and 1933, when he took office, were years of going backward. He figures that at the beginning of his Administration the country was thirty years behind the times. "In five years I think we have caught up twenty years," he says. "If liberal government continues over another ten years we ought to be contemporary somewhere in the late Nineteen Forties."

Mr. Roosevelt's strongest personal conviction is that he is safeguarding the American system by applying overdue reforms to adapt it to present conditions. He holds that few Americans oppose the ends he has in view, that most of the quarreling is over the means or the tempo he employs to attain them.

To the criticism that the social legislation of the New Deal is improvised and ill-considered his reply is that the American Government, by the time it got around to measures like old-age insurance, had the experience of thirty years of trial and error in other countries to draw upon in preparing its own bills. The Wagner Act was carefully drafted, Mr. Roosevelt insists, as the result of three years' experience of NRA. So, far from rushing ahead in contrast to the gradual pace of England, he says we are much more deliberate. Lloyd George a quarter of a century ago put through in two years a greater body of radical reforms than the New Deal has attempted in five.

If you ask whether every grant of power to government should not be weighed, especially in these days, with reference to its effect on the democratic system, and whether that

system is not weakened as the margins of individual liberty
are narrowed and the citizen loses power to defend himself
against too much government, the reply is another question.

"Just how much personal liberty have you lost under the
New Deal? Have the citizens lost their power to control,
criticize and change their government or not?"

Democracy, in Mr. Roosevelt's view, is a process—not a
static condition we have attained. "It is where we in the
United States are going now; also it is the way we are going.
It means relative security for all in a free society."

Centralization of government, he contends, has little to do
with politics, the New Deal or his own desires or ideas. Science, speed, motors, radio, corporate ownership, the far-
spread spiderwebs of power, industry and business have done
more to undermine States' rights than all the legislation trying to catch up with the technical revolution. These are the
facts of life which the law must recognize. Any control that
can be exercised locally should be left in local hands, but an
ever-widening field of activities cannot escape national regulation in the national interest. To face that honestly, he
argues, is the best way to avert the chaos that does lead to
"overcentralization and the super-State."

The President admits, moreover, that he is in a hurry. He
is moved by the sense of urgency that presses on all the rulers
of our time, and also by a sense of personal urgency to get on
with his program and leave his mark on history. There is no
doubt, convinced democrat though he is, that he is irked by
the slowness of democratic procedure. As a typical instance
he cites the eleven-year fight in Congress for an airport to
take the place of the small and poorly placed field the President considers a danger and disgrace to the capital. This
Summer, by means of personal initiative and the PWA, the indefinitely postponed project has been started and Mr. Roose-

velt is able to present Congress with a fait accompli. He will take great delight, when the legislative body assembles, in announcing: "Well, here's your airport!"

He is irked, too, by the rising tide of protest against the cost of government. "It is the cost of improvement," he protests in turn. "If you live on a dirt road ten miles from a paved road you have to pay the price if you want the road paved to your door. Everybody wants the road without footing the bill. Also, it's the cost of insurance for the system the critics of the cost accuse us of undermining. If we really wish to save the system we must accept the fact that relief and unemployment are not temporary accidents. They are varying but fixed charges, to be dealt with on a permanent basis."

The President's impatience to take personal short-cuts and push things through by any means is what most disturbs a good many worried citizens. In his own eyes he is merely seeking to effect and hasten a compromise, or, rather, two fundamental compromises. The first has been mentioned. It is a coordination of controls between local, State and Federal authorities so that their fields are clearly marked and non-controversial. This implies larger scale Federal administration, which might be countered, he suggests, by the "localizing" of some Federal bureaus and by a more intelligent approach to a modern problem which a Federal system has to solve.

The second goes deeper. In Mr. Roosevelt's social philosophy "the submerged third" of the population does not enjoy the freedom of choice which is the essence of democracy. Nor, he admits, do the millions on relief or engaged on public works. The object of most of his non-emergency program *—

* Wages and Hours Bill, June 25, 1938, provided minimum wages, forty-hour week.

National Labor Relations Act (Wagner-Connery) created NLRB, July 5, 1935. This Board had power to determine appropriate collective bargaining the Wages and Hours Bill, the Labor Relations Act, social security, SEC, profits taxes, housing, resettlement, trust-busting—is to strike a balance between the freedom of the two-thirds above water level and the necessities of the fraction underneath. He recognizes that American democracy functions through free enterprise or the capitalist system. The question he asks is: How far is this system willing and able to bear its own burdens? How far, in other words, can it support the costs when government guarantees not only the right to life, liberty and pursuit of happiness but to a modicum of economic security?

This is the compromise—between political liberty and economic security—the New Deal is really after. The search represents the riskiest and most urgent political adventure of our epoch, and the hardest. The chief reason Mr. Roosevelt is alternately charging ahead and drawing back, lambasting business and calling it into conference, veering from one labor front to another, spreading confusion with each shift of weight, is that he himself does not know how to do what he thinks should be done. He has come to doubt whether anybody really knows anything about economics, or can know enough, in a world where the elements of change work so incalculably, to guarantee that any prescribed economic treatment will produce the effects intended.

Nothing in the President's conversation supports the idea that he is playing with the thought of a third party, with himself as the leader in a new alignment. His effort in behalf

---

unit subject to elections they supervised at request of the workers, to certify the duly chosen trade union, to take testimony about unfair employer practice, and to issue cease-and-desist orders.

Social Security Act, August 14, 1935, created a board to administer old-age benefits, etc.

Security and Exchange Act, June 6, 1934, established Securities and Exchange Commission and required licensing of stock exchanges and other functions.

of New Dealers against old-line Democrats and his statement
that he would favor liberal Republicans in preference to conservative Democrats might indicate that he was making a
test of personal strength, but it is more likely that he was
actuated in these fulminations by the same motives that inspired the move to reform the court. He is ready to go to
great lengths to remove obstacles to the realization of his
plans. His persistent attitude toward opposition is that its
motives are selfish and its objective is to turn the clock back.

More and more, as his Administration lengthens and resistance to his leadership develops within the party ranks, he
recalls and quotes "T. R." The first Roosevelt has always been
a model for the second, and the extravagance of his boyish
admiration for his kinsman in the White House has not diminished with the years. The Square Deal is not only the ancestor of the New Deal but the key to its methods and manners. But this does not mean that the President intends to
emulate "T. R." in splitting his party.

On the contrary, the emphasis now is on the Democratic
party as the liberal party. As to the chances of his seeking or
accepting a third term as the party candidate, this is a subject
Mr. Roosevelt will not discuss, and it is fair to assume that it
is actually an open question in the sense that he has not seriously considered it. He lives too intensely in the present to
cross bridges before he comes to them. He is a man to whom
two years is a long time, to whom the current topic is the
absorbing topic and the present battle is "the" battle.

In foreign policy, Mr. Roosevelt is torn between the desire
to play a resounding role in the world as the leader of democracy and a natural caution against involvement in the power
politics of the other democracies. The caution is more than
a reflection of the isolationist sentiment of the American people. It is partly native suspicion and partly a hard-headed
knowledge of the world. In dealing with other nations the

President is not likely to stand aloof; nor is he likely to be taken in or to affix the signature of America to something he cannot carry out.

At the moment caution is uppermost. Whether or not Mr. Roosevelt approves of the Chamberlain policy,* he thinks American help was necessary to help to save the peace of Europe at this juncture. But perhaps the real clue to the direction American policy is taking under his guidance is to be found in the declaration made in Canada in August. This had a direct effect on the European crisis. In essence it gave notice to the world that the American hemisphere represented a cooperative self-defense system. Undoubtedly the major tendency of this Administration is to build up this system. The "round-the-table" parley of world leaders has always appealed to the President. It was he who first threw out the idea. Just now, however, in foreign affairs he is increasingly careful to restrain his natural impulses. In all fields of policy, indeed, the outstanding fact of the present hour is that all signs point "home"!

This compound of bold impulse and cool caution is what makes the President baffling to the analyst and understandable to the simple. If there is danger in his leadership, danger because he has deep designs to centralize power and extend the control of government over all private enterprise, or danger because a shallow light-heartedness blinds him to the implications of his policies, the rank and file of America cannot be frightened into thinking of him as dangerous. They refuse to believe that the persuasive conversational voice of the fireside chatter is the voice of a revolutionist. They laugh at the notion that there is anything of the Hitler or Mussolini complex in a man who never frowns in public and otherwise

* Representatives of Britain, France, Italy, and Germany met at Munich, September 30, 1938, and agreed to the dismemberment of Czechoslovakia. Chamberlain returned to London with "peace in our time," later called appeasement.

doesn't speak, look or act like any current image of a dictator. They question or resent specific acts, like "fooling with the Supreme Court" or "muscling in on local politics," but can't be convinced that he aims at changing the form of government.

To the mass of Americans Roosevelt seems a pretty typical American—of the first families, to be sure, but friendly, even folksy, and uncommonly steeped in the tradition, lore and fluid spirit of this land. He is, besides, the husband of Mrs. Roosevelt, and no one should underestimate the reassuring effect on public opinion of the figure of the many-sided father of a family who slips in and out of the diary of the accomplished White House chronicler who manages to sublimate the typical American woman in the person of the First Lady of the land.

[31]   1942   *January 25*. AT 60 HE IS STILL A HAPPY WARRIOR. *Mr. Roosevelt's birthday finds him facing his titantic task confidently and cheerfully*

WASHINGTON

When he was a candidate for the Presidency in 1932, Mr. Roosevelt named for a curious interviewer the characters in history he most admired. On the eve of his sixtieth birthday the same interviewer, still curious, ventured to recall to the President that ten-year-old question. Without hesitation or prompting, although he had not thought of the matter since, he named the same all-American list—Benjamin Franklin, Thomas Jefferson, Benjamin Thompson (a little-known genius of Revolutionary times) and Theodore Roosevelt.

But whereas the reason he gave ten years ago for his admiration was that his heroes were versatile men, of wide-ranging and universal minds, this time he added another. They were all happy men, he pointed out, happy because they were always interested, eager for new experience. Any one of them would have found plenty to excite him on a desert island.

Facing the desk in the Executive Office is a big, brightly colored map of the world, and as he talked his eye followed the line of his thought as it traveled from Mozhaisk to Singapore, from Corregidor to the coasts of West Africa. Under his hand were a few sheets of notepaper on which were written the agreements he had just reached with Mr. Churchill during lunch in the White House study. He was absorbed in the crushing problems of the present, although he remarked that since Dec. 7 he often has the sensation that he is living in a previous existence, wrestling again with the same questions that came up when he was Assistant Secretary of the Navy in the last war.

Compared to the global dimensions of the present struggle, that old war was not a world war at all, but a local and limited conflict. Everything has changed in scale in the cataclysmic decade since Mr. Roosevelt first ran for the Presidency. His own position has vastly changed. At 60 he is at the apex of a career that is already projected into history. Whatever happens hereafter, his placed is fixed in the compendiums where epochs take the names of men and only the momentous dates are recorded.

There are leaders who fail to perceive the proportions of the drama in which they play decisive roles, but he is not one of them. His sense of history is his sixth sense. When the chronicler of the future seeks the key to the Roosevelt policies, domestic and foreign, he may find it in the fact that the President consciously rides the currents of time in the direction in which they are going.

He is quite aware that he is the first third-term President

of the United States because the war elected him. During Winston Churchill's stay in the White House some one remarked that Mr. Churchill could never have become Prime Minister if a supreme emergency had not pushed him to the top. The President was quick to reply that Churchill was chosen because he was prepared to take the lead, the one man in public life in England who knew the world well enough to understand the crisis; and it may be inferred that Mr. Roosevelt considers his own leadership equally inevitable, and for the same reasons.

His sixtieth birthday finds him facing tremendous new tests and experiences. He has to run the biggest war in history, a war of uncertain course and unpredictable consequences. He has to work in close partnership with the head of another government, in cooperation with Oriental minds like those of Joseph Stalin and Chiang Kai-shek, in the interests of more than twenty other assorted nations, and with constant reference to the special problems of this hemisphere.

It is a titanic responsibility, an Atlas load of headaches and heartaches laid upon the shoulders of a man who detests, he says, being a war leader. Mr. Churchill, in his youth a soldier who went looking for good fighting as far afield as Cuba, India and South Africa, may derive a certain grim enjoyment from the war command, but Mr. Roosevelt declares that the job "sickens" him. Until he ordered troops to take over defense plants last year, his proudest boast was that in eleven years as Governor and Chief Executive he had never called out the Army or the National Guard except on errands of mercy.

Yet he is cheerful still, the image of the happy warrior. He sits at a desk piled up with somber or nagging reports from many fronts, as calm and confident as the candidate of a decade ago. The years have thinned his hair, drawn lines around his eyes, set his jaw more firmly, but neither time nor the hammer blows of defeat in the Pacific have shaken his steady self-assurance. Mr. Roosevelt is more at ease in all circumstances, more at home in his position, than any leader of his time. His nerves are stronger, his temper cooler and more even. If he worries, he gives no signs of it. If any doubt of victory ever stirs in the recesses of his mind, it never gets to the surface.

At 60 the President looks as well as he did at 50. He can be haggard and hollow-eyed at the end of a hard day and come up brisk and smiling after a good night's sleep. But his physical rebound is less remarkable than his mental resilience under killing strains. Maybe because the uncertainties are resolved and the great debate is over, his mood seems brighter, if anything, than it was a few months ago.

Mr. Roosevelt has reached the chronological but not the psychological age when men begin to look backward. Despite his keen interest in the public record, evidenced in the accumulating mass of documents in the Hyde Park library, he will probably never write his private memoirs. He is not a reminiscer, even on anniversaries, as one discovers in trying to focus his attention on the personal past.

He describes himself truly as "the least introspective man in the world." He is likewise one of the least retrospective. He never has time, he says, to survey the road behind and speculate on what he might have done if he had not devoted his life to politics, or what he would do in any given set of circumstances if he had a chance to do it again. In nine crowded years in the White House he has presided over a period he considers as revolutionary as the struggle for independence or the Civil War. But now it is all just background, interesting only as related to the overwhelming present. All other reports to the contrary, one feels that in the mind of the No. 1 New Dealer even the New Deal has become like a "little business," pushed aside by the great and urgent priorities of today.

The President has always turned gladly from the smaller to the larger aim. A case in point is that of Mr. Nelson, selected to be the full-powered boss of war production because he "passed the exams best." It takes a year or two of trial, in Mr. Roosevelt's view, to find out whether a business man can make good in Washington. Most people would say the difficulty lay in slow-paced bureaucratic methods and tangles of red tape, but the President's explanation is that a manufacturer or executive accustomed to concentrate on one line or one article is bewildered when he has to change his methods or deal with many things at once.

Mr. Nelson had to pass the test, but this is not the complete explanation of the President's delay in giving up sole control over the arsenal. It's a fair guess that he waited to take this step until we were actively engaged in the war because until then production was the chief function of the United States. As soon as this country became a full participant, however, strategy on a world front became the business of Washington. The arrival of Mr. Churchill signified that the headquarters of the conflict was transferred from the Thames to the Potomac. Thereupon Mr. Roosevelt resigned the lesser job to devote himself to the bigger business of Grand Strategy.

Here enters the highly interesting question of the relations between the two Grand Strategists. It is a vitally important question, besides, since never before have great issues and events been more dependent on a few persons and the way they get on with one another. For the best part of three weeks Franklin Roosevelt and Winston Churchill worked together long hours every day in the White House. They had to make the most difficult and delicate decisions two men have ever had to make in the name of two great nations, the most sensitive in the world regarding their independence and their sovereign dignity.

Both men, moreover, are orchestra leaders by temperament. Both like their own way and are irked by interference. Both exercise almost dictatorial power. Nevertheless they worked in extraordinary harmony. It may be a relief for both not to have the last word. "It's lucky we got on so well," commented Mr. Roosevelt, who holds to the theory that two people can always agree if they wish to agree. If negotiations are blocked by an unacceptable formula, he adds, it is possible to find a new set of words and start over again.

On the personal side the President and the Prime Minister have much in common. Both are great talkers, Mr. Churchill with more flash and Mr. Roosevelt with more fluency, and in the intervals between the endless and wearing discussions on the conduct of the war, they "kidded" each other unmercifully, discovering in the process many similar tastes, interests and experiences. Mr. Churchill began life as a soldier, but he is a sailor at heart and shares the President's passion for ships and the sea. They met for the first time during the last war, when as First Lord of the Admiralty Churchill dealt with the young Roosevelt as the representative of the American Navy.

Both have great zest for life and people and their minds range over the world with the same inexhaustible curiosity. When Mr. Roosevelt began exploring it, about the age of 9, he recalls that he developed a fascinated interest in Egypt— not Cairo, the Pyramids or the Valley of the Kings, but the wild reaches of the Upper Nile. For years he read everything he could find on the subject, including an early book of Churchill's, called "The River War," but never met anyone who shared his interest. He looked up the old two-volume copy he had read as a boy and asked the author to auto-

graph it, and discovered that he was the first person Church-
ill knew who had read the book that inspired the Prime
Minister's interest in the Sudan—Bruce's "Travels to the
Nile."

How far this personal congeniality colors their official exchanges it is impossible to say, or to what extent their political and social outlook can be harmonized when the time
comes to build the new world order forecast in their joint
declarations. During the parleys they set up a number of
coordination boards in London and Washington, each composed of American and British members, to make decisions
on military operations and allocations of all kinds of supplies. Roosevelt and Churchill will be the "supreme umpires"
for these boards, and if you ask either who will be final um-
pire in case of disagreement, both answer with a shrug that it
is a "50-50 proposition."

People who talked to the two men in Washington got the
impression that if there is any division of labors, the emphasis is on Churchill as military leader and Roosevelt as
political leader. For the duration of the war that distinction
will be largely academic, since the stake of both countries in
every major operation is so great that there must be joint
decisions.

But the President, though he speaks with a grimace of 60
as "the dark age," is nearly eight years younger than the
Prime Minister. He has more chance, perhaps more inclination, to be the peace leader. His answer to critics of the war
production program to date is that it moved faster between
Dec. 7, 1940, and Dec. 7, 1941, when we were not at war,
than it did between April 1917, and April, 1918, when we
were at war. He is determined that it can and will reach
"the sights" he set in his message to Congress on Jan. 6.

But how he would enjoy reconstructing the world! His eye

lights up when he turns for a moment from the dreary planning for war to speak of a world without passports, of a Europe with federalized public services, of the ever-normal granary on a world scale, of international control of rubber and other essential raw materials, of a world police force. In answer to complaints that the Atlantic Charter is an inadequate and out-dated program, he insists that he would write it again in the same words.

"You can't have a finished plan for a building and subdivide the floor space into rooms," he argues, "until you know when and how it will be occupied."

As long as he lives Mr. Roosevelt will continue to look forward and avoid looking back. He saw the war coming before most statesmen and he is now searching for the outlines of peace. His place in the record will be in the line of the war Presidents, but the role he covets is that of the great peacemaker.

Looking back, it seems clear that this has been in his mind ever since he took office—coincidentally with Hitler—and began to envisage the shape of the struggle that lay ahead. Talking to him after returning from Germany in that year, this writer saw crystallizing in his mind the idea that the basic conflict was between Hitler's solutions and his own.

The South Americans greeted him as a symbol, and that helped to deepen a feeling that he was called upon to assume the leadership of the democratic cause. From that point, as the storm broke, it was a short step to the conviction that he is responsible for a democratic peace. Our entry into the war, followed so swiftly by our election to war leadership, has given substance and reality to that belief.

Of course, it means winning the war first. Since his talks with Churchill, underlined by the disasters of the Pacific, Mr. Roosevelt has a heavy realization of the cyclopean job that will be. He does not flinch at the prospect because he never for a second doubts the end. But he is already looking beyond.

Years ago, asked why he aspired to be President in a crisis, his answer was: "Some one has to!" When the war ends some one has to work out a New Deal for the world, and it would not be surprising if he feels that he will be elected to that job too.

[32] 1 9 4 5 *April 22*. HIS "UNFINISHED BUSINESS"— AND OURS. *A final interview with Franklin Roosevelt, who saw San Francisco as his career's crowning act.*

WASHINGTON

Others may say of President Roosevelt that his great work was done. But he would not have said so. He led the nation to victory, and saw it near, but he was looking beyond victory. He was looking to the inauguration of the San Francisco Conference as the crowning act of his career. This was his project. He proposed it, set the time and place of the meeting, speeded up the preparations in the belief that it was supremely urgent, for the United States and the world, to project into the picture of victory a design for peace.

If he desired one thing more than any other in the last days of his life,* it was to see the Grand Alliance enlarged and reshaped into an armed security system while the forge of war was still hot enough to fuse the nations together. He dreamed of going down in history as the President who had succeeded where Woodrow Wilson failed in making the United States the great bastion of this system. If Benjamin Franklin's saying about America representing the interests

---

* President Franklin D. Roosevelt died April 12, 1945 at Warm Springs, Georgia.

of mankind was often on his lips, it was because he had aspired for a long time to be the American who would lay the cornerstone of a new world order which would insure longer spaces of peace and gradually render war obsolete as an instrument of national policy or international change.

This was the outstanding impression left by a talk with the President less than three weeks before his death. The crash of Germany breaking into pieces was all but audible in the quiet of the executive office. Bulletins kept pouring in telling of brilliant advances of the Allied armies on every front. Mr. Roosevelt was excitedly aware that the climax was at hand. But he hardly spoke of the war; all his thoughts were fixed on the meeting at the Golden Gate.

It was strikingly evident that in his mind this was the most urgent business of the moment. He talked at length of his experiences at Yalta, but always as the exchanges there and the developments thereafter—which disturbed and puzzled him—related to the success of San Francisco. He referred to the Flynn mission in Moscow and Rome as one of many "exploring expeditions" he considered useful as a preliminary to the conference.

He asked more questions than usual, about conditions in Italy, the political outlook in France, popular feeling in England toward America, the mood of liberated people, especially in smaller countries. He listened with unusual interest to the answers, again with reference to their bearing on the central problem of organizing international security. Never had his naturally discursive mind seemed so concentrated on a single theme.

Ordinarily the President's conversation was a fascinating medley of digressions, anecdotes, illustrations drawn from an immense experience with people, places and human events. His mental world was crowded with persons he had met and concrete examples to illuminate almost any question, so that discussion with him always tended to dart from the general to the particular, from the complex to the simple, and often from one topic to an entirely different one.

This time he hewed to the line. No one ever accused Franklin Roosevelt of having a single-track mind, but for once he hardly deviated from his subject. And he developed it from every aspect with a clarity and vigor that belied his look of weariness and convinced his listener that all his hopes of success in life and immortality in history were set on getting an international security organization in motion. He did not speak in terms of moral fervor, but in his grave and sober words, in a smile touched with a strange wistfulness, in the deep anxieties he revealed, one detected a new note of feeling and of urgency.

The San Francisco Conference is the unfinished business of the Roosevelt Administration. It is also the unfinished business of the life of Franklin Roosevelt. It was clear in that final interview that this was the thing he was straining his strength to accomplish. It was the objective of the hard, perhaps fatal, trip to Yalta. As his first term was devoted to the battle for recovery and reform on the home front, the second to charting and directing the sinuous and difficult passage from peace to war, the third to the prosecution of a two-front battle against the most powerful military conspiracy in history, the fourth was to have been a fight for the organization of peace.

There was an interval, from 1941 on, when the President refused to think of anything but winning the war. At the beginning of his third administration—long before we were attacked—he told this reporter that he had no thoughts beyond the immediate present and the instant problem. "I can't see more than six inches beyond my nose." he said. But at the end he was back where his imagination dwelt in the early years of his Presidency, looking beyond the present scene of destruction and chaos to the future, seeing himself as chief architect of a new structure rising out of the wreckage.

He talked like a man in a hurry. Looking back, one might surmise that he had a premonition that his time was short. But he gave no such impression at the time. On the contrary, though he appeared shockingly gray-faced, gaunt and tired to a visitor who had not seen him for many months, he seemed exhausted rather than sick, and no doubt he counted on a few weeks' rest at Warm Springs to restore the resilient energy that had never failed to respond to the monstrous demands he made upon it in recent years. Although he was grave, subdued by a weight of responsibility he carried lightly in former years, the old flashes of gaiety colored his talk, and his manner was as cheerful and assured as ever.

Certainly he gave no sign of worry over his health. He fully intended to go to San Francisco for the opening of the conference. He referred several times to the speech he was going to deliver on the occasion, and said he thought of keying it to the struggle for the American Union, not only because of the application to the present undertaking but because it would direct the attention of the assembled delegates to a chapter of history most of them knew nothing about.

The reason he was in a hurry was that he believed the time was short for translating the Dumbarton Oaks proposals * into reality. He admitted that the other two great sponsoring powers did not feel the same sense of urgency.

Asked if the enterprise might not get off to a better start if more time had been allowed for preparation, for ironing

---

* Dumbarton Oaks conferences held in Washington, D.C. First between U.S.S.R., U.S. and United Kingdom, September 29–October 7, 1944. Proposed establishment of an organization of nations for maintenance of World Peace. This led to the calling of the United Nations Conference on International Organizations at San Francisco in 1945, where the charter was signed June 26 by fifty nations.

out differences, he answered that he regretted that the conference could not have been held in March, as he wished, because a shorter interval between Yalta and San Francisco might have prevented many misunderstandings. Delay, he added, was the dangerous element in enterprises that were launched at the moment of high tide in the affairs of men or were not launched at all. "I am not afraid of being too early for the rendezvous," he smiled. "I am afraid that the appointed moment will roll by and we shall be too late."

There were two main reasons for the President's urgency. The first was the necessity to insure the support of the Soviet Union for the world organization. The attack by Germany drew Russia into the military coalition, and ever since American entry into the war the Administration has made a consistent effort to overcome the Soviet Government's deep-seated suspicions and draw it into full political partnership.

This explains Mr. Roosevelt's persistent efforts to get into personal touch with Stalin. To this end he was ready to make all the advances, to ignore rebuffs, to take long journeys, to offer concessions and accept compromises. He acknowledged that he did not like these compromises, but he weighed them against the alternative. Since without Russian cooperation there could be no international security, he argued, every lesser consideration had to be subordinated to that essential aim.

Until the President died Stalin manifested a half-hearted interest in San Francisco. He was in no hurry to invite the lesser powers into council and acceded to a conference at this time mostly out of deference to Roosevelt's wishes. The key to Stalin's policy is determination to insure Russian security first by his own means. The key to Roosevelt's was determination to win Russian confidence in the general security system by every means possible, and the Soviet decision to send Foreign Minister Molotov to the conference is a sign of American success. The Russians evidently expected Roosevelt to carry the meeting by his own power, in his absence they show themselves sufficiently interested in the fate of the enterprise to give it backing and prestige by raising the rank of their delegation.

The President had also to insure American support of the international organization. This, of course, superseded all other objectives in his mind. His overall aim was to secure the ratification by the Senate of the Dumbarton Oaks charter as modified and accepted at San Francisco. If there could be no collective security without Russia, certainly there could be none without the United States. It was for this reason that he pressed for an early meeting. He believed that American public opinion was as nearly unanimous in favor of participation as it ever would be and that delay and differences over war settlements might cause a recession of popular sentiment.

"We must strike while the iron is hot," he declared. "We can't afford to let disappointment over specific solutions pull us back again from the course we have to take, however hard it is. If we all go our own ways, there will be no guarantee of peace or justice for any nation."

He desired to have the conference in this country to provide a New World setting and atmosphere for the discussions. By starting the new system here, moreover, it was hoped to dramatize it for Americans and strengthen the feeling of American responsibility. The choice of San Francisco was made with the idea of emphasizing America's world-wide interests by directing attention to the Pacific battlefield.

Mr. Roosevelt was also thinking of reassuring and encouraging China. The creation of a strong China remained to the end a focal point of his policy. It is due to his insistence that China was a member of the Big Four, and he joined with

Britain, it should be added, to turn the Big Four into a Big
Five by supporting the inclusion of France.

The President's sense of timing and his quick sensitiveness
to the ebbs and flows of popular feeling warned him that the
Big Three should be divested of some of its power, at least
ostensibly, by giving a voice and a feeling of responsibility
to smaller nations. This was another reason for his urgency
in calling the United Nations together. He liked power as
well as any leader. He was certainly not averse to the secret
sessions war makes necessary for the men who decide its
strategy. All his life he took a boyish pleasure in "secrets."

But in large issues, and especially in world affairs, he was
a man of clear vision. Small and shortsighted as he sometimes was in his political deals at home, his "farsight" was
keener than that of any statesman of his time. So was his instinct for reading the minds of men. People everywhere
trusted him above all others because they felt he was their
representative in the high councils of the world.

In his own mind he was. The chief motive that impelled
him to hurry up San Francisco, to override the objections of
the "postponers"—his colleagues at Yalta who wished to wait,
the counselors who advised more preparation—was a strong
sense that the Big Three phase was over and it was high time
to merge exclusive authority in something larger. The President believed that next week's meeting was the first step toward what he called "a democratic organization of the world."
He insisted, with unwonted vehemence, that that step could
not be taken too soon. He did not expect great results from
the meeting. It was only to lay the framework, he said, so
that "it would be there, for all men to see," but this seemed
to him of immense and instant importance.

Franklin Roosevelt will not be present at the conclave he
called. But in the most literal sense he will be conspicuous
by his absence. His voice will be the loudest there; the vacant

seat will overshadow all the occupied chairs. It may well be that the speech he does not deliver—the speech his mind was full of when he fell—will be more effective in carrying his dream toward reality than anything he could say in person.

[33]   1 9 4 5   *May 6.* SAN FRANCISCO: BATTLEFIELD FOR PEACE. *There, 46 nations are trying to find something better than an enemy to unite and hold them.*

SAN FRANCISCO

San Francisco stands midway between two battle-fronts. As the conflict in Europe comes to a crashing close, this city cannot forget that the fighting is not over. What appears from here as the "war beyond the mountains" ceases, but the "war beyond the ocean" goes on.

This is as good a reason as any for choosing this Pacific port as the place where the organization and planning of peace begins. San Francisco used to be the Far West, the end of the American trail. On Dec. 7, 1941,* its position changed; it became not merely the gateway to the East but the central point in that grand jumble in which East is West and West is East and the twain are always colliding.

As the globe turns, the view is better here. The perspective is clearer. But that is not the sole reason why San Francisco seems a more suitable place than it did a month ago for the inauguration of a new international order. This is the New World—new compared to the ancient lands of the Orient, reawakening from centuries of stagnant sleep; new compared to the exhausted countries of Europe; new compared even to New York, Washington and the settled States of the Eastern Seaboard.

* Pearl Harbor, Hawaii, U.S. possession, was attacked by Japan, December 7, 1941.

New enterprises flourish here. Great dreams, unblurred by too much bother about details, by worry about ways and means, are as indigenous as the tall redwoods, the oversize rhododendrons, the roller-coaster terrain. Nothing seems too big to try or too impossible to accomplish. Making deserts bloom, beginning over again from scratch, are just part of the day's adventure.

Less than forty years ago San Francisco was a ruin.* The charred wreckage of the gold-rush town tumbled down the perpendicular planes of its seven hills, so steep, sharp and separate compared to the softly merging hills of Rome. Today a new city rises out of the bay, one of the world's great cities, its heights crowned with towers and solidly encrusted with buildings, ivory-colored or rose-tinted by the strong sun. Its harbors are jammed with ships, its streets swarm with sailors and GI's, its suburbs spread down the coast and push into the crevices of the lupin-carpeted hills.

San Francisco is a lusty city, with youth in every line of its uplifted profile and vigor in every breath of its brisk trade winds. It must be a sight for the sore eyes of delegates who come to the world security conference from London and The Hague, Belgrade, Chungking and all the shattered cities of the war zones. More than any other city, it is a sign of promise of resurrection.

Most of the statesmen gathered here are tired—tired of war, tired of destruction, tired of exile, tired above all when they contemplate the ruin of their world and think of the superhuman tasks of reconstruction that lie ahead. The peoples they represent are wearier still, drained dry by long-drawn-out suffering and suspense. It is impossible to understand the muted mood of the conference, its rather spiritless speeches, its undertones of doubt, without remembering the background from which many delegates come. Neither the

* San Francisco earthquake and fire, April 18–19, 1906.

great victors nor the liberated feel elation because never was victory won at so high a price and never did war leave so many problems in its wake.

It is not a mood or a moment a good psychologist would select for the work in hand. The statesmen who have borne the strains of the war are not the men to supply the fresh energy, the resourcefulness, even the physical strength needed to rebuild the world. Some, moreover, occupy the anomalous position of speaking for countries with which they have had no direct contact during the years of the war. Others cannot be sure they express the will of the nations they represent.

Of the big powers the United States is the only one that attends this conference with a fresh and direct mandate from the people. The election last November was a vote for President Roosevelt: especially it was a vote to carry out the policies he advocated, and therefore, since this was the dominant issue in the campaign, for participation in the enterprise this assembly is engaged in.

The commission of the American delegation is clear and bi-partisan. British sentiment undoubtedly runs parallel and ahead of ours, but for ten years there has not been a general election to prove it. The Russians have no means of registering their opinion that we would recognize; China has had no election and the European Governments present are all provisional. In fact one of the remarkable features of a meeting that is in effect a constitutional convention called to draw up a charter for international organization is that a considerable proportion of the delegates are without popular mandate or are creations of temporary regimes that may or may not represent nations.

This makes for uncertainty and caution. The statesmen here are mostly figures of transition from a world in convulsion. They are little men, as all men must be when they are measured by the events they have to deal with. Our days are too big for giants. The picture of the delegates assembled in the brightly lighted opera house for the plenary sessions is a panorama of anxious, somber faces not too attentive to the scene before them because their eyes are filled with visions of conditions at home and their minds with nagging questions concerning the future.

This frame of mind is another good reason for holding the meeting in San Francisco. There is hope and life in this western air. It is no more like the atmosphere of old international conferences than Mr. Molotov's manners conform to the traditional etiquette of diplomacy. It is nothing like Geneva or even Bretton Woods or Dumbarton Oaks. Whatever it is, it is not stuffy. New York is a receiving station, a port of reception into which Old World currents flow but San Francisco is a sending station, a port from which the currents move outward rather than inward. It is a point of departure so palpably a starting place that it should goad the United Nations to look forward instead of backward if any place can.

The delegates need all the courage they can draw from environment or circumstance. It is not necessary to go backstage at this juncture to know that peace making is much harder than waging war. On the actual battlefield the issues are simple and means and end are crystal clear. When you get to the fighting line the only realities are life and death. All other problems fall away before the stark imperative of pushing forward against your enemy, of driving him out of the next house, the next street, the next field, of killing or being killed. General Patton, poring over a map at his headquarters, said the hardest thing he had to do was to work up the American soldier to the mood to kill.

"But look how straight-aimed and simple is the duty of a soldier," he added. "We just have to get to this point tomorrow. We know exactly where we want to go, what means we have to get there, and what we have to do if we miss. The politician never has such clear objectives or directives."

Behind the fighting line are vast problems of logistics, so staggering that the mind of the reporter reels when he contemplates the delivery service that works like a giant conveyor system to supply the insatiable needs of modern armies. And behind this global network of factories, rails, ships, air ferries, trucks, bomber runs, oil and ammunition dumps, storage depots as big as towns are the problems of strategy. These involve decisions as delicate and difficult, as nerveracking and responsible, as human judgment can render. In a coalition they are concerted decisions, which multiplies and compounds the difficulties to the nth degree. Anyone watching this titanic conflict, fought with all the resources of the earth, fought with Eastern and Western forces that made their first contact after four years of combat, would say that nothing could be so hard to manage.

But the over-all purpose of the fighting Allies is the same. They are united in the single aim of defeating the foe. As in the case of the individual soldier war for the nations that wage it is a simple struggle for survival. When they join together it is because each needs the strength of the others to overcome the common danger. On the battleground there may be differences. Usually the soldiers bicker, the various commands are often like rival camps, the Governments strain at the leash, the supreme strategists are sometimes at odds on the most vital questions—on the choice between invading Italy or the Balkans, for instance, or on the allocation of military supplies.

Yet danger unites them. The enemy unites them. While national resources are pooled for the use of all, as they are in this conflict, there can be no serious break in the solid front. While a supreme commander uses all the armies as one army, as General Eisenhower has done on the Western Front, they are one.

If there is a place where great military operations seem simple and all the harnessed forces appear perfectly synchronized and under control it is in General Eisenhower's headquarters. He never speaks of the divisions or generals under him as American, British, Canadian, French or Polish but always as the "Allied Armies." He is the complete internationalist in his dealing with the varied members of his staff. The battlefront is international too. The troops are all fighting for their country, but on the dividing line between life and death they fight as a close community.

It is always a shock to go from that line of clear issues and ultimate values to the areas where other problems begin to press for solution. You don't have to go back very far to see how much easier is the work of destruction than the job of reconstruction. To blow a town to bits is an affair of minutes or hours; to put it together again takes years. And structural rebuilding is the least of the complications. Anyone who has seen the ruin left in the wake of this war knows how small a part of this immense devastation is physical.

The confusion comes from the obliteration of moral, social and political landmarks. The signposts are gone that marked direction, the clocks that told time, the framework that held communities together, the sense of continuance that gives life its shape.

In the purely obituary view that the historian takes of the long-buried dead, perhaps this process will appear good. Perhaps it will be easier to build a new order on the wreckage of the old. Perhaps it will be simpler to make peace when the destruction and cruelty of war are so monstrous that nobody can escape it or face it again.

War, the worst war in history, is the background of the San Francisco conference. The delegations gathered here are united by war. Many come from countries laid waste by war. Even the light of victory cannot brighten the drab pictures they see when they look back upon their homelands. Inevitably their views are colored and their minds are distracted by their immediate anxieties. For many the cessation of hostilities is the beginning of another struggle, as stark as war, for mere survival.

This shadows the atmosphere of the conference. But it does not alter the fact that as soon as the war partners begin to think in terms of peace they tend to think separately. They are nations again, met to lay the foundations of an international system, but as member nations rather than as people welded together by a common danger. To wage war is to concentrate on one end, but to make peace, and especially to create a peace system, is to try to harmonize a lot of diverse aims, interests and ideas.

The enormous complexities of this effort appeared in the first week of the conference. "Let this be the last battlefield," cried General Romulo of the Philippines in one of the plenary sessions. His words only emphasized that the conference room is a battlefield. The initial engagement was a contest among the sponsoring powers over an "agreement" that Russia interpreted in one way and Britain and the United States in another. Out of that grew a tactical contest for position, first for the chairmanship of the convention, then for a showdown apparently designed to prove that if the Soviet Union and its satellites form a "bloc," so do the States of the Pan-American Union.

All this sparring proves, provided the great powers are resolved to go along together despite differences, is that the struggle to maintain peace is immeasurably more difficult than any military operation. But if it is relaxed for a moment, given up for any reason, there is war.

In San Francisco two worlds, two systems long kept apart

by mutual fear and suspicion and forced into conjunction by a common enemy, are trying to adjust themselves to a new system that will enclose them both. Forty-six nations are attempting once more to find something better than an enemy to hold them together. Now that the enemy is crushed, is no longer a power or a threat, it requires more will, more sacrifice, more statesmanship, more patience, to forge the bond. Here is where the New World spirit of San Francisco comes in.

And where the desperation of the peoples of the world beats upon the Golden Gate. For if the forum does not take the place of the battlefield this war is lost and the next begins.

INDEX

i

Index

A NOTE ON THE

T Y P E

IN WHICH THIS BOOK IS SET

THE TEXT of this book is set in Caledonia, a Linotype face that belongs to the family of printing types called "modern face" by printers—a term used to mark the change in style of type-letters that occurred about 1800. Caledonia borders on the general design of Scotch Modern, but is more freely drawn than that letter.

The book was composed, printed, and bound by The Plimpton Press, Norwood, Massachusetts. Paper made by S. D. Warren Company, Boston. Typography by W. A. Dwiggins. Binding design by Charles E. Skaggs.